THE IGBO–IGALA BORDERLAND

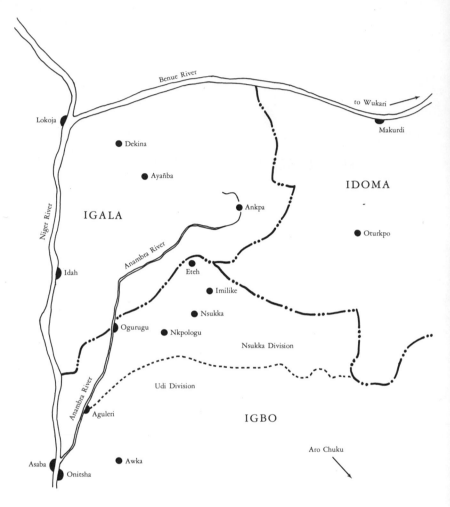

MAP I. *Igala and Nsukka Districts*

AUSTIN J. SHELTON

The Igbo-Igala Borderland

Religion & Social Control in Indigenous African Colonialism

STATE UNIVERSITY OF NEW YORK PRESS

ALBANY · 1971

Published by State University of New York Press
Thurlow Terrace, Albany, New York 12201

© 1971 by State University of New York
All rights reserved

ISBN 0-87395-082-8 (clothbound)
ISBN 0-87395-182-4 (microfiche)
Library of Congress Catalog Card Number 70-141493

Designer: Richard Hendel

Printed in the United States of America

This book is dedicated to my friends and teachers,
Ugwuja Attama and Ugwu Nnadi Eze,
and to all my borderland friends alive and dead

Contents

Illustrations

Introduction

THE BORDERLAND AREA of the northern Nsukka District of East Central State and Kwara State of Nigeria presents several problems relatively uncommon in the literature either of traditional religion and social control or of social and cultural change. Like many ethnic frontiers it manifests the usual peculiarities of higher frequency of loan words on either side of the border, syncretized institutions strong in the borderland and diminishing with parallel steadiness as one moves in either direction away from the border, and notions of mixed ancestry. There are other traits, however, peculiar to the Nsukka borderland. First, traditions on either side of the frontier speak of the political domination of northern Nsukka Igbo villages by the Igala, particularly after the wars of conquest led by Onojo Ogboni. Second, these two societies living in relatively close contact show marked differences in their structure and social organization. The Igala, on one hand, possess a centralized kingdom with delegated authority formalized to the degree almost of enfeoffment, and have a combined form of family organization with a ranked agnatic descent system with matrilateral descent under some circumstances. The Igbo, on the other hand, possess no centralized government but rather village autonomy characterized by gerontocratic rule, and have had until recently a patrilineal form of family organization with less strictly agnatic descent. Third, the non-European cultural influences affecting the peoples of the borderland include not only mainstream Igbo and Igala, but at least two others. From the far southeastern area of Igboland came the widespread although here not very powerful influence of the largely Igbo Aro Chuku people of Bende, who established settlements south of Nsukka District on important trade routes, in the neighborhood of central markets, and in certain rich farming areas for the gathering of slaves (see Ottenberg, 1958:299–306). Much more important, from the area of Awka, east of Onitsha, stemmed the important influence of Umunri, whose language and culture are largely Igbo but whose political organization is divine monarchy with a specialized caste system. To these influences, as well as contact with the Idoma in the north and the Tiv in the east, all overlaid by the European conquest, Nsukka has been subjected, so it provides a fascinating area for investigation of cultural borrowing, retention, and syncretism.

The problem struck me shortly after I began work in Nsukka in 1961 that in view of all the cultural influences upon the northern Nsukka area, in view of the relatively recent (18th–19th centuries) Igala conquest of Nsukka and the establishment of Igala occupational personnel in key village positions—particularly as shrine priests—and in view of the reputed Igbo adaptability to change, why were the control forces in the Igbo villages now Igbo rather than Igala? These questions in turn suggested other problems concerning culture change particularly in the tropical West African context: what are the factors which might determine the extent and quality of cultural substitution and replacement rather than simple cultural borrowing and addition—the pattern emphasized by Bascom and Herskovits (1959) and many other researchers? Are these always intensity of contact, length of contact, special prestige of one contact agent as contrasted with the other, special motivation of one party aroused by the situation, or what?

The Igala conquest of Nsukka resulted in definite substitution of Igbo shrine priests by Igala *attama* and the addition of Igala lineages of diviners and priests to Igbo clans and villages, and although these very Igala in their descendants became Igbonized, typical Igbo shrine priests did not reappear. Furthermore, whereas *alusi* typically had been relatively supportive earth spirits the term in Nsukka came to refer to particular hostile and generally wide-ranging spirits, a definite switch in the meaning of those beings for whom the alien *attama* ministered. A strengthening of ancestral worship in the form of *arua* was an expected Igbo reaction to the invaders' having assumed the office of intermediary between the people and the *alusi* and, even as the *attama* became steadily more Igbonized, *alusi* worship increased in importance while *arua* worship remained virtually static.

The present study is intended to do the following: first, and most important, to present a body of ethnographic materials focused chiefly on the religious control forces in a selected group of northern Nsukka villages, along with my brief analyses of some of this information; second, to describe and assess the effectiveness of the Igala-Okpoto mode of social control in northern Igbo villages; third, to investigate briefly some ramifications of the social and cultural changes, reversions, and syncretizations involved in the alterations of religious institutions in the area. Hopefully the work will contribute to other work being done, particularly by such capable individuals as J. S. Boston who piloted the Nri-Awka Project and who has contributed more than anyone to Igala studies, J. C. Anene who until the Nigerian civil war had been involved in the Eastern Region History Scheme, the Igbo anthropologist Victor C. Uchendu, and my colleague, Simon Ottenberg. At this stage I would also like to thank the Research Foundation of State University of New York for the research fellowship and grant which enabled me to complete this work.

A Note on Methods

The materials of this study were gathered during a three-year period from 1961 to 1964 in the borderland area of northern Nsukka. By 1962 I had acquired a practical although largely passive knowledge of Nsukka Igbo which enabled me to maintain close checks on my informants and translators in the gathering of data. I used a large number of persons as Igbo and Igala translators, some among these in perhaps a natural way appealing more to me and thus being used more frequently than others. Among these, especially, I must single out the following:

Malachi ' Yacubu Onu Ankpa, the fifth son of the Okpoto-Igala chief of Ankpa, a very intelligent boy of sixteen whose truthfulness and tact despite his youth and the inclination of some of his elders to glorify their history were such to impress anyone favorably.

Mallam Baw'allah Momoh, a Nupe politician and man of all sorts, who was my personal friend and son-in-law of the ruler of Ankpa, Onu Yacubu. Conniving and clever, Momoh nonetheless interpreted honestly and accurately, and the proud knowledge that his own grandfather had formerly been ruler of much of the borderland led only to minor embellishments.

Elias Owuchi Eze of Imilikenu, a young man who was a clerk in the University of Nigeria Accounts Department. Elias was lovable and extremely loyal to his own people, thus a careful observer of the ethnographer's actions. We first met when I was returning to my car which I had parked near the *ofo* tree in the village square of Ameegwu while I was visiting my friend and teacher of divination, Ugwuja Attama. Elias saw me and, throwing his right hand against his chest, exclaimed: "Good afternoon, sir! I had no idea you ever visited the suburbs!"

Joseph Ugwu of Ejuona-Oba, a teacher in the Roman Catholic mission school who, ever suspicious of my motives, was faced constantly with the conflict between such distrust and a personal predilection for the spread of knowledge about his people as well as friendship with me personally. His knowledge of Europeans gave him fine adeptness in interpreting many Igbo events.

Francis Eze of Ihe Owele, Nsukka, who was my household steward, a gangling lop of a boy of nineteen who suffered perhaps unjustly far too much culture shock by accompanying me on some visits and stays in villages far removed from his own and accordingly wildly alien to him. Sincere in his feeling that he was employed by a madman, Francis not only translated well but accompanied this work with detailed (and often erroneous) commentary, including numerous value judgments, about the peoples concerned.

Okeke Attama of Umugoji, the senior son of the late *attama* of Ngwumadeshe, who was of great help in my understanding of the interplay of control forces and the initiation of shrine priests.

Many other persons as well have been of great help in the gathering and interpretation of materials, including persons at the University of Nigeria, Nsukka. Particular among these have been my friends, B. Enyi of Eha Amufu Nsukka and Bennett Ukeje of Awka, Isaac Eya of Enugu-Ezike, and Rev. S. Ezeanya.

Pre-field preparation for this study was perforce rather scanty. It consisted of my reading the few works available, consulting government records for Nsukka District, and interviewing missionaries and government officers. Missionary authors such as G. T. Basden (1921, 1938) include interesting and often valuable ethnographic data in their writings, although it is advisable to double-check all such secondary sources, for often underlying such reports are normative attitudes such as the following expressed by Jordan (1949:37): "Nri, the headquarters of juju and voodoo and pagan priesthood for the whole Ibo tribe." C. K. Meek (1937), on the other hand, is a more authoritative source except when he discusses "Hamites" and, unlike others, he deals specifically with Nsukka District. Generally, however, it is safe to say that there are no really useful primary or secondary sources concerning the subject of this study: the Nsukka-Igala borderland has been a politically and economically neglected corner of Nigeria. Many historians preferred to deal with the peoples of the north, who possessed centralized governments which could be reduced to the sort of order the European mind often prefers, and ethnographers have focused their efforts either on those areas of Igboland where kingship exists because of culture borrowing or colonization (e.g., Onitsha) or which typify nuclear Igbo culture (i.e, that away from frontiers with other cultures)—with the exception of Simon Ottenberg, who has conducted the most definitive high-level studies of Afikpo Igbo in the northeast. I hope that this study will contribute to further understanding of the area and that it will be followed by other more conclusive works than it pretends to be.

Oral Traditions
Like much oral testimony and data based upon oral traditions, there is a wide range of quality in the data concerning the borderland. It

ranges from the official version of an extended village group to the official version of a narrower group such as a secret society (e.g., *omabe*), an Igbo descent group jealous of an Igala group or vice versa, and individual interpretations some of which are accurate while others are sheer fabrications of the worst poppycock imaginable. It became known by early 1962, of course, that a European was seeking to "learn about our forefathers," and this naturally affected much of the testimony, some groups and individuals making quite conscious efforts to glorify their own while ignoring or deprecating others. Some informants, furthermore, suspected that what was elicited might be used against them by the Nigerian government, particularly when testimony concerned such matters as headhunting, blood feuds, village law enforcement, tribalistic attitudes, and relations with other groups, so much testimony had to be carefully sifted in order to get to the "facts".

In the borderland, furthermore, there is little if any institutionalization of customary knowledge, no professional historians such as the *griots* of the Western Sudan, not even professional story-tellers, so that each descent group maintains its own traditions in its own way and, presumably, to its own advantage. There is not even a highly developed formalism of literary types in the borderland. Most commonly, traditions are handed down the generations as prose statements to be embellished as the given teller sees fit. The proverb is common, and is a more tightly structured form, but contains little that is historical, unlike proverbs in some cultures. Praise names are scanty, and certainly not developed as containers of historical materials such as the *oriki* among the Yoruba or the *maboko* of the Tswana. Thus what is considered important in the past of a borderland group is not normally maintained through formalized structure which could keep it from changing greatly, but depends instead upon the interests of succeeding generations. (See Shelton, 1969 b.)

Some Problems of Definition and Concept

Preliminary to proper understanding of the ethnographic data from the Nsukka borderland is a clarification of terminology. The present study deals largely with what one refers to as the "religion" of the borderland, and the term "religion" has posed problems of definition to many researchers. In the Nsukka area, "religion" can best be understood by reference to certain expressions of belief and to particular rituals dealing with the maintenance of calm on the part of aggressive spirits and the acquisition of positive forces (*oke ogwu:* male medicine) and the removal or neutralization of negative forces (*icho aja:* to offer a sacrifice). Thomas has generalized that

> Nature in Africa may . . . be defined as a community of powers, which are most of the time intentional and likely to be expressed by an organized body of signs or intentional symbols. . . . The African conception of the world amounts to a set of connections (participative thought) and antagonism (separating thought) linked to a classification of beings that are forces (1961:131).

Many of the "powers" to which Thomas refers, in Nsukka might be called "supernatural beings" or "gods" insofar as they are personified in belief and treated as special sorts of persons in the ritual and ceremonial behavior. But these terms are vague and not terribly useful for our purposes: first, "super-natural" denotes that which is above nature, and connotes awe and a kind of mystical majesty surrounding a divine person—not always the case in Nsukka religion, which is often strongly pragmatic and much less emotional than religious observances are said to be in other parts of the world.

Horton (1967:52) has rightly pointed out that "each category of beings has its appointed functions in relation to the world of observable happenings," and that Africans think of the spirit-world when confronted with the unusual or uncanny, sometimes in the face of anxiety-provoking or emotionally charged situations, and sometimes when crisis theatens the society (1967:59–60). But the "spirit world" in Nsukka is peopled not simply with personified beings, but by spiritual force (*mmuo*) itself: which is not always distinguishable as "supernatural," but is "natural" in only a slightly different manner from the way the term "natural" might be applied to, say, the growth of the yam crop. "Gods" also connotes beings which are definitely personalized, and does not include completely spiritual force existing in itself. (See Evans-Pritchard, 1965, 120 and passim.)

The foregoing remarks are not meant to suggest that there is no "religion" in Nsukka, nor that religious belief and ritual are chaotic there. It can help understanding if one observes that to Igbo all things and events which utilize or expend energy in any manner are somehow empowered by what might be called an ultimate energy-source. Second, not all things which utilize or expend energy can be directly witnessed through the senses, but are mentally constructed as empirical results of observed sense happenings. For example, the wind obviously has power, but it cannot be seen, even though it can be felt and its effects heard. A tree, on the other hand, can be seen and touched but not heard. Some beings, furthermore, appear to possess more power than others: the leopard obviously has far more power than does a man, although on certain occasions man's power can overcome that of the leopard—mentality itself exists and empowers a person, yet it is removed from sensations. Out of the myriad experiences of observed reality thus arises a very basic notion: the strongest power is that which empowers other things which have and manifest powers, and that power clearly is not simply a physical force, although it manifests itself most commonly by means of physical beings and actions.

This force or power—one may call it *vital force* or *dynamic force* or *spiritual power*—possesses, in Nsukka thought, several characteristics. Most important, it can be manipulated by those who know the means of manipulating it, and it can empower an object. The making of medicine is the empowering of an object. It radiates waves of force, as it were, in all directions from itself, so many sacrifices are laid at crossroads, and some of the most potent of all medicines are located deep inside sacred groves upon the precincts of which villagers will not dare intrude. Force is contagious and extremely dangerous: medicine meant to serve one purpose can become a source of evil to anyone who even "inadvertently" interferes with it. Force appears also to vitalize or empower various beings which are more or less personalized: the *arua* (lit., "spears") which represent the dynamism of the ancestors although not the ancestors as persons; the High God, *Ezechitoke* ("Chief-Creator-Male" who is also known more commonly as *Chukwu*) (see Talbot, 1926, II:43 on *Eze Chite Okike*), who is considered much too vast and powerful to be very personalized but who is nonetheless worshipped regularly and is not nearly so distant as some writers have argued; the *alusi* "something dangerous spoken": i.e., that which, when it speaks, manifests great power), which are non-familial and aggressive spiritual beings; *Ane*, the deified Earth; the *mmuo* which are spirits in general, or ghosts, or the risen dead, according to context; the *ndichie* ("group who return") or spiritualized forefathers, including the *nna* ("fathers"); assorted other spiritual beings, and certain special classes of human beings such as diviners, blacksmiths (who are believed to have magical powers), medicine makers, sorcerers, and shrine priests.

The term "religion" as I will use it refers to the various activities (including beliefs) having to do with the manipulation or avoidance of spiritual force—usually personified in the form of one of the numerous spiritual entities or beings. In rural Nsukka a nice dichotomy between "natural" and "supernatural" does not seem to exist, although the people do make common sense distinctions. Thus one distinguishes clearly between the *nna* or forefathers and the *ndigbo* or "first men, ancestors of ancient times," between the ordinary world and the land of the spirits, or between a calabash which is "medicine" (*ogwu*) and a calabash which is merely a dried gourd. "Religion" and ritual activity associated with it make up only a small part of the daily life of the Nsukka borderland traditionalist, although beliefs and events related at least obliquely to religious behavior and needs pervade his life: if nothing else, he is always aware of them with one part of his mental faculties. He is not a terrorized individual by any means, but he lives in a world inhabited by forces, many of them easier avoided than gotten rid of, better fed regularly than appeased when angry. He can be called, then, a practitioner of his religion in the truest sense of the word, but besides this he is a resident of a village and of a world in which other forces besides spiritual ones affect him. The remainder of this study is therefore focused upon the interplay of some of those political and social control forces with religious activities.

PART ONE

Background: History & Social Structures

1. The Nsukka–Igala Borderland

TOPOGRAPHICALLY, Nsukka is characterized by a central plateau rising approximately 1500 feet above sea level, referred to as the Nsukka Escarpment, running from the extreme south of the Division to the northeast (which was also one of the main trade routes: *uzigbo*, "road of the Igbo"), the slope rising gradually from the Anambra River plain in the west and falling off sharply into scattered hills in the east. The terrain varies from densely forested or intensively cultivated valley and bottom lands rich in oil palm, raffia, plantain, and tuberous food crops under hoe cultivation, to upland savannah where a limited amount of grain cultivation is carried on, as well as even more limited pastoral activity, the livestock consisting mainly of the dwarf cattle called *efi*. The majority of the people, as one would expect, are engaged in subsistence agriculture, with fewer than ten per cent of the population employed in such activities as trade, smithing, and other non-agricultural livelihoods.

Nsukka Division is the fourth largest and northernmost administrative division of formerly Eastern Nigeria and Igboland, the last area of Igboland to be effectively conquered and occupied by the British (in 1921, Nsukka town was made a divisional headquarters —see Abangwu, 1960:32). Approximately one hundred miles long by forty miles wide, it encompasses important trade routes which have increased contacts between Nsukka Igbo and other peoples to the north, east and west (see Map I: *Igala and Nsukka Districts*). To the west and north of Nsukka lies Igala country; to the north, northeast, and east, Idoma. Non-Igbo groups also are residents of Nsukka District, aside from the "Igbo" descendants of Igala shrine priests installed after the Igala conquests of the area: at Eteh in the north (pop. 13000) and in the Anambra valley (pop. 10000) the people are mostly Igala. The Igbo population of the Division, approximately 500,000 or 350 per square mile (Census, 1953) falls into several groups or clusters of villages. The eastern sector consists of the Uzo-Agu group, which generally does not concern this study; similar is the Igbodo group in southern Nsukka. Much more important for our purposes are the westerly group of Uzo-Uwani, which as I mentioned consists of some Igala settlements although it is largely Igbo; and the important central and northern group of villages clustered about Nsukka town, from Opi in the south to Enugu-Ezike in the north, and from Edim in the west to Obolo in the east—the group known as Igbo-Omabe (compare Talbot, 1926, IV:39).

The actual borderland people living on either side of the frontier, but especially those of the Nsukka borderland on the "Igbo" side, overlap socially and culturally (although not politically) in so many ways that it is difficult to isolate any one group and discuss it without reference to the others. Important cultural groups nevertheless exist, and it is to these that we must look for ethnic configurations illustrating the area's past.

The Igbo

Igbo in general are sedentary hoe-culture agrarian peoples numbering perhaps six million and inhabiting the area now referred to as the East Central State of Nigeria, although Igbo are also numerous in other areas, particularly in the Mid-Western, Rivers, and South-Eastern States. Their general population density is 200–300, although this figure is deceptive as averages often are, for some areas of Igboland are unoccupied badlands, so that higher population density results in occupied areas than this number indicates. Such is the case in Okigwi, for example, and in Nsukka itself. (See Forde and Jones, 1950:10–11.) Igbo societies are typically acephalous segmentary units, usually no larger than a village group, and there seems to have been no broader organization in their history (but consult Ottenberg, 1958). Igbo language in general is fairly unified at least in the expression of basic ideas, although it has several dialects which are not mutually intelligible except for such basics (see Armstrong, 1967: 1–6).

According to the Igbo historian, Dr. Modilim Achufusi, in an address on the origins of the Igbo to the Historical Society of Nigeria in December, 1963, the Igbo people possibly migrated to their present locale in eastern Nigeria from the area about Lake Chad during the first millennium after Christ, having become relatively settled well before 1500. This is the older theory of origins, which is not so widely held as hitherto. According to this notion, the Igbo of Awka and Orlu were among the earliest migrants, along with Cross River groups eastwards, and the northeastern Igbo of Abakaliki and Afikpo possibly later.

Uchendu, on the other hand, citing more recent theory, holds that the belt of Igboland formed by Owerri, Awka, Orlu, and Okigwi Divisions constitutes a nuclear area from which there was early migration into the Nsukka-Udi highlands in the north and into Ikwerri, Etche, Asa, and Ndokki in the south. There are also traditions of peoples who migrated into Igboland: the Umunri, Nzam, and Anam, who show traits of Igala and Bini culture; and the Onitsha and Oguta groups who claim affinity with the Bini (Uchendu, 1965:3). The northern Nsukka groups were possibly originally non-Igbo or transitional groups who became Igbonized, for as we shall see, while Okpoto were moving southward toward Nsukka under the pressures of other peoples north of them, it is very likely that, at the same general time, Igbo groups were expanding northwards into the same area.

Ukpabi (1965:27) argues that the high population density in northeastern Nsukka might result from refugees from the Igala and Okpoto areas in the 19th century who moved southward because of Fulani pressures from the north and northwest of Igala, although actual Igala and Okpoto migrants were relatively few. Enugu-Ezike, he believed, was a center of dispersal of Igbo peoples. From the lower Anambra valley and the area between Onitsha and Awka came direct influences of and perhaps even some colonization by Umunri peoples.

The borderland with which we are concerned was not simply an Igbo-Igala contact area, for Igbo are not a neatly homogeneous people; the Nsukka Igbo especially have derived from and have been influenced by other peoples, including the Aro Chuku slave traders and the Umunri (See Map II). As Cohen and Middleton have said, "ethnic units as clearcut entities are sociological abstractions from situations that very often, especially in Africa, involve multiethnicity both traditionally and in the contemporary setting" (1970:9). The aboriginal peoples of Nsukka and their exact culture are unknown to us, but it seems most likely that they were Igbo-like with segmentary societies rather than Okpoto-like with semi-centralized societies, for all the borderland traditions—of Igbo clans and of Igala-Okpoto clans—refer to the traditionally Igbo clans as the "senior" or "eldest." This of course may only mean that of these two groups the Igbo arrived at that locale earlier than the Igala, not necessarily that the Igbo were the aboriginal people there.

The term Igbo itself gives us no useful clues to the origin of these peoples. Ìgbò (older spelling: Ibo) refers to the language spoken by ńdÌgbò ("the Igbo people") who claim to be descended from their own ńdìgbó ("group of old ones") or forefathers. The 1841 commissioners wrote that "we ascertained that the name Ibu belongs to a large tract of country lying on both sides of the Niger, but it is more extensive to the eastward of it, and containing possibly many independent tribes" (1841 Expedition, I:233), which gives us little help. Jeffreys said that, to the Yoruba and Umunri people, the Igbo were considered simply people of the forest (Jeffreys, 1946:88; 1956:127; and see Horton, 1868: Chapter 13). Meek wrote that "among the Igala, neighbours of the Ibo, the word for slave is onigbo (oni=person)" (Meek, 1937:1; see also Nigeria, 1957:275; and Forde and Jones, 1950:9). The Igala word for slave is adu, as distinct from one, a freeborn person; onigbo in Igala means "an Igbo person."

Meek's interpretation reflects a bit of the tribal antagonism which sometimes exists on the two sides of such a frontier. Talbot similarly argued that to the Asaba Ika and Sobo the word *Ibo* means "slave" (1926, II:404; see also Green, 1947:6). *Igbo* seems to refer to people of the forest, in their own classificatory scheme, for it is common although not universal to hear Igbo make the distinction between *ndigbo*, the Igbo people ("of the interior" or "forest" is implied) and *ndolu*, "the waterside people." Regardless, most Igbo traditionally referred to themselves regionally (and quite narrowly) or according to kinship ties, rather than tribally or linguistically.

Because typically Igbo-speaking peoples possess no centralized government but rather gerontocratic village or village-group autonomy, there are few origin legends except in Nsukka which are shared by more than a village group. Origin legends in general deal with the founder of the particular village or clan, this First Man invariably having lived in *mgbe* (*igbwe*) *ndichie* ("time of the ancestors"). Usually, it is said, "He came from the land of the earth spirits" or "He came from the sky." The strong emphasis given in traditional rural Igbo life to reincarnation within the family line helps to explain the relative disinterest in history. The present becomes more important than the past or the future when it is repeated throughout time. So just as one does not overemphasize last year's yam crop, but concentrates upon consumption of this year's crop, one similarly de-emphasizes the historical past in favor of the present.

Important for understanding the mixed population and history of the Nsukka borderland area, nevertheless, is the character Omeppa, who appears in several Igala, Idoma, and northern Igbo legends. During the wars between the Jukun and the Apa, who were fleeing from them perhaps in the 18th century, the Apa chief's son, Ayegba om'Idoko (later founder of the present Idah Igala dynasty), fled to Awulu Market near Ankpa in the land of the Okpoto, whose chief was Omeppa, a man influential among the Nsukka Igbo (see Seton, 1928:270). This chief is the mythicized founding father of Nsukka peoples, and is referred to as Ezuugwu Owuru ("famous chief of Awulu") and by other related honorifics. Omeppa received the title, *ashadu* (referring to Igala kingmakers) from Ayegba, and in turn called Ayegba, *attah*, which is the title of the king of all Igala (see Temple, 1965:147; Boston, 1969:30). Thus a close link was established between Igala and Okpoto, who already were linked by many ties with the borderland Igbo.

Whether of varying stock or not, of course, the dominant peoples of Nsukka seem to have been aboriginal Igbo, despite the many influences upon them from various directions.[1] Certain special groups of Igbo people should be mentioned in connection with these influences. Among these are the Onitsha and the Aro. The Onitsha have a monarchial government possibly reflecting Umunri influence and resulting also from colonization by Bini from the Benin Empire about 1630 A.D., according to Dike (1956:25–26). Egharevba, however (1960:30), citing Benin tradition, places the time of founding the Onitsha colony during the reign of Esigie (1504–1550). These colonists, interestingly, bypassed the Asaba area of midwestern Nigeria to gain control over or at least to establish their initial colony in the trade center of Onitsha, thus blocking Umunri expansion—real or imagined—westwards (see Thomas, 1914, IV:8). Perhaps the hostility of the western Igbo, rather than worries of Umunri expansion, influenced the founding of the Onitsha colony, for Benin tradition tells of much warfare with western Igbo. Like Umunri, if they originally were not Igbo (a possibility, for *ngwa onye igbo*, "son of an Igbo," is a term of contempt among Onitsha), the Onitsha became Igbonized, retaining mainly their original form of monarchial government.

Another southern influence upon Nsukka came from the Igbo of Aro Chuku in the Cross River country of Bende Division. The Aro Chuku (*aro*, "spear" [of] *Chukwu*, "God") possessed an influential oracle shrine called *Ibini Ukpabe* or "the long juju." As shrine agents and astute traders, Aro traveled and traded extensively in Igbo and Ibibioland, specializing in the acquisition of slaves, and

1. The name *Nsukka* further suggests such influences: from *nsu* ("stammer") and *ka* ("like those who"), it means: "People who speak like strangers." Alternately it is *Nsoka* ("what follows discussion is better than. . ." i.e., warfare) and *Nsuka* ("those who came later," referring to later migrants into this area).

establishing colonies (Wood, 1959:122–123). Anene, following Ottenberg's study of intergroup relationships and Igbo oracles (1958:299–307), writes that "trade routes dominated by the Aro radiated in all directions, running northwards to the Ibo of the North and Ida, north-eastwards to Obubra, south-eastwards to Itu, southwards through Aba to the coast, and westwards through Awka to Onitsha and Oguta (1966:16, 17–18). Reflecting rather outdated diffusionist theories based upon notions of culture supremacy (i.e., those cultures with kingship being considered superior to those governed gerontocratically), Margery Perham wrote that

> The Aro-Chuku priesthood, which spread its influence like tentacles from the north through the greater part of Iboland, reaching even to the coast, may have derived its dominating conception from still farther north, though it seems that to-day the Aro are indistinguishable from the other Ibo except that they are said to show superior intelligence (1937:230).

G. T. Basden (1938:251) argued for the importance of Nri over Aro Chuku, particularly in relation to the spread of cults and largely for diffusionist sentiments similar to those expressed by Perham: "Spiritual domination in those days [two generations past] emanated from Nri *not* Aro-Chuku."

Judging from the traditions, it seems that "spiritual domination" or diffusion was equally ineffective in Nsukka whether from Aro Chuku or Umunri, although institutions and people of both groups certainly affected our area. Ottenberg indicates that the Aro influence reached Eha Amufu in southeastern Nsukka, and Aro trade routes connected with the Nike-Ogurugu-Idah routes, but strong Aro influence certainly did not extend to the borderland area (see Ottenberg, 1958:300–307). In the 19th century Aro traders made treaties with a number of relatively well known Nsukka leaders. Among these were Odo Nwokoro of Ukehe in the south, who was named warrant chief by the British in 1912; Ugwu Manu of Aku (warranted in 1912 also), which is on the *uzigbo* ("road of the Igbo"—a north-south communication route) from Ukehe to Nkpologu, a very important center of Igala influence; *Attama* Eze Ugwu Oye of

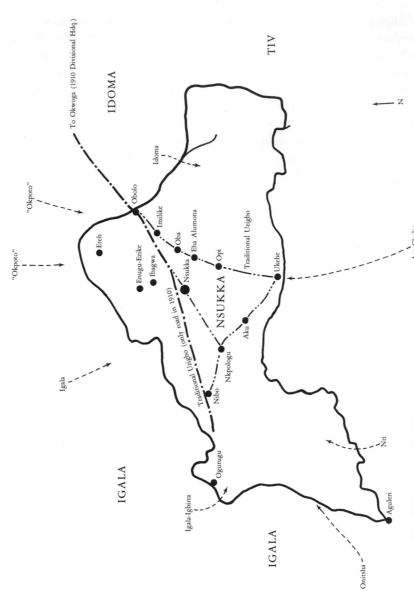

MAP II. *Alien Influences on Nsukka*

Eholumona, which is on the road from Ukehe northward; and Ohabuenyi Ugwu Aboyi of Obolo, much farther north on the same road and at the junction of the northbound route into Idoma country and the northwest route to Enugu-Ezike and Igala-Okpoto country (see Map II: *Alien Influences on Nsukka*; consult Abangwu, 1960:29, 42–43).

The Umunri

Umunri is derived from *umu*, "children of" and *Nri*, the eldest son of the First Man, *Eri*, who came from the sky; thus it means "the Nri people." Modilim Achufusi argues to the non-Igbo origin of the Umunri, whose government (divine monarchy) certainly differed from that of nuclear Igbo. Thurston Shaw's tentative dating of the Igbo-Ukwu complex, particularly of what appears to have been the grave of a divine king or a priest-chief, places these or closely related people in the general area of Onitsha-Awka about 840 A.D. (1966:21). In another place Shaw said, "It is inviting to associate the finds at Igbo-Ukwu with the institution of *Eze Nri*, the priest-king of the Umueri clan of the Ibos . . ." (1967:72), but he is cautious about making any definite connection. Political differentiation of the Umunri continued until recent times even though they became otherwise Igbonized. Boston (1963) has argued rightly, though, that the Umunri complex could be explained not by diffusion or by migration but by invention within Igbo groups (see also Lewis, 1967:32, on the dangers of diffusionist interpretations).

There have been many contacts between the Umunri and the Nsukkans, but their influence has not been everywhere very strong. C. K. Meek considered Umunri influence to have been greater than it probably was:

> At Niebo the first Eze was the person who brought the Agbala cult from Nri, and at Nsukka the first (and the only real Eze Nsukka ever had) was the person who brought from Nri the iron staff which is the symbol of the Ezoguda cult. At Eha

Alumona it is said that Ezokpaka, who introduced the cult of Ezqwele from Nri and, like Ezoguda of Nsukka, was a son of the Eze Nri, was made Eze of half the town of Eha Alumona (Meek, 1931:5).

Umunri influence in other parts of Igboland has also been emphasized.

Blacksmiths and other craftsmen from Awka, as well as Umunri medicine makers, traveled extensively as smiths, doctors, purveyors of cults, circumcisers, and agents of the Awka oracle called *Agbala* (see Meek, 1937:18). Jordan, quoting Father Duhaze's notes of his trek in 1906–1907, wrote that

> The religious influence of Nri once extended over the whole Ibo country. The Nris were the high priests of the idols, and from their hands the chiefs loved to receive the insignia of office. They regulated even the building of huts for fetishes (Jordan, 1949:42).

Much more recently, J. S. Boston in explaining the Nri-Awka historical project said that Nri-Awka is the

> centre of the ikenga cult, which can usefully be studied in relation to the ideas underlying ancestor worship and the cult of personal spirits (*chi*). When this complex has been analysed it can be compared with other less closely connected forms of worship, such as the earth cult and the cults of different nature spirits (*alosi*) and the part they play in the total religious system (Boston; 1963:11).

This too is overstated; so far as Nsukka goes, there is no "system".

The northward migrations of the Umunri bypassed most of northern Nsukka, spreading eastwards from Nibo, which has traditions of having been founded by an Umunri man, Dimaleke, who fled from his homeland to avoid having to undergo *ichi* facial scarifications. Chieftainship—not a typically Igbo institution—south of Opi and in the area of Nibo was derived largely from the Umunri, where it does not have its origin in more recent British colonial warrants, although in Eholumona there is one tradition (among others contrary to it) that chieftainship came from the Umunri (see Ukpabi, 1965:26–28, 35). Ugwu argues that the more southerly areas of Nsukka were outside the Igala influence and thus were mostly influenced by Nkanu and Umunri, and (repeating Meek) says that even Nsukka town itself was directly affected by the Umunri (Ugwu, 1964:13). This contention is supported by my own findings among Nsukka villages, particularly in Ihe-Nsukka (see Chapter Five below).

Some Umunri seemed to have gotten deeper into the borderland than Nsukka town. I have written at length elsewhere on this topic (Shelton, 1965), so there is no point in repeating, although I might here add a few further points about Umunri influence in the borderland. One village, Umu Mkpume of Oba, claims that the chief forefathers of both clans were *nshie*, the word for Umunri in the borderland. The First Man of Ohebe, another village in the Oba complex, was the medicine maker who brought the *alusi* named Amanye. Saluted as "leopard," a common Igala and Idoma praise title, although here in Igbo language, he carried the name Eze Ikpoke Eze Nshie ("chief who was called king of Nri" or "chief who speaks as king of Nri"). Special male medicine shrines—*nche onye* and *akwari*—are said to have been installed by the Nshie when they came visiting the area some fifty years ago and met with the tragic circumstances of their visit to the village of their presumed offspring, Umu Mkpume. In Imilikenu is the clan of Umu Ogodo ("in-laws of the past"), itself originally an adopted Okpoto group, which contains one adopted stranger lineage called Umu Nshie ("children of the Nshie"). The present elder of the lineage (1963) is *Attama* Ugwu Egere, who claims that he and his people are nshie descended from Eze Nshie ("chief of the nshie"), who fled from Umu Mkpume that fateful night some fifty years ago and apparently gained refuge in Imilike, traditionally the enemy of the Oba people. Attama Ugwu informed me that he used the title *attama* because his father had used it, but that his "proper" title was *Eze Ike* ("strong leader"), a more distinctly Igbo title than *attama*, which in the borderland is almost always associated with Igala shrine priests. He traces his ancestry as follows:

Eze Nshie, who was given refuge in Imilikenu.
Ugwuoke Nzeza, his son.
Okenya Onyishi, son of Ugwuoke.
Ogbonna Okenya, a collateral male relative of Okenya.
Eze Ike, the present Headman.

This lineage possesses the main *ofo* tree in Imilikenu, and its members consider themselves to be "brothers" to the people of Umu Mkpume, who according to them and most people in Oba also descend from the Nshie.

In Eholumona there is a shrine to the old sacred tree (*ofo*) of the chief of the Nshie (*Okpaka Ezenshie*), and in a large number of villages there is wide agreement that Nshie people were the forefathers of the two clans of Umu Mkpume and the one adopted lineage in Imilikenu. Accordingly, references are made to the Nshie as powerful medicine makers in prayers to the tutelary spirits throughout much of Oba. There are, then, good reasons to believe that in part of the Nsukka borderland at least there was considerable influence from Nri.

The *attamas* of the two clans of Umu Mkpume, moreover, unlike *attamas* elsewhere in the borderland, steadfastly refuse to consider their origins to have been Igala or Idoma, although both of them claim that most of the other *attamas* in the area are the direct male descendants of Igala. When I attempted to pursue this, and asked why they did not then refer to themselves as *Eze* Mkpume and *Eze* Iyi Akpala—the more typically nuclear Igbo titles for shrine priests —they informed me that their fathers had taught them that their title was *attama*. A dead end here, accordingly; neither of these men knew that a class of Umunri were referred to as *adama*, and when I pointed this out to them they said I must be in error, for *attama* was a shrine priest title which came from the Igala.

Lack of millet prohibition also may support some of the claims of Umunri origin made by some borderland villages. The people of Umu Mkpume have no taboos against the consumption of millet (Igala: *okodu*, which is *Pennisetum* or bulrush millet), but consume it with gusto, to the general horror of many of the borderland people.

Most shrine priests and many ordinary people of the borderland maintain a taboo against the eating of millet or the drinking of millet beer, considering the grain to have a powerful antagonistic spirit because of those with whom it was originally linked—the Fulani. Usually it is not referred to as *enene*, its Igbo term, nor by its Igala term, *okodu*, but by the circumlocutory, *ekum eha* ("not to call its name"). The argument is that the *attamas* and people avoid consuming millet because the *alusi* will bring sickness and death upon them; thus it is associated with *alusi* hostility, and its name is not called lest one thereby also call the *alusi*.

This prohibition is, however, very limited. Samuel Crowther reported large farms of guinea corn in the vicinity of Idah (Schön, 1842:291, 295) and said that the northern Muslims abhorred guinea-corn beer even though they drank other beer and liquor (328). Schön (1842:143, 217), however, pointed out the abundance of guinea corn at Muye above the confluence and the popularity of guinea corn beer at the Model Farm site near the confluence. Seton (1929:42) said that the Igala claim millet was given to them by God. But apparently such prohibitions, whether very old or not, are widespread in the borderland—definitely among those holding the *ama* title; and the people of Umu Mkpume and others claiming Nshie ancestry do not follow the taboo at all, and openly speak against it, perhaps in their overall reaction to Igala political control in most villages.

Although references are made to the Nshie in general in ancestral prayers in several borderland villages, there appears to be no special listing of forefathers believed to have been Nshie. Indeed, they are referred to probably because the Umunri are so widely known as medicine men. As ancestors of Umu Mkpume and other such groups, however, they are no more personally identified than the *arua*, all objective details of their persons (if any ever existed) having become lost over the generations. It is unlikely, furthermore, that such groups were colonies of Umunri, for village elders consistently argue that *arua* ancestral forces existed before the Nshie came. Whatever the notions of origin or degree of likeness they may believe they possess with the Nshie, the fact remains that aside from their not observing the millet taboo the people of Umu Mkpume do not differ either in social organization or ritual and ceremonial practices from their neighbors in the borderland, although they do manifest the problem of the name shift which has been occurring for the past few years and which is a direct result of Igala occupation. The worship of *alusi* spirits, in the control of the shrine priests who were Igala and Idoma, like the worship of ancestors and *arua*, moreover, do not show marked differences between those villages who claim Nshie ancestry and those which claim Igala or Igbo ancestry.

The spread of various titles further indicates the demographic complexity of Igboland in general as well as the Nsukka borderland. Titles among Igbo people are acquired by one's joining a title society, which normally requires a large outlay of money and goods for payment and feasting of the existing title holders. The title confers on the holder special status, and sometimes privileges, but requires of him particular behavior—consisting of some proscribed behavior or taboo as well as certain exemplary demeanor—prescribed by custom. Igbo titles are not inherited, so they are distinct from many Igala and even Umunri titles, which are inherited. In the borderland there are both inherited and voluntarily-acquired titles, some of them shared by other Igbo groups, others shared by non-Igbo groups to the north and west, and still others which use Igbo terms but which have non-Igbo application. Epelle writes that

> The title *Eze-Nri* is common in Nri in Awka Division. This title goes back to the last century. Many Igbos had claimed Nri town, the home of a priestly cult, as their ancestral home. A representative of the *Eze-Nri* was usually present during the taking of an Ozo title [*Ozo* is not, however, an important title of northern Nsukka]. A similar title is that of the *Eze-Aro*—the supreme head of Aro Chuku, an area composed of nineteen villages. Each village is ruled by a chief and the *Eze-Aro* is saluted as *Mazi*.
>
> Of the three most important chieftaincy titles in Igbo land *two* (the Ndichie and the Ndiama) are foreign—the former deriving from Benin and the latter from Idah (Epelle, 1966:5).

Neither *Eze-Aro* nor *Mazi* are used in northern Nsukka; and *Ndichie* is used in its primary meaning as "returners" or "ancestors," rather than in its Onitsha meaning as holders of a title. *Ndiama*, on the other hand, deriving from Igala, is understood, for the *ama* title is common in the borderland. Indeed, influence upon the borderland Igbo was far more strongly Igala and Idoma than it was Umunri or Aro.

The Igala

What we call Igala at present are a people compounded of several groups whose social organization and value systems are generally similar and who recognize the one paramount king, the *attah* (literally, "father"), at Idah as their political ruler.

Numbering about 500,000, the Igala inhabit the area of Kwara State south of the Benue River and east of the Niger in an area of about 5000 square miles, in what was formerly Kabba Province of Northern Nigeria. On the east they are bordered by the Idoma, and on the south by the Nsukka Igbo; because Igala Division extends southward between the Niger and Anambra Rivers, the Igala border the Igbo along the Anambra as far south as Ogurugu, the base from which Onojo Ogboni invaded and conquered Nsukka. Consequently, much of the northern and western borders of Igbo-dominated Nsukka Division of East-Central State touch Igala country. On the south the Igala hegemony diminishes in the Anambra River forests, but it is through this region—into which Umunri influence extends northwards—that Igala and Umunri may be geographically connected (see Jeffreys, 1960:54).

The present day Igala appear to be a mixture of several peoples who are generally Igalicized, although my own studies of the "Igala" from Ankpa to Ogurugu indicate that the Igala melting pot is still extremely lumpy. A major group of people—possibly the aboriginal "Igala" and actually an offshoot of the Idoma people—who are largely although not completely absorbed are the Okpoto peoples speaking the Igumale and Orukpa dialects of Idoma who inhabit the eastern part of Igala, their tribal area extending southward well south of Ete District of Nsukka Division (see Command 505:114). Almost all accounts agree that the people native to the area now referred to as Igala were the Okpoto. In some cases their language is referred to as Igala, and in other instances it is said that Igala or Ogala was the name of their chief. It is probable that the western influence on Idah is mainly Bini (see Boston, 1962:373; 1968:7; Sieber, 1965:80), but other groups probably influenced the interior regions. During the vague and indefinite predynastic time (possibly between the 15th and 17th centuries) the Hausa of Zazzau also made their presence felt in Igala country, mainly in response to demographic and military pressures of the Zaria region to the north and the spread of the powerful Jukun Kororofa Empire in the northeast. Other peoples, too, came into Igala country—small groups fleeing the Jukun, and possibly some Jukun themselves, in successive waves of people moving down the Benue River well into the 19th century (see Clifford, 1936; Jeffreys, 1951:91; Meek, 1931:21, 141). During this period, of course, the aboriginal Igala were being conquered, and while some of them were assimilating their conquerors, others were responding to the demographic pressures on the north and west by moving southward and eastward into the Igbo-occupied Nsukka area, whose people even then perhaps consisted mostly of Igbo and some other peoples, possibly aboriginal, in the process of being Igbonized.

Many cultural modifications point up the overall influence of the Igala upon the Nsukka borderland:

> In many settlements the lineages have Igala names, while many also have an *Ama* title system, derived from Igala, as opposed to the *Ozo* system. They also have *Odo* and *Amaba* "dodo" cults in addition to, or instead of, *Mmo* dances. Other Igala elements are the weaving of cotton cloth, and the use of circular baskets or calabash basins in contrast to the typical rectangular basket of the Ibo and Ibibio (Forde and Jones, 1950:35).

Why such modifications developed is in part the subject of the following chapter.

2. Onojo Ogboni, the Conquest of Nsukka, and Later Borderland History

FROM THE TIME of Ayegba onward (possibly 17th century), the Igala became steadily more powerful, extending their tribute-collecting and slave-gathering empire (often by means of the spread of Igala control over trade centers and routes) until the great *jihad* of the Fulani during the 19th century. During the early and generally pre-dynastic period the pressures of Jukun Kororofa imperialism in the upper Benue River valley pushed other groups southwestward while the similar spread of Hausa empires pushed even more groups directly southward. In the meantime, the steadily developing Benin Empire kept populations from moving in too great numbers into the area southwest of the Niger-Benue confluence. These factors, along with control of the confluence perhaps were the more important reasons for the settling at Idah of several migrant groups, and the consequent displacement of aboriginal "Igala" or Okpoto peoples. These Okpoto moved in the only direction they had open to them: eastward and southward, and they very possibly account for some of the mixed Igbo and "Igala" population of the Nsukka borderland.

The Igala conquests of Nsukka, however, were military as well as the result of migration. Most accounts (see Appendix I) consistently point out the existence of actual war between the Igala and various Nsukka villages, and the long-standing trade between Igala and Nsukka groups particularly in horses from the north and slaves from the south. They also emphasize two personalities: a real Idah Igala hero named Onojo Ogboni who was probably one of the later conquerors of Nsukka; and the somewhat more legendary Okpoto mythical founder of Nsukka, Omeppa.

Onojo Ogboni and the Conquest of Nsukka

Despite numerous embellishments and mythification, Onojo Ogboni appears to have been a real war leader, an Igala probably related by uterine ties to the ruling family at Idah yet either not able or not willing to reside there. The constant references in all accounts to his struggle against "heaven" (the gods) and "earth" (the ancestors) suggests his opposition to custom. Baikie remarked that "not far from Ada-mugu is a town named Onuja, which was built by the son of a former Atta, who was compelled to leave Idda, being too fond of thinking and acting for himself" (1856: 291).

From Ogurugu he led his armies eastward in wars of conquest continuing Igala imperial expansion which probably intended to secure trade routes at the expense of the Aro Chuku traders rather than to colonize the area with actual Igala settlers. In the northern borderland there was also fighting among the more mixed populations (Igbo and Okpoto) against Idah Igala, largely for the same reasons. As we have seen, population pressures had long caused Okpoto peoples to move southward and eastward at the same time similar although not identical forces (perhaps population growth rather than confrontation with alien groups) were causing Igbo to move northward and westward.

Ukpabi reminds us that the Igala Empire was in its golden age in the 18th and early 19th century, and says that

In attempting to determine when the Igala soldiers invaded Nsukka and built their fortifications which stretch from the north (around Ete) of the Nsukka-Udi scarp down to Opi and then to Anambra, it is only natural to assume that this invasion which was so effective as to leave its mark on the culture and history of Nsukka must have taken place in the hey-day of the Igala Empire when the Attah's word was law and his soldiers could be sent to the limits of the Empire on wars of conquest.

One such conqueror, Onu Ojo Ogbonyi, the son of the Attah of Igala, after devastating the Okpoto territory, moved southwards and after establishing his base at Ogurugu, invaded Nsukka and penetrated as far as Opi (Ukpabi, 1965:29; compare Ugwu, 1958:12).

He goes on to say that like the Umunri, Onojo Ogboni did not invade the eastern plain of the Nsukka-Udi ridge, but remained at outposts on the ridge itself. For example, Inenyi Ogugu, an Igala war leader of the late 18th century, made Opi his base of operations (Ukpabi, 1965:31).

Floyd places the time of conquest before the Fulani *jihad*. Speaking of terraced hillsides in Nsukka, he says that

the originators of the terraces were probably Igala settlers who, under the leadership of successive chiefs or "Atas," invaded and colonized this area of the plateau from the vicinity of Idah, in the second half of the eighteenth century (Floyd, 1965:60).

He fails to show why the terracing of the hillsides is Igala rather than Igbo, but he is probably close to the truth in his time reference, although one suspects that the "conquest" and settlement of Igala agents continued for quite a long while, even into the middle 19th century.

In response to my queries about the general conquest of Nsukka villages by the Igala, the gathered elders at Ejigbo Village near Ankpa explained:

At first, in the olden times, Igala would take horses down to Nsukka and sell them to the Igbo for slaves, and then our fathers would sell the slaves to river people at Idah, who would take them down the river to *Beke* [i.e, White Man—white slave traders at the seacoast]. Horses were ridden and taken from

Ankpa to Nsukka and Ibagwa. The Igbo wanted the horses for sacrifices to their spirits. During that early trading some Igala lived near Nsukka and Ibagwa, and they built their own compounds to protect themselves and their women from the Igbo.

On another occasion the elders said:

Igala and Igbo first came together at a place called Eteh, near Nsukka, north of Enugu-Ezike. In the olden times the Igala were very strong warriors, so the Igbo sometimes still fear us, although this is now all past, because we live in peace. The Igala had bows and arrows and special spears which were very good for war, and most important, they had horses and they had medicine. Our fathers had special war uniforms made of ordinary cloth [ili] made magical with a medicine called echi, so their enemies could not see them, and thought they were spirits [ambekwu: ancestral spirits]. In those olden days the Igbo had only cutlasses, which they obtained from the Ibibio who live south of them.

At first the Igala had their own special war medicine [ogwugwu], but when they joined with the Yoruba who hunted with them, the Igala learned more medicine from them, and in turn they gave some of their secrets to their Yoruba friends. This started with Egbele Ejuona whose husband was Yoruba.

There were many forts built in those days, and they used to be all over Igala. All Igala and Igbo know about these, which were built so that the Igala chiefs could be protected from enemies. This kind of construction came from the Jukun people originally. That fort at Nsukka was built by Igbo as a place for them to protect their chiefs from enemies.

This account does not clarify matters of time except for the details of the arms: the Igala with spears, bows and arrows, and tip-poison, the Igbo presumably armed only with cutlasses. This is supported by the following Igbo account. Near Nsukka town, on the grounds of the University of Nigeria, are the ruins of an old fort, consisting today of little more than a circular (ca. 200 meters diameter) earthen wall, one of eleven forts running from Unadu to Ogurugu probably used by the Igala as slave pens (Hartle, 1967:136). The eldest man of Amuukwa Village of Ihe-Nsukka, named Eleje Nw'Asogwa, said that the name of the place is *okpe'gara,* "the Igala wall."

A long time ago the people from Idah lived in this place. There had been some war with the men from the north, the Igala. They were not all from Idah, for some came from Ogurugu, under the one called *Onoja.* The Igbo had only cutlasses to fight with, so the Igala conquered them. But when they [Igala] left this place, long ago, the walls remained.

My own studies in northern Nsukka indicate that the "factories" (actually forges) for the manufacture of Dane-guns (flintlock muskets) did not become established in the district until about the 1870's, and that guns were extremely scarce in the area before the 1850's. If this is the case, then, the conquests by the Igala must have occurred well before the 1850's. Most likely Igala control over Nsukka villages was gained in successive conquests, and Onojo Ogboni has attained renown chiefly because his conquest was among the last.

The Igala brought well developed concepts of political and social hierarchy based upon factors other than personal achievement, which were thus foreign to the Igbo, although not completely unfamiliar. The Igala wished to control the Igbo so that tribute might flow from the people through Igala-appointed chiefs in major population areas (e.g., Enugu-Ezike), but perhaps even more important they wanted to prevent the people from combining effectively (possibly with Aro mercenaries) to wage war against the Igala side of the frontier which would interfere with Igala trade. Accordingly, they installed in the subjugated villages shrine priests with the Igala title, *attama,* who were the major intermediaries between the Igbo villagers and the *alusi* spirits. These *attama* became the major agents of Igala social control.

The installation of chiefs and *attama* by the Igala was doubtless intended to solve the problem of local control. But it has become a truism that the solution of one problem can be the creation of another, and in this instance the installation of chiefship among people without chiefs, and the displacement of Igbo shrine priests by Igala shrine priests, brought repercussions which seriously affected the mixed borderland and northern Igbo culture in general. How the northern borderland Igbo adapted to these and related situations is one of the focal points of this study.

Later Borderland History

The Igala reached the apogee of their power during the 18th and 19th centuries, building much of their wealth and influence upon the control of slave trading centers, their power stretching south to Adamugu (north of Onitsha), east almost to Oturkpo, across the Benue River covering Igbirra country, and across the Niger to encompass Kakanda country (*Nigeria*, 1964). Allen and Thomson suggest that the Igala were not actively involved in the trade:

> In answer to my many inquiries, it could not be elicited that the Eggarahs make inroads on other states for the purpose of taking slaves. They depend more on defensive warfare, but all captives are retained, or sold as slaves (1841 Expedition, I:326).

One way or another, they certainly collected many, for Laird and Oldfield (1837, I) earlier reported having met coastal slave-buyers in Idah itself.

The Fulani *jihad* emanating from Sokoto in the early 19th century, and the widespread extension of Fulani suzerainty in northern Nigeria brought steady and rapid contraction of Igala imperial power in the north and west, causing some peoples hitherto subject to the Igala to switch their tribute payments completely to the Fulani. Dr. McWilliams of the 1841 Expedition wrote that "Gori pays an annual tribute of 360,000 cowries to the Filatah King; and to the Attah of Iddah a mere nominal tribute, being only a horse yearly" (1841 Expedition, II:85). Under the Fulani threat to Igala, the Igbirras at Panda seceded from the Igala Empire, and some Kakanda were driven to the right bank of the Niger while others were forced to submit to the Fulani. Laird in 1837 wrote of the

Felatah raids on Kakanda (Laird and Oldfield, 1837, I: 246–248), and Oldfield reported that the *attah* had informed him that the Felatahs were intent on taking Idah (II: 22, 193, 235). *Attah* Ochejih himself told the commissioners in 1841 that the Fulani had driven the Igala from Adakudu, the Igala colony south of Lokoja (1841 Expedition, I: 300, 368). Angwileh, the country directly across the Niger from Idah, then rebelled against the authority of Idah, and declared themselves henceforth tributary to Benin (I: 307).

Despite the inroads made upon their empire, the Igala of the heartland from Idah to Ankpa suffered little, nor did their self-confidence as a nation of rather warlike and usually successful conquerors diminish. Nevertheless, one can observe decline in the central authority of the Igala Empire from this general time onward (see Ifemesia, 1962: 302). The main cause, of course, was the success of the Fulani conquest: as subject peoples in the west and north either seceded or switched their tribute payments from Igala to Fulani, other peoples in the east were tempted to declare themselves free of the Igala of Idah. Dr. Baikie wrote that in October, 1854, the Igala were warring with rebellious Okpoto, and said that Idah was definitely on the decline (1856: 283–286). During this same period the thirteenth *attah* broke up the *Igala Mela*, the representative body through which important clans of Okpoto people had some influence in Igala government, and this act increased conflicts and resentment in the eastern interior regions. War was still going on against the Igbirra, who were finally defeated during the reign of the fourteenth *attah*. But as Captain F. Byng-Hall wrote,

> The country was, however, over-run at this time by the Agatu, Idoma, Bassa-Komo, and Nge, who were driven out from the lands they were occupying north of the Benue by Nupe raiders, in consequence of the great Filane occupation. The Bassa-Komo came in friendliness, and were at first given land by the Ata, but on receiving reinforcements from their own clan, they made war on the Igara Onu [Chief] of Igga, and, after six months' fighting, established their independence. The Ata was hard pressed for means to continue this constant warfare and, in

return for their services, gave fifty titles to small Chiefs, together with complete independence.

This contributed to the break-up of the kingdom, and when the British occupied the country they found that there was little combination under Oboni, but that it was broken up under a series of small Chiefs, who possessed little authority (Temple, 1965:150).

This breakup of the empire enabled British military patrols to fight a large number of small groups rather than requiring the capitulation of one well organized empire, as had been the case in Goldie's conquest of the Nupe. The Ankpa elders made reference to the coming of the Europeans as follows:

In the time of *Beke* [here referring to William Balfour Baikie, mid-19th century, but usually meaning "European"], some European missionaries came to Idah, just a few of them, to visit the Igala. Later was the time of Lord Lugard of the North, who sent Hausa and Fulani to teach indirect rule to the Igala, and the English came with Fulani, Hausa, Yoruba, and some Nupe soldiers to make war against the Igala. They even came as far as Ankpa and *Ayangba*, which means "Where the People Make War," because the people were fighting among themselves.

In April, 1898, the agent-general, William Wallace, R.N., fought the Igala near Idah (Perham, 1963:384), and British forces moved inland. Lord Lugard noted in his diary that Major A. Festing was on an expedition (May 19, 1898) against the "Ibos of the Anambra Creek with 100 R.N.C. I had to lend them 100 of our men with officers and N.C.O.'s and also 4 extra officers to work Maxims and to help" (Perham, 1963:409). Lugard's first attempt to subdue the most easterly Okpoto and especially the Idoma was a catastrophe, the entire force of 95 officers and men either killed or captured and enslaved (see Geary, 1927:221). In 1903 A. D. C. Boyle and an escort of twenty men were attacked on their way from Idah to the Anambra by the forces of Chief Adukukaiku, who "had closed all the routes in his territory to trade and barred both Hausa and Yoruba adventurers who attempted from Idah to tap the resources of [his] domain" (Anene, 1966:246). The result of this, as the result of the Okpoto-Idoma loss, was a punitive expedition: in the case of the Anambra River "pacification," a military garrison was established at Ogurugu, Onojo Ogboni's old stronghold. About 1910 British patrols first visited Nsukka Division, and in 1914 a military patrol from Okwoga, Idoma District, visited Opi and Ekwegbe (Wilmer, 1965:41). Eleje Nw'Asogwa in 1963 told me: "I was twenty years old when the white men came. Only a few whites, with Hausa soldiers, from the direction of Ibagwa-Ani and then Obukpa. This was about forty years ago [i.e., about 1923. Nsukka actually was made a district headquarters in 1921, so he is referring to a punitive patrol]. They burned Ibagwa and Obukpa. They didn't burn Nsukka."

In 1917 some villages showed hostility toward the advent of British administration and were therefore burned by the district officer and some soldiers. Mr. Aaron, the district officer, gained the name *Otikpogbodo*, "Destroyer of Towns," for such deeds. In 1918 war broke out between the colonialists and Imilike because of a harsh district officer, Arthur Whitman (who was saved from the enraged Igbo villagers by an Igala shrine priest), and the people of Enugu-Ezike in the same year reacted violently to British conquest. In 1918 the influenza fairly effectively ended opposition to British colonialism because of the widespread death it caused in Nsukka (see Abangwu, 1960:33–34). By 1920, then, the Igala and Nsukka Igbo areas were colonialized by the British, and the history of the area takes a different form. With changing social forces resulting from colonialism (e.g., the naming of warrant chiefs in 1912), traditional social control forces in many places atrophied, and new politics resulted in new expressions of ethnic and regional identity.

3. Nsukka Igbo Temporal, Familial, and Spatial Organization

THE NORTHERN Igbo world view is at once exceeding complex in its organization and relatively simple in its categories. The Nsukkan world, like Igbo world-views in general, is one in which extension moves in every direction "into an invisible world filled with spiritual beings of all kinds; the deities of the sky and the earth, the spirit of the local land and river; the dead members of his family waiting, perhaps, to be re-born; evil spirits ready to do him harm, and the spirits of animals. Society is set within this spiritual world, and for its advantage or defence, is ritually linked to it on every side" (Perham, 1937:235).

Most simply, the Igbo world is divided dichotomously into the simple categories of "we" and "they," the "we" virtually always referring to a tightly related consanguineous group extending its membership hesitantly and with numerous serious reservations affinally, usually within a non-exogamous village-group called a "town" in English, and the "they" referring to all other peoples not of the consanguineous familial group, nor of the affinal and "town" groups. Differing from nuclear Igbo, however, the Nsukkans are somewhat ambivalent about ethnic purity of the kin-group, largely because of the admittedly different influences upon them from other peoples (none of the villages in which I worked claims that their ancestors were absolute natives of the area, for example). It is not the usual Nsukka manner to say,

N'anIgbo nine n'eli ji ahube'em ihe deka nkea.
"In the land of the Igbo who eat yam have I never seen thing like that" [i.e., "I have never seen such a thing in the *land of normal human beings*"].

"Normalcy" in such a saying is defined as the Igbo yam-eating custom and, although Nsukka Igbo eat yams as a normal pattern, they are not nearly so isolated from non-Igbo cultures as are the nuclear Igbo of the heartland. Much more inclined are they to say,

akanri kwoo akaekpe.
"Right hand washes left hand" ["The good hand (of the in-group) washes or tolerates and accepts the bad hand (of the outsider)"].

As one result of conquest, some of the more prestigious households had an Igala father and Igbo mothers, and the children avoided some of the divisiveness that would result from a normally Igala patrilineal loyalty by overstressing the idea that

Madu agaire nneya muru.
"A person must not sell mother his who bore him" [i.e., "A man should not give up his own mother, no matter what the reason"].

But this strengthening of uterine descent in reaction to occupation eventually brought further divisiveness.

There is nevertheless a general concept of Nsukka-ness, if one might call it this (preferably borderlandness, an impossible word), for where almost every village has shrine priests descended from Igala occupational personnel whose progeny have become Igbonized without losing their ability in the main to speak and understand Igala or their personal identity as the offspring of what were originally Igala men, and where these shrine priests have become accepted as part and parcel of the rest of the village society, the resultant society tends to have become tolerant of differences in its midst.

Time

The northern Igbo concepts of time (*oge*) are important as the basis for understanding the kinship and household structure of Nsukkan society. As with most rural societies the world over, among the Nsukkans time is classified in several ways related to growth seasons and natural phenomena. The year itself (*aro*) is divided into two seasons: *udummili* ("fullness of water"), the rainy season, and *okochi* ("hot days"), the dry season, which is characterized by the harmattan wind blowing southward from the Sahara Desert. The year begins with the harvest feast of *Ishiji* ("head yam," also called "the new yam festival"). This harvesting of the new yam crop is the renewal of the major food store for the coming year, and is the expression of masculinity, the reassertion of Nsukkan manhood, for the harvest festival celebrates the male ancestors and the renewal of life. During the dry season which follows, while there is abundance of yams, a number of festivals, special rituals, and appearances of secret societies occur, and with the coming of rains once more planting is resumed. From late June until September, sometimes October, is a period of hunger called, simply, "famine": *unwu* (compare Leith-Ross, 1939:92—at Okigwi, this period is from April to July). Yams have been planted by the men, but they are not ready for harvesting, whereas the older crop of yams has been exhausted. At this time, which is not truly a period of great hunger but merely yam hunger, the men eat women's crops which are raised by their wives and daughters, and look forward to the resumption of yam and kokoyam in their diets. This is an important time in the annual life of the borderland farmer, for he is dependent upon women who normally are relatively dependent upon him, and his masculinity at this time is not expressed in his diet, for yam is undoubtedly the crop of men.

Igbo say: *kw'aro, kwa'm* ("As year, so I"—"As the year continues, may I have life"). Annual life flows cyclically in the alternate seasons of dryness and rains, of dormancy and growth. This is the basic pattern of the northern Igbo world view, the model of the universe in which dwell the dead, the living, and the unborn.

Other natural phenomena which lie at the base of Nsukkan time concepts are the cycles of the moon and of the sun. The moon, aside from the growing seasons, is the most important subdivision of the year, setting the pattern for women's menstrual cycles which themselves parallel the ebb and flow of annual life and the seasons in which Earth, *Ane*, who is female, alternately gives forth life and is unproductive. The moon or month itself is divided into seven weeks of four days each. Names of the days of the week also denote the names of markets: *eke, oye* (*ede* in Igala), *afo, nkwo* (*ukwa*). The development of the "big" and "little" weeks is not so common in the borderland as in nuclear Igboland (the "big" week having eight days), although now and then this usage is applied to markets.

Aside from this more or less "natural" time of the Nsukkan world, there is the equally important *ritual time*—a term which I use here to signify the time determination of ceremonial behavior and actual rituals, and "time" which arises from aspects of the belief system which bear directly upon the family structure. Ritual time as the time determination of ceremonies is governed as much by seasons as by other rational determination. Accordingly, harvest festivals occur when the crops are harvested; secret societies for the most part conveniently operate in the dry season when farm labor slacks off and the young men have more time on their hands; and worship of the ancestors, a daily affair, is conducted at dawn before anything else. But ritual time varies from this insofar as in many instances it is governed by the spirits rather than by humans, so it must be determined by divination. For example, what is the proper *time*—aside from that which is regularly scheduled—for sacrifice to particular spirits to whom worship is not regularly directed? The diviner will tell this; no one else can. This sort of ritual time, however, is perhaps less important in relation to family structure than the cyclic pattern of human existence conceived broadly, for time becomes in this an endlessness in which one focuses his temporal attention upon that period between attainment of adulthood and death.

The Family

The first point one must make about descent systems in the border-land is that they are a mass of confusions; although mainly patri-lineal, there are some groups tracing descent through a maternal line, and others tracing descent strictly agnatically and patrilineally. This situation results from the introduction of Igala and Okpoto lineages among the Igbo, Igbo reactions to Igalicization and loss of political and economic control despite their priority on the land, and the eventual partial Igbonization of many Igala.

All this is deep beneath the surface, however, for the simple reason that the reaction to Igala occupation caused not only the shift from typically Igbo patrilineal and agnatic descent to frequent matri-lateral descent reckoning but also an emphasis by Igbo upon Igbo-ness, if you will, so that terms which elsewhere give relatively decent clues to the nature of a kingroup, in the Nsukka borderland are quite deceptive. What at first glance seem to be standard Igbo terms turn out to have variant references; for example, whereas in central Igbo, *umunna* ("the fathers") will encompass one's patrilineage, in much of the borderland the same term refers rather to one's mother's *umunna* rather than to one's own. In a later chapter we will consider in more detail the complications resulting from the introduction of Igala lineages among the Igbo.

The largest family unit in Nsukka consists of the *ukwaarua* ("great *arua*," which are bundles of spears representing the powers of the spiritualized ancestors), an exogamous clan the members of which presumably are descendants of a single male ancestor, usually of EGO's father, but often of EGO's mother's father. Such a unilineal unit possesses an *onyishi* ("head person") who makes daily sacrifices (*igaarua*: "offering to *arua*") for the sake of all the lineages. This unit is sometimes referred to as *etarigba* ("many are joined together"), although this term is more often used to designate villages consisting of more than one exogamous clan.

Ottenberg (1968:28, 78) uses the terms "major patrilineage" and "minor patrilineage," the latter being segments of the former, in reference to Afikpo Igbo. In the Nsukka borderland, family structures differ from this, the *arua* group being different in name and meaning from the lineage. The patrilineage is the next smaller unit, called *umunna* ("Children [of the] Fathers"). They are typically (in Igbo patrilineages as distinct from mixed lineages) the descendants of a son or brother of the founder of the *ukwaarua* and possess an elder and an *ulonna* ("house [of the] fathers") in which the statues representing the lineage forefathers are kept. The compound family and the nuclear family are the units smaller than the lineage.

The essence of the family is blood relationship, all consanguines being referred to as *ikwu* (although often this is used chiefly with mother's people), and falling into two classes from EGO's point of view: the *umunna*, having reference to father's agnates; and the *umune*, which refers to mother's agnates, although is often extended to include all mother's consanguines. *Umunna*, in the typical Igbo situation is the male and dominant group for EGO, and that kin group to which he owes major filial obedience and from which he inherits, whereas the *umune* would be that group with which he would have affective relationships. One is reminded, for instance, of *igba n'ikwunne* ("running to mother's relatives"), the flight of refuge to mother's people when one is in dire straits with one's own patriline. But in the northern Nsukka villages agnation and patrilineality are less well defined. Where alien lineages were founded by Igala shrine priests married to Igbo women, Igbo reckoned descent overtly through the male line (*olokpu* or, more specifically, *omenekele*, Igala "descendants of males," or father's agnates) but covertly through the line of mother's father (EGO's *umune* or mother's *umunna*) in order to maintain Igbo control over Igbo goods and persons. The descent system also at times was simply bilateral (compare Uchendu, 1964:48). In either case, emphasis is placed upon maleness in lineages and upon filiation as the basis of the actual kinship terminology (compare Henderson's study of Onitsha kinship, 1967:20). Blood relationship—real or putative—determines the membership of the family, within which power or force is extremely important, so the males of the family take precedence over the females. The ancestors about whom one talks, furthermore, are male, and even the language often equates old age and strength and goodness and maleness.

This returns us to our definition of time in the borderland. Time as related to the family structure is divisible into three broad categories: the time of the dead, or the past and transcendant (*mgbe ndichie*); the time of the living; and the future, which is partly conceived as the time of the unborn progeny.

1. The Dead and Eldership

Nsukkans believe, like Igbo in general, that the dead continue to exist although in a changed condition from that of their existence on earth. They tend to be much less personally identifiable than are ancestors in some other African cultures, yet they can nonetheless be identified in any of several ways. Most commonly, if calamity should strike someone and if it were known or suspected that someone in his *umunna* had committed any offense against the forefathers, against the *arua*, the High God, or the spiritualized Earth (*Ane*), divination might indicate that the ancestors in general or, sometimes, a specific ancestor are thereby punishing the offender or anyone in his *umunna*. It must be understood, however, that when a specific ancestor is identified by such divination, it is only because he is remembered in the fragmentary genealogies characteristic of most *umunna*. The second method of identifying a specific ancestor is the recognition of certain distinguishing features or character traits in a child, who is thenceforth presumed to be that ancestor returned; in such a case, divination usually confirms the family's suspicion. So the ancestors are spiritual beings rather vaguely defined as persons, but usually not personified nearly as thoroughly as some of the *alusi* spirits.

The ancestors are called *ńdíchìè* ("the returners" from *ńdí*, "group" and *ichìè*, "returning" or "to return", not to be confused with *ńdí'ichí*, "group [marked with] *ichí* [facial scarifications]," which are the marks of having taken the *ozo* title in Onitsha and central Igboland (see Jeffreys, 1951b: 93–94). The ancestors are sometimes also referred to as *ndimo* (*ndimwo* farther south), "group of spirits," which describes their status and suggests the source of their power, for the

unseen is invariably considered to be more powerful than the immediately material. They reside in *aneezi* ("land of the family,") insofar
as their shrines are located within the geographical confines of the
patrilineage; they are also said to reside in *ane mmuo*, ("land of
spirits") which is inside the earth, linking them closely with Ane,
the spiritualized Earth; and they are said to reside, again as spirits,
n'igwe ("in the sky,") thus close to the High God, Ezechitoke.

The ancestors possess several important functions in the borderland family systems. They are reincarnated through both the male
patrilines of their progeny and quite often among their *okele*
(mother's agnates and daughter's descendants), thereby renewing
and maintaining the family lines and linking them inextricably to the
past, or the past to the future, depending upon one's point of view.
This certainly focuses attention of the living upon the present
life, and particularly upon the role of male elders in the present
life.

Nsukkans claim that respect is to be accorded to the elders largely
because of their proximity to the ancestors, for they soon will possess such powers themselves. Nearness in spiritual matters means
greater power, for a principle of spiritual contagion applies to all
beings which possess vital force. Certainly a closeness to sacred
precincts causes a being or a thing to take on some of the awesome-
ness associated with the vital force of the precincts—the vulture, for
example, appears on sacrifice days at shrines and shares in the offerings made to gods, so it thereby acquires some of the force. Even
more so is the case of the closeness of elders to the ancestors.

The elders are, first and foremost, the *ndichie*, who are either the
dead ancestors or, depending upon the context in which the term is
used, the living elders of the most advanced age. The important
elders of one's family are grouped into the two mentioned earlier,
the *umunna* and the *umune*. In the first, "father's children" or "children of the fathers," the more important elders are:

THE FATHERS
Nna, "Father."
Nnaukwu, "Great Father," Father's senior brother.

Nneukwu, "Great Mother," Father's senior sister. She will reside in another *umunna*, and thus is generally out of contact.
Nnanna, "Father's Father."
Nnenna, "Father's Mother," given a great deal of ritual accord.
Nna Ochukwu, "Father Aged Great," FaMoFa, a very important person to EGO.
Nnanna oche, "Father's Father Aged One," FaFaFa or FaFaFaFa.

In the second group, the *umune* (alternately *umere, umele nne*) the more important elders are:

THE MOTHERS
Nne, "Mother."
Nnaukwu (nne), "Great Father" ("mother"), Mother's senior Brother, who is very important to EGO.
Nnaoche, "Father Aged," Mother's Father, who is also very important to EGO as the link to an ancestral group.
Nnenne or *Nne oche*, "Mother's Mother."
Nna Ochukwu, "Father Aged Great," MoMoFa.
Nne Ochukwu, "Mother Aged Great," MoMoMo.

In both sets of elders, the men are considered to possess the major share of both importance and responsibility in the system, while the women—particularly in one's *umune*—have a more affective relationship with EGO.

2. The Living: Azi

EGO's generational group is the next category of living family, again divisible into two distinct categories according to relationship either with the *umunna* (or Igala *omenekele*) or with the *umune* (or Igala *omonobule*, "sons of females"). The smallest family unit is the *onama* ("mouth of the compound"), children of the same mother who are full siblings and are referred to as *umunne* ("children [of] mother"; singular, *nwanne*, "child [of] mother"). Mother's brother junior to EGO often is referred to as *nwanne*, too; mother's senior brothers are *dee*. All of mother's agnates, including those of EGO's generation, are EGO's *umune* or *okene*. The second group of family in

EGO's generation are his *umunna*, "father's children," who are half siblings, referred to individually as *nwanna*, "child [of] father." The family as it extends both vertically and horizontally within the *umunna* is referred to as *imenna*, meaning "inside the fathers" or within the group of those agnatically descended from a given male ancestor.

The generations younger than EGO constitute the third temporal unit of the living family. Like others, they are *azi*, the present generation of people, and are called more specifically *azi*, "children," and *umazi*, "children [of] the generation". Of course, like all the living vis-a-vis the ancestors, they are *umu*, "children," or "people." The senior son is *eya*, although here and there because of nuclear Igbo influence the term is *okpala*, but without the institutionalized ritual descent and authority which that term elsewhere connotes. Junior son and junior daughter are both referred to as *osobe*, "he/she follows," describing the role of the younger children in relation to the elder. Senior daughter is *ada*, and any woman of the consanguineous family is referred to by the singular term, *nwada*. *Umuada* refers especially to a woman's organization, but also as in Onitsha (see Henderson, 1967:27) consists of all those "daughters" of the *umunna*, one's female agnates, as distinct from *umu mgboto*, which terms refer to all women of EGO's *umune, umunna*, and in general all females related to EGO.

Small children are referred to as *umutakiri* or *umutakili*, "children small"; a small child, usually not yet talking, is *ize* ("toothed"); until perhaps the age of four or five, when it appears that the child "has decided to remain among the living," a child is called *nwandu* ("child [of] life"). After mother has conceived again, the child is called *nwaaka* ("child [of the] hand"), indicating that the child is no longer carried but can follow or can walk holding another's hand.

3. The Unborn

The third group of persons within one's vertical family broadly considered are those yet to be born, including newly born infants and very small children who have not yet "decided to remain among the living" or who might be changelings or trickster spirits in human form. The *ogbanje* or *okpakachi* is the more common of the latter tricksters who get themselves born in the guise of children, but then die, only to be reborn to the same woman (who becomes *nwayi ome n'omumu*: "woman repeatedly gives birth"), tormenting her constantly with the tantalizing hope that she will have a child who will remain among the living.

What is particularly important about the not-yet-born members of the family is that, in a very real sense, they partly pre-exist as ancestral spirits. They constitute the group not merely of *ikwu*, "relatives," but more importantly *azu (azo)*, "back," or *azummo*, "The spirits who are behind one." The word "back" here is used symbolically to express a very important Nsukkan notion, that those who are "behind" one support one, as in the proverb, *azu bo ike*, "The people giving support to a man are his strength." Indeed, the to-be-reincarnated ancestors, the "unborn" in large part are those who support one: they are "behind" EGO and "ahead" of him. In their original selves as *ndichie* they are of the "past," and in their forthcoming selves as *umu* they are of the "future." It is understood that "new" children can be born within the family line, although I found no one who would specify a person within his knowledge who was so considered.

In Igbo time, obviously, the past is tied to the future, which might indicate that Igbo would be solid traditionalists who are not very amenable to change. This is not necessarily the case. The present generation, *azi* (and *azu*), are reincarnate ancestors, and if they change their culture or society they are not simply living children changing immutable patterns established by the ancestors; they are certain "ancestors" themselves changing things, although not specifically as *ndichie*. They are those for whom the *ndichie* hoped and waited and those who will be accountable to fellow ancestors when they are again ancestors. They are equally accountable to the unborn, who can neglect them drastically in offerings and sacrifices if the changes which they institute have negative effects on the future generations. Time in the northern Igbo family is cyclic; the past does not necessarily repeat itself but family members of the past return to life on the surface of the earth where they perhaps undo some wrongs of the "past," or perhaps make new mistakes for the "future."

The Household and Affinity

1. Affinal Relations

Marriage generally in Nsukkan rural culture is arranged when the girl is quite young, although her consent is later required in most families. Ideally marriage is polygynous, although the poverty of the land and the difficulty of accumulating sufficient bridewealth have made monogamy in practice the most widespread form of marriage. It is largely the shrine priests (*attama*) who, possessing a superior position for accumulation of goods and actual money, most consistently enjoy polygyny. The household, by which I refer to the residential, affinal, and domestic institution (see Bender, 1967:495, 498), consists of the husband, his wife or wives, his unmarried daughters, his unmarried sons, and his married sons and their wives and children.

Husband is *di*, wife in general is *nwunye*. A number of terms, largely descriptive, are understood and occasionally used in reference to the wives, but most common are the following. The senior wife, a very important person in the household, is *obonoko* ("she who prepares the way for wealth"), or *obonokwo* ("female-great," not to be confused with *obonuku*, which Seton, 1928:267 refers to as a garment). She is *ishi nwayi*, "the head woman" of the compound; *nnekwu*, "mother of the kitchen," and in some localities *nwayi ishichi*, "woman of the head *chi*" (i.e, personal spirit of the male head of the household). The junior wife might or might not be *nwunye mma* ("woman of love," meaning that she is sometimes so much younger than her husband that he can love her as he loves a child); indeed, although a number of my own friends and acquaintances have quite young "special" wives, such girls seem to be playthings (sometimes admittedly so by the men themselves) as distinct from the *obonokwo*,

who in any serious value judgment would be classed as the man's
"favorite wife." The junior wife is referred to as *nwa nkponobi*
("child of the heart") insofar as she is usually selected by the man
himself (sometimes with the cooperation of his *obonokwo*, but usually
not), and as *obunwa okwu* ("she is large child"). Otherwise she is called
nwunye osobe ("wife who follows"), particularly if she is the junior
wife of an Igala. In the latter situation, of course, she has considerably lower status than the senior wife or than the junior wife of an
Igbo man.

2. The Household

The typical Nsukkan household, *mbala ezi* ("breadth of the family"),
properly the compound family, although the term is used to refer to
more than the people, consists of several interfunctioning units.
First among these are the family shrines, which function for the
members of an *umunna*, to which the wives of course do not belong
but under whose protection they are subsumed. It is understood,
however, that they have their own *umunna* which is more important
for their welfare than is their husband's and which is the important
kin-group of their children, who view it as *umune*. Here the borderland system differs from that of nuclear Igbo, where wives are
usually considered in the care of their husband's forefathers and
other protective spirits. Under the Igala occupation, the woman's
allegiance tended to become strongly linked with their own *umunna*
rather than that of their husbands', the latter being in some cases
actual Igala; and the men even now emphasize their *umune*—the line
of their Igbo mother's agnates—at least as strongly as the line of
their fathers.

The important shrines of the household will be discussed later,
but for the present they might be briefly described. First is the
onuchi ("mouth [of] god"), the shrine dedicated to one's personal
spirit-protector. The *chi* shrine is definitely a household rather than a
personal shrine. A child, for example, does not possess his own
onuchi until he grows up and has his own house. At that time he installs an *onuchi* in his sitting room or close to an entrance, but inside
the dwelling. Until he has grown up, while he is still patrilocalized,

he remains under the aegis of his father's *chi*. When he marries, his wife is subsumed under his *chi*, although she has her own staff which is set in his altar; if she divorces him, or vice versa, she returns to the protection of her father's *chi*. A woman thus does not, as a rule, possess an *onuchi*, but is protected either by her husband's or her father's *chi*. Another important shrine of the compound is *onu Anyanwu* ("mouth" here meaning "altar" of the "Sun"), which is the altar to the High God, Chukwu, who in Nsukka is more commonly referred to as Ezechitokc ("chief god creator male"). The High God is believed to be the ultimate owner of all chi (see Shelton, 1965b), but prayers to chi concern one's immediate personal and household affairs, while prayers to the High God are also prayers for the broader residential units such as the lineage and the village. *Onu Abere* ("altar [of] *Abere*"—i.e., the "Maiden") is the shrine to the *alusi* who guards each compound. She is different from *chi* insofar as *chi* is one's alter-ego, part of one's spiritual makeup derived from the High God, Chukwu, whereas Abere is a distinct and alien, potentially hostile spiritual being. There are other lesser shrines in some households, usually depending upon a certain need which arose within a particular family. Common to most households, however, although definitely of a lesser order than the shrines mentioned above, are the *ekwu*, which are small breast-shaped (although ideally so if I may compare them with the actual models which I have observed among most Nsukka women) and at times breast-size mud cones which are used to support the women's pots in the kitchen. They of course represent breasts, the source of food and life, and are empowered to prevent poisoners or evil spirits from tampering with the food of the household and causing death (compare this with the similar *omanne*, another breast-shaped mound set near the kitchen wall and representing mother's power as a life-giver and feeder—in Henderson, 1967:43). Shrines are thus located in each important area of the household compound: at the entrance, so that enemies cannot enter; at the entrance to the man's house, through which anyone going to the women's and children's quarters must pass; in the open space of the *ezi* or compound; and in the kitchen where food is prepared.

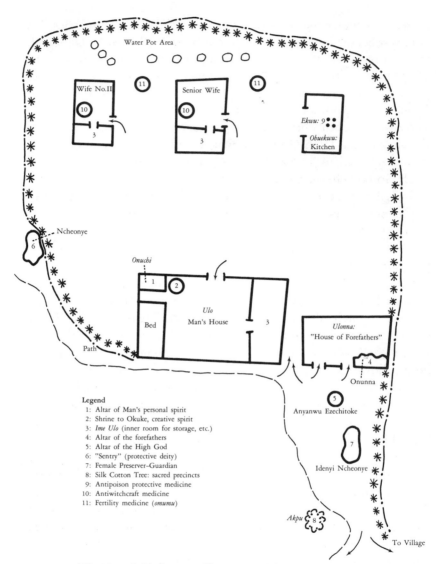

CHART I. *The Household Compound: Lineage Head*

The household consists of several other units (see Chart I: *The Household Compound*) located on *aneezi* ("ground [of the] compound") —the human beings and dwellings protected by the shrines. The house group is referred to as *ime obi* ("inside the family"), meaning the compound family to include the wives residing in their husband's lineage area. The term *ebeinu* ("place [of the] house") refers to a smaller unit, usually of a grown son and his wife who are residing patrilocally while the son's father is still living and is head of the household. A smaller house group than this is *onama* ("mouth [of the] compound"), consisting of one wife and her children. This latter, with the husband, is the nuclear family in Nsukka.

The Village and Village-Group

Many villages in northern Nsukka are single clans (*ukwaarua*) consisting of two or more patrilineages (*umunna*) and possessing but one *onyishi* or headman. A much larger number of villages, however, contain more than one clan, and it is these which require some explanation, for community is obviously more easily maintained within a single descent group than when two or more such exogamous groups are combined.

1. Village Structure
The largest grouping referred to by Nsukkans, aside from *uwa* ("world") is *mba* ("country") which is applied indefinitely to virtually any large area inhabited by a single people. The next smaller unit is the *nkpulu*, "heap," meaning a number of villages constituting what in English is called a "town." Examples of this are Nsukka town, Ehalumona, Oba, Imilike, and others (see Chart II: *Village Organization: Umu Mkpume*). Such a town or village-group is also called *ogbodo*, although this term is used more extensively to mean "village." Villages are grouped together because of real or putative relationship of their founders in the mythical past; in some instances, different villages were founded by brothers or sons of a major origin hero;

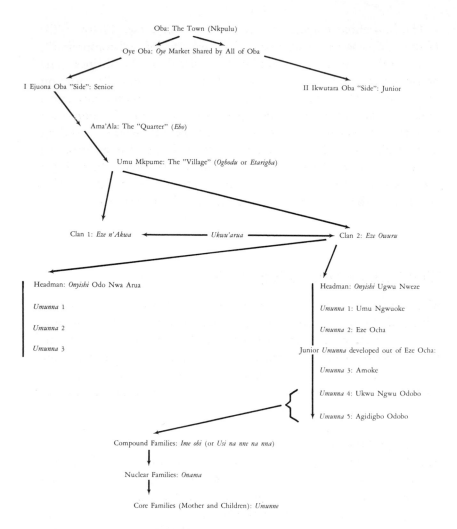

CHART II. *Village Organization: Umu Mkpume*

in other cases, the villages were founded by men who traveled together as friends to those districts. This is not to imply that within the villages there is ethnic consistency—some lineages, for example, were supposedly founded by Umunri, whereas others were Igbo (see Shelton, 1965)—but that such origin legends and their implications constitute ritual history which satisfies non-historical needs of the societies.

The village proper is the *ogbodo*. Structurally, it is divided along the lines of component *ukwaarua* clans, boundaries of the land being defined according to such social criteria as occupation, traditions of ownership, tenure of settlement, location near untouchable land such as sacred precincts, etc; according to notions of senior and junior sections; and in some instances according to the proximity of one section to the "outside" or adjoining village territory (see Maps III, IV, V: *Spatial Relationships: III Imilike; IV Umune Ngwa; V Oba*).

The senior section, which is usually Igbo, is called *ezi*, an Igbo and Igala word designating this section, or *enu* (Igbo: "upper"), as in Imilikenu, the senior section of Imilike. The junior section is *ifite*, Igala for this reference; *ane* (Igala: "earth"), *ana* or *ani* (Igbo: "earth"), as in Imilikani, the junior section of Imilike. (Compare Jeffreys, 1946:87). The other mode of spatial division is into two "sides" (*ibe*). *Ibe ama* (*ama* or "path" side) is that half or section of the village which adjoins another, where there is usually a common path or road. *Ibe owele* ("side farther removed") is the more interior section of the village, usually more removed from places where the people will commonly encounter neighboring villagers.

The latter division into "sides" functions mainly for convenience in making reference to residential neighborhoods, although in the past those people dwelling on the path side had to bear the brunt of raiding headhunters and, especially, slavers, so that many of the war shrines as well as many of the protective medicines are located there. Another division not very different from this is made between "house" and "farm." The term *uno* ("house") is used in conjunction usually with a name to signify the group living in the original dwelling area, whereas *ago* ("farm") designates the group who, because of population pressures or other forces, settle a new location. The

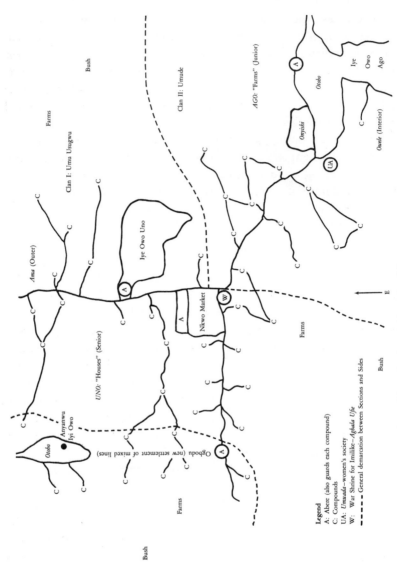

MAP III. *Spatial Relationships: Umu Inyere Village, Imilikenu*

Legend
A: Abere (also guards each compound)
C: Compounds
UA: *Umuada*—women's society
W: War Shrine for Imiiike—*Aghala Ufie*
– – – – General demarcation between Sections and Sides

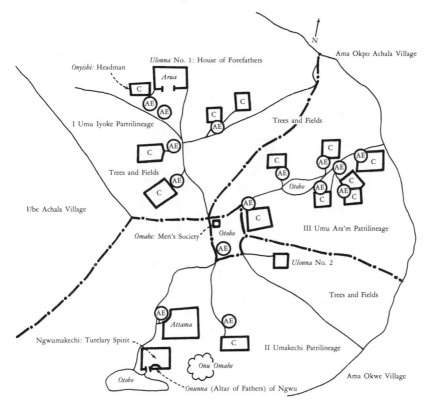

Legend
AE: Anyanwu Ezechitoke, the High God
C: Compound
Otobo: "village square"
Onu Omabe: Altar to spirit of men's secret society
Heavy lines ━━●━● indicate three lineage areas
Light lines ——— indicate paths

MAP IV. *Spatial Relationships: Umune Ngwa Village. Nsukka*

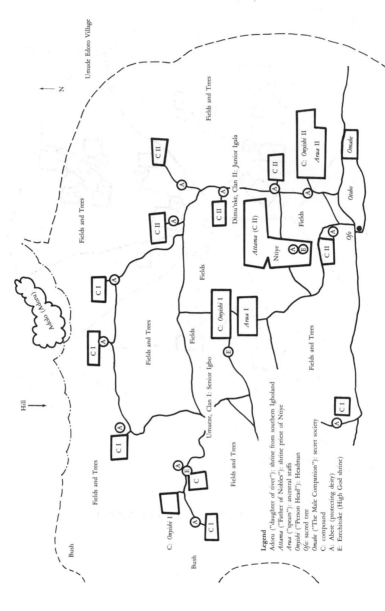

MAP V. *Spatial Relationships: Oba Ameegwu Village, Owele-Ezeoba*

Legend
Aduru ("daughter of river"): shrine from southern Igboland
Attama ("Father of Nobles"): shrine priest of Ntiye
Arua ("spears"): ancestral staffs
Onyishi ("Person Head"): Headman
Ofo: sacred tree
Omabe ("The Male Companion"): secret society
C: compound
A: Abere (protecting deity)
E: Ezechitoke (High God shrine)

village of Umu Inyere in Imilikenu, for example, is so divided, its protective deity carrying the different terms. Some generations ago, when villagers had to extend their dwelling area, the *alusi* named Iyi Owo was carried along to protect those going to the new area. As the present day elders put it, Iyi Owo's "son" was sent. Regardless, the name was not changed from *Iyi* ("female god"), so the goddess who remained was called Iyi Owo Uno ("Iyi Owo of the compounds") and the goddess who accompanied the settlers was called Iyi Owo Ago ("Iyi Owo of the farmlands") (see Map III: *Spatial Relations—Imilike*).

The division into senior and junior sections is perhaps as important as this sectioning into sides or areas, for the senior section (*ezi, enu*) usually enjoys the privileges of land and ritual seniority or priority over the junior section (*ane, ani, ana*). Such seniority is normally rationalized by origin legends which indicate that the founder of the *ezi* side was senior to the founder of the *ane* side. Sometimes other legend is used to explain the distinction between the sides, which in fact are complete lineages when the village consists of only one *ukwaarua* clan (as in Umune Ngwa—see Map IV), and are complete clans when the village is composed of more than one *ukwaarua*. For example, it is often argued that the senior section was the only village at one time, but it was decided that strangers would be permitted to join the village on the agreement that they would aid in mutual defense, cooperate in the rotation of certain farmlands, and in general respect the seniority of the originators of the village. Very often, indeed, the junior clan or lineage was an Igala or Okpoto group who took over control of the village *alusi*, and are still considered to be adopted or "stranger" groups. The whole system, then, contributes to community unity despite the division of people into distinct social groups.

2. Association and Community

There are other factors as well which tighten the bonds of different lineages and clans within the northern Nsukka villages. Uchendu, discussing nuclear Igbo, referred to "persuasion, cross-cutting marriage ties, the respect of common taboo and the willingness to con-

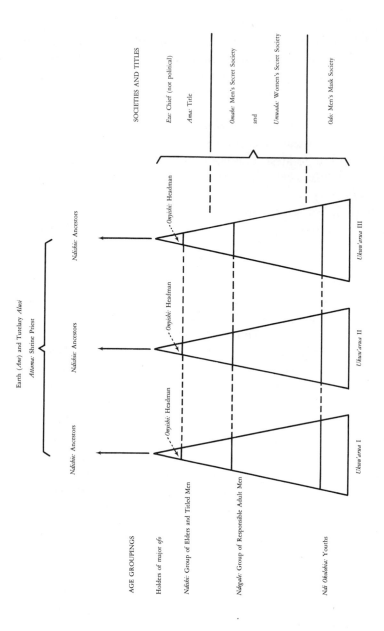

CHART III. *Vertical and Horizontal Allegiances*

cede points to a villager without losing face" (1964:48). Among northern Igbo, certainly, there are other factors. There are title societies, most important of which is the *ama* title system derived from the Igala (see Forde and Jones, 1950:35), which is manifested commonly in the cult of *inyiama* and the title of *attama,* but with other membership comprised of men from villages throughout a village group, regardless of the individuals' particular lineage or even village affiliation, so long as they are free men and not slaves. I will discuss this and related societies later. Within a village, also creating horizontal strata to offset some of the inter-lineage rivalry, are the age groups (*azi*: "generation"; *ogbo*: "age grade"; *owa*: "age group") such as the elders (*ndishi*), the grown married men (*ndegale*), the youths (*nde okolobea*), and boys too young to have been initiated (*ndezuukwu*).

Certain non-title societies as well as the general association of persons of the same age groups increase the ties which bind vertical lineages together (see Chart III: *Vertical and Horizontal Allegiances*). Chief among these are the *omabe* ("village males") men's society and the *umuada* ("children daughters") women's society, the latter having cross-village and cross-lineage functions even though its membership consists only of the women born within a patrilineage. These societies have no control over shrines save their own: to the *omabe* spirit, and to the spirit of fertility in the case of the woman's society.

Shared geographic areas also contribute to the maintenance of community in Nsukka villages. There is invariably a common meeting area or public, cleared place called *otobo* (central Igbo: *ilo*) where public negotiations and meetings can be conducted and where other inter-lineage or inter-clan matters can be performed or transacted. Often the *otobo* is located between the various clans comprising the village. In this "village square," or quite near to it, normally grow the sacred trees, particularly *ofo* from which the *ofo* staffs of authority are taken, and *akpu*, the silk-cotton tree. The village market is also held in common and is usually located in a different section of the village, sometimes near another village which shares it, thereby creating even broader possibility of peaceful cooperation at least once a week (i.e., every four days). Forest areas or bush are normally shared and, where potential farmland appears to be diminishing because of growth in population, agreement on the rotational cycle of bush lands is reached by meetings of the elders of the various clans, who gather together in the *otobo*.

Discussion

The foregoing material on time, space, kinship, and social structures in the northern Nsukka borderland, in conjunction with the historical relationships of the Nsukkans with other peoples, might be summarized briefly to bring one or two problems into sharper focus.

Ardener's summary of the four salient features of the southern Igbo kin system applies fairly well to the Nsukka borderland, with a few altered stresses. These features are: the extension of terms to cover the wide range of kin; the emphasis on seniority rather than generation, and the tendency for relationships with little seniority to be subsumed under sibling terminology; the importance of the distinction between full siblings and half siblings; and the durability of the ties with mother's and mother's mother's patrikin (Ardener, 1954:97–98). The emphasis upon seniority in the case of the typical Nsukkan family can cause intergenerational rivalries, such as that which LeVine describes: "The knowledge that the advancement of [the son] is dependent upon the demise of the [father] causes the relations between the leader and his prospective successor to be strained, despite the high degree of respect paid to the aged" (LeVine, 1965:190). Such conflict was largely minimized by the methods sanctioned for successful seniority among the northern Igbo: to become *onyishi* one normally had to survive longer than one's peers, over whom the headman had no authority, regardless, for his peers in fact were his immediate counsellors; and to take a title one had to work hard to accumulate goods, and develop and maintain an exemplary character, so no one was particularly favored over others. But to become a shrine priest, on the other hand, one had to be born Igala and also to be "called," after which elder Igala-controlled divination would determine if the "vocation" were valid (consult also Shelton, 1969), for succession to the title was not automatically from father to son. So traditional tensions between fathers and sons, among Nsukka Igbo or within Nsukka Igala clans, were relatively reduced. Hsu's description of the typical father-son relationship applies:

> It is continuous because every father is a son and every son, in the normal course of events, is a father. Therefore every father-son relationship is but a link in an everlasting chain of father-son relationships. It is inclusive because while every son has only one father, every father actually or potentially has many sons (Hsu, 1965:643).

This continuity, in the traditional northern Igbo family (kin and household) system, normally led to stability within the family, EGO's loyalties to his *umunna* not often clashing greatly with his loyalties to his *umune* because his relations were of a different yet expected kind: affective with mother's father's people, filial with his father's father's people. Because seniority counted most, his place in the generational and age-group scheme—to whatever degree formalized—was clearly understood, and he had little justification for revealing hostility toward close relatives. Furthermore, the open title systems (non-hereditary) and secret societies enabled him to assert his personal abilities, which have always meant much to the Igbo living in politically uncentralized societies. Those problems which arose in borderland Igbo village life under the Igala colonization were mainly the result of introducing Igala lineages particularly of shrine priests and diviners.

PART TWO

Nsukka Religion

4. Sacred Precincts

TO UNDERSTAND the several aspects of interculturation in the Nsukka borderland it is necessary to study those particular means whereby the Igbo over a long period of time (certainly more than a century) developed new methods of coping with the different kinds of familial and societal problems which arose with the establishment of non-Igbo control personnel in Igbo villages. These new or adapted coping techniques, in turn, can be properly understood only in relation to institutions and networks in the Nsukka villages upon which social control turns. Such networks are numerous: familial, local and territorial, occupational and, particularly in the case of the borderland, religious (see Back, 1965:337). It is this latter network to which I will devote most attention.

Nsukkan religion can be most clearly comprehended by understanding distinctions between the kinds of beings or forces with which this religious behavior is concerned. These forces may be divided generally between familiar (familial from the point of view of borderland Igbo, or usually benevolent ones, such as the High God and creator gods, personal spirits, and ancestral forces) and those which are essentially different, alien, and potentially hostile (particularly *alusi*) and which are usually in the control of Igala shrine priests. Both sets of forces create or reside in sacred precincts, which the present chapter will describe by way of introducing the topic of Nsukkan religion.

I am indebted to Rev. S. N. Ezeanya, a devoted student of traditional Igbo religion, for his study of "The Sacred Place in the

Traditional Religion of the Igbo People of the Eastern Group of Provinces of Nigeria," a paper published at Nsukka and consequently no longer obtainable. In this work he discusses the general nature of sacred places, defining "sacred place" as

> any place set aside by the people for the performance of acts of religion—offering of sacrifice, prayers, oath-taking, performing of certain initiation rites. . . . What is important is that the place be chosen either by the express directive of a divinity or an ancestor or by an individual or a community, as a place *set aside* solely as a dwelling place for a particular deity and/or a place where it may be consulted with the concomitant rituals or simply as a place set aside for the performance of certain religious functions, like making offerings to ancestors (Ezeanya, 1966:1).

Ezeanya classifies sacred places as public (nature oracles, gods with widespread reputation and powers, sacred trees, etc.), quasi-public (ancestral shrines, localized tutelary gods, medicine of restricted groups such as lineages, etc.), and private (shrines belonging to individuals, such as the *onuchi* and women's "inner room" fertility shrines) (Ezeanya, 1966:3–6). Although such categories may be useful, we might at the same time remember that a nice distinction between "public" and "private" is rather difficult to achieve. For example, the Nsukka crossroads sacrifice[1] is placed by a private individual, yet it creates a sacred precinct, indeed a dangerous precinct chosen expressly for its publicness, since a person disturbing the medicine whether intentionally or not will thereby become the sufferer (see Figure I: *Ebeeto at Obimo*). Thus the crossroads temporarily becomes a sacred place which in different respects is both "private" and "public." Furthermore, certain precincts are sometimes public and at other times private rather than always semi-private or quasi-public. But to belabor the point is needless. Let us

---

1. *Egba eja* ("to tie sacrifice") or *ebeeto* (*ebeito*) "place untying" or "place exchanging"), referring to the function of the medicine to remove evil influences from the people responsible for setting out the medicine at the crossroads, which is often used to drive off *okpakachi* or *ogbanje* trickster spirits.

FIGURE I. Ebeeto (Egbe aja) Crossroads Medicine at Obimo-Ejuona
The red feathers are stuck in yam fufu that is mixed with kola as medicine, around which is wrapped a piece of red cloth; all is set with pieces of cut yam in a shallow dish. This medicine is meant to cause tricksters to leave a woman.

instead examine the nature of Nsukkan sacred precincts, distinguishing them according to their danger as sacred precincts.

The Nature of Spiritual Power

What separates sacred from ordinary precincts in the borderland[2] is

2. The villages upon which I will focus most attention are
   Ameegwu, of Owele-ezeoba, which displays Igala and Okpoto influences;
   Nkpologu-attah and Obimo-ejuona, which were strongly affected by Igala invasions from the west, particularly from Ogurugu;
   Umu Egale of Imilikane, most strongly affected by Okpoto but with some more central Idoma influences; *continued on next page*

simply the presence of special spiritual force. If one finds an egg in the farmland or in the bush, it is not extraordinary; if one finds an egg lying beside the High God shrine or at a crossroads, he dare not touch it, for it is not ordinary at all. The difference is that the egg of the farm is there because a hen laid it there, a perfectly normal occurrence. The egg at the shrine, however, is there because a person intentionally put it there to be temporarily protected, or as an offering to the shrine. In either case, the High God is protecting the egg. The egg at the crossroads is possibly there because some foolish hen laid it in that unlikely spot, but which Nsukkan will take the chance that it is *not* a sacrificed egg? Heavy odds lie against the fool who touches it that it is medicine and that he will take on the sufferings of the person who made the sacrifice. Thus the motive for action determines to some extent the ordinariness or sacredness of a thing or area. But there is more to the point than this. In the case of the egg at the High God shrine (*onuChukwu*), a kind of power existing at, in, and near the shrine protects it, circulates about it and can affect anyone who bothers it. Similarly, and worse, at the crossroads: the common use of a crossroads for "exchange" medicine to remove a curse or an evil from one's shoulders to some other victim causes the area to possess potential power, almost actual power, in itself. When a sacrifice is made there, the crossroads definitely possesses such power, which radiates from the sacrifice itself, flowing outward to affect seriously a careless or unlucky passerby.

The first characteristic of any sacred precinct, therefore, is the existence of spiritual power in and about it—power which need not be personified, although it often is among the borderland people. From what does this contained yet radiating spiritual power derive? Here one is on unsure ground, largely because the people themselves have not systematized their ideas about spiritual force. Certainly

continued from previous page

Umu Inyere of Imilikenu, which reveals Igala, Okpoto, and some Umunri influences;

Umu Mkpume of Ejuona-oba, which displays strong evidence of Umunri influences despite my own earlier argument to the contrary (see Shelton, 1965);

Umune Ngwa of Ihe-owele, Nsukka, which is an amalgam of Igala and Igbo with some Umunri influence.

it is held that *ogwu* ("medicine-power") exists in itself, spiritually, not as any sort of personalized being or thing, but rather as a vast and ultimately mysterious source of power from which the appropriate rituals can draw spiritual power into more concrete things in the practice of sorcery and the making of medicine which can serve human beings. In other cases, the sacred qualities of some precincts depend upon spiritual force derived from a personal being, such as the High God or a creator godling, an *alusi*, or ancestral powers considered collectively in the *arua* staffs.

In virtually all cases, however, the generally understood process is the same: there is some *source* of power from which, somehow, power emerges to reside in and radiate from or to make similarly contagious some being or object. It might be well to distinguish diffusion and creation, though, from emanation, as slightly varying modes of transference of power.

Creation is a deliberate process by which a personal being such as a god intentionally causes a thing or being to exist, that is, to have some degree of force, which can range widely in quantity although there are no changes in the quality of the spiritual force passed from creator to creature.

Diffusion is a less deliberate sort of outward flow of spiritual force. Typically the word refers to a "spreading out," as in the transmission of elements or features of one human culture to another. As I use it, the word refers to the act of transmitting spiritual force from its origin to a being or object *by means of contact* between the two. The sacralization of a shrine, for example, involves a great number of activities which are ritually ordered, but central to the process is the blood sacrifice which is made atop the shrine altar. The altar is called, appropriately, *onu*, meaning "mouth," and is the particular area through which the spirit resident in the shrine "eats;" the blood sacrifice, accompanied by appropriate prayers and other ceremonies, "calls" the spiritual force into the altar and shrine area by this first act of "feeding" the spirit, after which the spirit (or part of its force) is believed to be forever resident in the shrine. Such transference of spiritual power from a source to a lesser residence of that power by means of establishing contact between the two things is common not only to such sacralization of shrines but also to the acquisition of powers by blacksmiths and shrine priests. Medicine (*ogwu*), similarly, is "made" by the transference of generally undefined spiritual power into specific objects ranging from amulets and talismans to small shrines, and usually has relatively specific purposes—to ward off witches, to counteract sorcery, to overcome enemies, and the like. The methods for such transference are customarily determined rituals where great deviation from prescribed form will result in failure, or can be used to rationalize failure (as in a ritually installed shrine priest's being later proved a consumer of taboo foods).

So called "accidental" contact with certain medicine or objects containing spiritual power can also cause such diffusion or transference of power, usually with quite unfortunate effects upon the recipient's peace of mind and health.

Contagion is a characteristic of spiritual force whereby its qualities can be catching and can infect anyone or anything negatively or positively, although the rule is that such infection is negative. The contagious qualities of sacred precincts vary from benevolence to extreme hostility, so the reputation of the precincts differs markedly.

Emanation means a "flowing out of," and for our purposes refers to the act of transmitting force because of "overfullness" of that power at its source. The emanation of God-substance to human beings, and the emanation of lesser medicine from some mysterious origin, are examples of this process. There need be no direct contact made between receiver and origin, as when a human being is conceived (or born, in some areas of the borderland) and receives his *chi* from *Chukwu*, the High God, whose name means "the great *chi*." Some Nsukkan informants claimed that Chukwu created or deliberately creates each *chi*; others scoffed at the notion, arguing that the High God simply cannot help the *chi* from going from him, although he can call it back; still others argued that the High God could withhold *chi* and call it back, but that by the nature of things all actual human persons (as distinct from trickster spirits) born did in fact receive *chi*. How emanation as an automatic outward flow of spiritual force really relates to creation as intentional activity in

Nsukkan thought is thus difficult to say—perhaps all three interpretations must be accepted. There is little disagreement, however, about the "overflow" of power which now and then characterizes the behavior of *alusi*, who occasionally run amok, slaughtering and destroying the people regardless of prayers or sacrifice or the most sincere acts of contrition and humility, apparently until their "excess" power is expended. Then they settle down, receive the grateful offerings of their human subjects, and through the diviners offer some advice so the people may in future suffer less terribly—e.g., making wider streets in the village, separating compounds so that much open space exists where the *alusi* can burn off its powers, and so forth. The case of Iye Owo ("Mother God") of Imilikenu, described later, is a good example of this.

It must be presumed, then, that spiritual power radiates from a sacred precinct, even emanates from it—some spiritual forces intentionally range about seeking victims, others await the unwary, and the piece of *ogwu* (medicine) made by a sorcerer which the junior clerk hangs beneath his supervisor's office chair has aggressive power flowing from it. But power need not always be aggressive and "hot" or "male," but can be "cooling" and "female," or can be the spiritual power of relatives within one's consanguineous family. It is therefore proper to separate sacred precincts according to the sort of powers which inform them.

Precincts of Familiar Spirits

"Familiar" spirits as I use the term refers to ancestral force, dead forefathers, the protective household and compound shrine spirits, the High God in his several manifestations, and the deified Earth. The most common familiar sacred precincts are the ancestral shrines, although every house owned and inhabited by a grown man has a chi altar (*onuchi*: "mouth [of] chi") usually in his sitting room near the entrance. Each compound has a forefather shrine (*onunna*: "mouth [of] fathers") and every lineage has a larger ancestral shrine in which major lineage offerings to the forces of the ancestors are made. Each clan has an ancestral shrine house set apart; this is *ulo arua*, "house

[of] spears," *arua* referring to ancestral force as it is symbolized by the ritual staffs and spears of authority. The rituals involving these familiar shrines have the secondary effect of reassuring the northern Igbo villager that he is indeed protected and watched over by those who care for him—his own blood relatives. Their primary, immediate effect varies: the ordinary day-to-day ritual is a simple kola and food offering with a wine libation, so the repetition of the prayers and the custom-ordered motions by the elder conducting the daily service is a constant reassertion of the customary, the ordinary, that which can be trusted because it is dependable and not surprising. Although the *arua* symbols are usually not consciously examined or thought about by most of the people, the meaning of the symbols can be sensed in part without discussion, and the symbols and rituals, too, order certain human experience whether they are analyzed or not. But what is important here is that the ritual activities normally maintain the usual. Special festivals, however, involve blood sacrifices, and at these events—usually annual ancestral festivals—the power of the ancestors is felt. For a while they, and their shrine areas, are somewhat frightening, for they are indeed eaters of blood, and being in their environs creates a certain degree of nervousness. This itself sets the proper tone of those occasions, for people need reminding that the forefathers are powerful, lest the living become complacent. Complacency leads to degeneracy in moral behavior, about which the ancestors—as older members of the family—watch their children carefully. The ordinary individual, therefore, under most circumstances, feels comfortable in the precincts of the ancestral shrine, for he is being observed and cared for by family forces whom he is caused to respect through annual reminders of their vast powers over him.

Ease in proximity is also the case with the *chi* shrine inside a man's house, which is sometimes contiguous with his forefather shrine: it is in the entrance room where visitors sit, and is where guests will place their title staffs so that they enjoy the spiritual protection of their host's *chi* and ancestors. One does not otherwise notice these shrines; they are present and available, but people come and go, sit close by them and socialize. People are similarly more or less non-

FIGURE II. Ezechitoke Shrine at Umune Ngwa
The wooden shaft atop the earthen mound is the actual altar (onu) *upon which sacrifices are made by the* onyishi.

chalant about the High God shrine, which is usually located near or about the *otobo* or village square, and to compound High God shrines where these are to be found. Because such gods do not normally "seek" offerings, do not deliberately cause diseases, "accidents," infertility, or other misfortune, they are not feared under ordinary circumstances and their shrine areas although sacred precincts do not arouse much awe among the villagers. Figures II, III, and IV (*Ezechitoke Shrine at Umune Ngwa, Onu Chukwu at Umugoji, Anyanwu Shrine at Imilikenu*) are examples of such shrines.

Closely related to the High God, Earth (*Ane*), and ancestral forces are certain trees and sacred groves, although the latter are by far more common to the alien *alusi*, than to the more parental familiar spirits. Somewhere close by, or actually part of, High God and ancestral shrines are the "life-trees" called *alaghaa* or *ogbu* (*Ficus elastica*). The tree can be cut down and chopped into pieces, then

FIGURE III.Onu Chukwu at Umugoji
The top of the earthen altar is the actual "Mouth of God"; the tree is a life-tree, ogbu.

FIGURE IV. Anyanwu Shrine at Imilikenu
Sacrifices are made atop this earthen mound, which is a High God shrine; feathers and pots represent old sacrifices; the life-tree, ogbu, grows nearby.

tossed on the earth, and the pieces will sprout and become trees. When it is near other vegetation it survives at the expense of its competitors, so its life power is considered to be unnatural and therefore supported by powers greater than human. Another life-tree, *ichikeri* (*Spondias monbin*), is used in burial ceremonies and in certain cleansing rituals such as washing the hands after handling a corpse. A typical life-tree, it springs back to life under almost any circumstance, so it suggests the powers of the "returners," the dead ancestors who return to life in their family line.

Certain other trees are, in a loose sense, "sacred" although they are more closely associated with ritual and political authority than with spiritual power. *Ofo* (*Detarium elastica*) is certainly the best known of these. From this tree, which is never cut, the peculiarly jointed branches fall off and are gathered; wrapped in copper wire and often tufted with the tail of a cow or horse sacrificed for the purpose of title-taking, they become the physical symbols of authority. *Ofo* is held by each *onyishi* for his lineage or clan group, and every *alusi* also possesses *ofo*. *Akpu* (*Ceiba pentandra*), the silk-cotton tree, is generally considered semi-sacred in the Nsukka borderland and in some areas it is closely related to the ancestors. Other large trees are revered for their sheer size which is thought to require much life power to attain. Among these are *oji* (*Chlorophora excelsa*)[3], *ugba* (*Pentaclethra macrophylla*)[4], *ube* (*Pachylobus edulis*)[5], and *ibobo* (*Adansonia digitata*)[6]. The larger of these trees, particularly *oji* and *ube*, are not planted but are said to have the power to grow where they please. Northern Igbo respect trees and often relate them to ancestral and spiritual powers, for what can do as it pleases is a free and powerful being, whether it be a tree, an animal, a man, or a god.

Precincts of Non-Familiar Spirits

By "non-familiar" spirits I mean those which from the northern

3. Also called *iroko*, the African teakwood.
4. The oil bean tree.
5. The "pear" tree, often associated with ancestral power.
6. The baobab, important particularly in Igala origin legends.

Igbo point of view are not usually related to or favorably inclined toward human beings, but are "different" and separated beings, although often tutelary spirits, who are potentially hostile toward humans. These fall into three broad categories: (1) beings with widespread powers who possess and inhabit precincts usually forbidden to all but a few persons; (2) medicine (*ogwu*) which can be manipulated, but which through creation has gained a certain degree of independent power; (3) *alusi*, who are independent spirits who reside in borderland villages as protectors and social controllers, and are under Igala control.

The more important beings with far-reaching powers are probably *Ekke* (Python-spirit) and *Igwe* (Sky) in their various manifestations, to be discussed in more detail in conjunction with *alusi*. Their precincts are usually highly sacred and quite restricted, sometimes in the midst of extensive forest areas from which are excluded women and children, ordinary village men, those in conditions of ritual impurity (e.g., having touched a menstruating woman, having committed some abomination against Earth, having offended and not yet "cooled down" one's ancestors, etc.), and strangers except in unusual cases—which did not, in fact, include those engaged in ethnographical study. Such precincts are considered frightening, and are carefully avoided by everyone save those few shrine priests and rainmakers who might have rights of access to the sacred forest; farmers whose land adjoins that of the sacred bush are usually very careful to observe proper boundaries, for spiritual power is believed to emanate all the way out to the very edge of the forest. The power, of course, is much more intense close by those secret shrines where major sacrifices are made for the installation of shrine priests, the making of war medicine, and the stopping or starting of rain.

Medicine, *ogwu*, can range from that which is no more than an amulet or the already-mentioned crossroads medicine (see Figure I: *Ebeeto at Obimo-ejuona*) to great, powerful, shrine-type areas which enjoy widespread reputation. Good examples of the latter are the great war medicine shrines, *Ogwugwu* ("medicine [of] war"), north of Enugu-Ezike; and *Ogwu dinama* ("medicine of the people") at Nkpologu. The latter is said often to kill people, and when it does

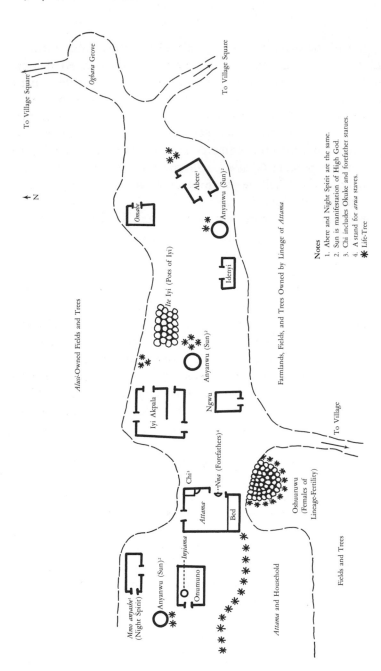

← N

Oghara Grove

To Village Square

To Village Square

Alusi-Owned Fields and Trees

Omabe

Abere[1]

Anyanwu (Sun)[2]

Idenyi

Ite Iyi (Pots of Iyi)

Anyanwu (Sun)[2]

Iyi Akpala

Ngwu

Farmlands, Fields, and Trees Owned by Lineage of *Attama*

To Village

Chi[3]

Nna (Forefathers)[4]

Oshuuruwu (Females of Lineage-Fertility)

Attama

Bed

Mmo anyasbe[1] (Night Spirit)

Anyanwu (Sun)[2]

Inyiama

Onumuno

Attama and Household

Fields and Trees

Notes

1. Abere and Night Spirit are the same.
2. Sun is manifestation of High God.
3. Chi includes Okuke and forefather statues.
4. A stand for *arwa* staves.
✳ Life-Tree

CHART IV. *Typical Shrine Compound: Iyi Akpala of Umu Mkpume*

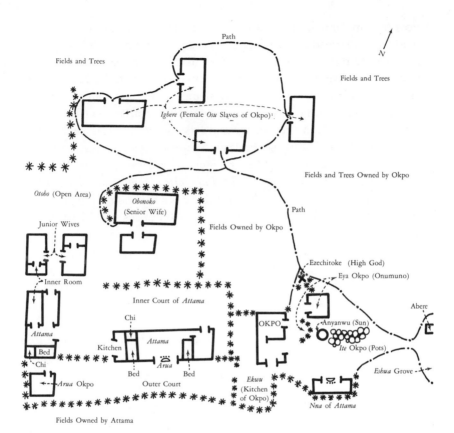

Notes

1. Houses of slaves, unlike those of free persons, are made of grass.
✱ Life-Tree

CHART V. *Typical Shrine Compound: Okpo of Imilikane*

no one can lament the death lest such attention-calling cause the
medicine to spread evil influences to the mourner himself. The shrine
area accordingly is a sacred precinct usually avoided as dangerous,
and when offerings are made to it they are conducted with a certain
amount of dispatch, no persons desiring to linger about the shrine.

The more common sort of non-familiar spirits are the village
alusi, each village in the borderland having at least one such spirit,
and most villages having several, with one being ascendant in various
respects over the others. The precincts of village *alusi* are normally
distinctive (see Charts IV, V, *Typical Shrine Compounds: Iyi Akpala
of Umu Mkpume, Okpo of Imilikane*): there is a central shrine "owned"
and inhabited by the parent spirit, smaller houses inhabited by the
spirit children, a small sacred forest in which some annual sacrifices
are made at the festival honoring the *alusi*, and assorted supplemen-
tary shrines including those which contain the spirit's ancestral
staves, those linking the spirit to the High God (usually through
the Sun, *Anyanwu*), and those linking the spirit to the *Omabe* secret
society.

Representation and symbolization of *alusi* tends to be more distinctive and widespread than with ancestors and other familiar
spirits. Whereas the latter are represented either by spearlike staves
(*arua*) or by small, generally poorly carved wooden posts (see Figure
V: *Forefathers [Nna] at Imilikane*), many of the *alusi* are represented
by statuary or other symbols. Ntiye of Owele-ezeoba is represented
by a small white-painted statue remarkably reminiscent of some
statues of the earth goddess occurring much farther south in Igboland; Okpo of Imilikane and Iyi Akpala of Umu Mkpume are
represented by tall wooden statues, their children by very small pyg-
moid carvings; Ezuugwu of Nkpologu, on the other hand, like
Adada of Obimo-ejuona, is represented by a great phallic figure.
(See Figures VI–X: *Representations of Alusi*.)

The life trees associated with *alusi* shrines are different from those
about the shrines of familiar spirits. Most common is *ejulusi* (*New-
bouldia laevis*).[7] They are respected for the same reasons, however, as
are the life-trees (*alagbaa*) around the ancestral shrines. Life trees are

7. Elsewhere called *ogilishi* or *ogilisi* (central Igbo) or *egbo* (Asaba).

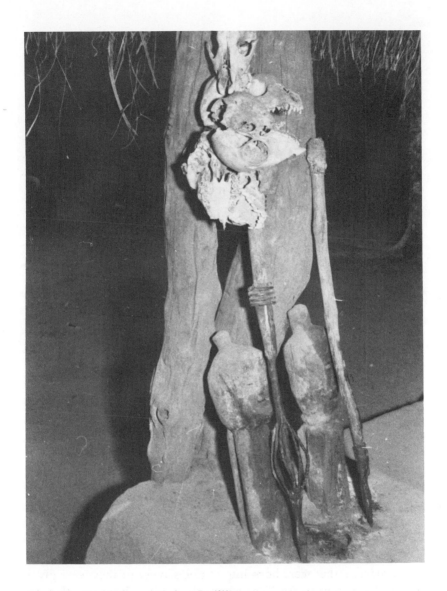

FIGURE V. Forefathers (Nna) at Imilikane

The statuettes represent the important founders of this lineage; the staves are their symbols of power; the skulls are those of sacrificed victims. Offerings are made in the "mouth"—the depression between the statueties.

often used as a living wall about the entire shrine compound, although there is no consistency in this; more often they are used in ceremonies, such as during the annual festival of the *alusi*, when a display of black cloth is hung between the life trees.

Houses inhabited by *alusi* and *omabe* (men's secret society) are distinguished from others by the presence of *kelekede* (plaited grass loop decorations) atop them, indicating that the buildings belong not to familiar beings such as humans or ancestors but to quite different spiritual forces (see Figure XI: *Kelekede and other Shrine Objects*). Similarly, *omu*, the green "heart of palm," is hung over entrances to such buildings during festival time, as indications that important sacred activity is being conducted. In front of shrine houses, at times taking up much of the open space in what otherwise would be the *otobo* of the spirit, lies a usually large bed of pots half-buried in the earth, existing as special offerings to the spirits (see Figure XI). About an *alusi*, further, one finds a wide assortment of paraphernalia, unlike the ancestral, High God, or earth shrines, which are as a rule plain and unadorned. The *alusi* spirits—or the shrine priest—will possess special sacred spears, *okwo*, ceremonial and ancestral staves, numerous musical instruments used in worship, clusters of bells (*oti*) used for summoning the spirits, *okwoji* which are tortoise-shaped lidded carved wooden containers which hold kola for sacrifices, *okwaju* which are wooden serving dishes in which food is served to the shrine priest, and assorted knives, matchets, and other weapons and tools.

An *alusi* shrine, furthermore, is attended by special persons: the shrine priest, *attama*, who is freeborn, descended from Igala and Okpoto patrilines; and slaves to the spirit, generically called *osu*, but usually more specifically titled *igbele* (Igala: "maidens") as females sacrificed to the shrine, or *akara* to designate the male slaves who serve the priest in making medicines and in cleaning the shrine area. These slaves either were born into shrine slavery or they were given to the *alusi* as human sacrifices on the demand of the spirit; they are not individuals who sought sanctuary by becoming slaves. Basden (1938:297) has referred to the *alusi* shrine as a place of sanctuary, and in the Owerri area the concept *igbana n'osu* ("running away to

FIGURE VI. Ntiye at Ameegwu

The small white statuette represents the goddess who is called "Little Mother," with the alternate name "Mother of Destruction"; skulls are those of sacrificed victims.

FIGURE VII. Okpo at Imilikane

The large statue represents the goddess; the smaller figure represents her senior daughter, Abere; the carved wooden figure in the foreground is a lidded vessel used for storing kola intended for sacrifice to the gods.

FIGURE VIII. Iyi Akpala at Umu Mkpume
The large statue represents the goddess; the smaller figure represents her senior son, Onumuno; on the far side of the wall is her altar, and above her are skulls of sacrificed victims.

FIGURE IX. Ezuugwu at Nkpologu-Attah

The large white-cloth-wrapped figure represents the god; the spears represent his powers; the altar is the blackened area on the right; as the father-figure of Nsukka Division, Ezuugwu is properly represented as a large phallus.

FIGURE X. Adada at Obimo-Ejuona

The large decorated phallic figure represents the goddess (?), the smaller one to her right represents her son, Onumuno, and the one to her left represents her daughter, Abere; the spears are symbols of her powers.

FIGURE XI. Kelekede and Other Shrine Objects (Number 1)
The figure atop the pole is a kelekede, which indicates that this shrine is dedicated to a nonfamiliar spirit.

FIGURE XI. Kelekede and Other Shrine Objects (Number 2)
The special pots are surrounded by life-trees, which are a feature at alusi *shrines.*

join the *osu*") may exist, but in the Nsukka borderland this notion is considered very strange. "If I want to run away from my people," Attama Iyi Owo once explained to me, "I will go to my mother's people. I would never become *osu*."

The precincts of an *alusi* shrine are never particularly inviting or comfortable for the villager, but rather excite nervousness or tension, and they are generally avoided. The ritual value of such precincts functions to reinforce the people's notion that the spirit is powerful and potentially dangerous, for the more avoidance they practice the more they rationalize their avoidance and the quicker they perceive that over-familiarity by anyone not especially attached to the shrine as priest or slave results in serious consequences for that person. The tension and fear aroused by shrine areas—especially of this class—strengthen the hold the priest and diviner (usually the same person) have over the community. This is important when one remembers that these priests, who are the sole intermediaries between the villagers and the often hostile *alusi*, were alien occupation personnel with political loyalties originally to the Igala and Okpoto rather than to the Igbo.

Function of Sacred Precincts

Geertz, speaking of religion as a cultural system, has said that sacred symbols function to synthesize a people's world-view, "the picture they have of the way things in sheer actuality are, their most comprehensive ideas of order" (1958:421, and in Banton, 1966:3). This appropriately describes the function of sacred places in Nsukka borderland belief: the shrine areas or environs associated with familiar spirits are treated familiarly, are places where one can relax and feel relatively comfortable; but places where medicine is deposited—such as crossroads—or *alusi*-inhabited areas of a village are dangerous and unpredictable, so people reflect anxiety around them. The sacred symbols and precincts in the borderland do less to synthesize the people's world-view than among groups with more consciously ordered religion and religious symbols, yet the precincts and symbols do reflect the basic dichotomy between things which exist and which possess vast spiritual powers: the known and the unknown, the predictable and the unpredictable, the usually friendly and the often hostile, the kin-group and the strangers. In the following chapters dealing respectively with the ancestors and familiar spirits, the *alusi*, and religious control forces, we shall see more clearly how these distinctions furnish one major pattern of the world as envisaged by the people of the borderland.

5. Nsụkka Family and Household Religion: Gods and Ancestors

As we saw earlier, "man" and "ancestors" are not terms which one can easily separate, for the living man is a reincarnated ancestor and, when he dies, will become a spiritualized ancestor with all the pertinent privileges and powers. Similarly, living man cannot be considered in isolation from some essentially non-human spirits which are integrally related to him, as distinct from other non-human spiritual forces—from whom he can be isolated, in certain respects—which are socially and extrinsically related to him. Those spirits somehow integrally related to man can generally be classified as "familiar" spirits and have as their priests and mediators the family or clan elders, as distinct from the *alusi* and non-familiar spirits for whom the *attama* is the priest. Outsiders have no jurisdiction whatsoever in family affairs, including the worship of familiar spirits, and the clan headmen jealously guard their rights as intermediaries between their kin groups and these forces.

Those familiar spirits without whom man could not come into existence as a physical being whose existence depends upon some spiritual intention, are *Chukwu* or *Ezechitoke*, the High God, and his manifestations as *chi* or personal maintaining spirit and *okuke* or maintaining and fertility creator spirit. Also important are a host of fertility spirits, including the spiritualized Earth, *Ane*, as the Female

Principle, but these are considered to be less directly functional in relation to a person's coming into being: that is, it is held generally in the borderland that, if Chukwu so desires, a child will be born regardless of the degree of cooperation by other spiritual beings.

Chi and the High God

The significance of the High God and closely related creator gods in Nsukkan religious belief was expressed most clearly in the following abstracts from field materials, drawn from several borderland villages (see Chart VI: *Relationships Between Man and Creators*).

Q. What is a man's *chi*?

A. This is not Chukwu, but the one who is inside a man. Every person has *chi* inside of him. Chukwu made it. Chukwu is the creator of man, and he owns you; when he calls you, it means you will die. The *chi* that you are talking about is *chi mmadu* [*chi* of the person], and it is related to a man's shadow. If a man dies, you can't see his shadow again.

Q. What happens to *chi mmadu* when the man dies?

A. Chukwu takes it back, because it is his and he wants it. If Chukwu calls for somebody's *chi* because that person did something, or only if Chukwu wants the *chi* back, then that person will be killed.

Q. Is *chi* the most powerful part of a man?

A. It is not part of him. It is in him somehow, but it belongs to somebody else [i.e., Chukwu]. The powerful things in a man are his *obi* ["chest"=heart] and his *ume* ["breath"= life], and especially his *mmuo* ["spirit"], but these things are not strong in a man without *chi*.

Q. Does a man's *chi* ever die?

A. It goes back to Chukwu, who owns it. He is too strong to die. *Chi* cannot die, because it is something that does not die.

Important about the foregoing is that because each man possesses

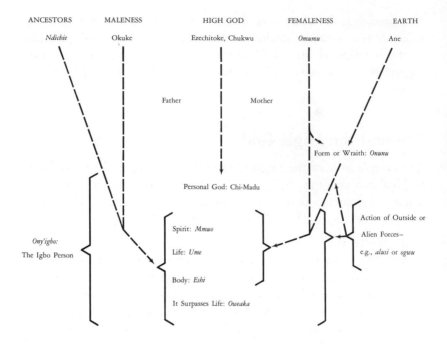

CHART VI. *Relationships Between Man and Creators*

chi, which is created and given him by Chukwu and which upon his death is reclaimed by Chukwu (and which also *is* Chukwu in one sense), the High God is always immediately present to the northern Igbo villager: the villager participates in the High God through the possession of *chi* (see Shelton, 1965b:16; Talbot, 1926, II:16, however, refers to *chi* as the High God in general among Igbo).

According to this set of beliefs, man is composed of a number of forces, as Meek (1937:53 ff.) pointed out in his study of southeastern Nsukkan groups. Among these are his body which has *ndo* or "life" in general. The person's existence depends upon *oweaka* ("it surpasses life"), which resides in the heart. Spiritually centered here is *mmuo*, which leaves the body at death and is that which survives as his spirit, and *chi*, which returns to Chukwu, its possessor (compare Basden, 1938:281).

Worship of the High God varies in Nsukka, although everywhere there is at least an annual festival for Chukwu, and in some villages the High God, rather than one of the *alusi*, is the "protector" of every compound (see Map IV: *Spatial Relationships—Umune Ngwa*). In almost all villages, moreover, there is a sun shrine, *Anyanwu*, which is specifically a shrine dedicated to the High God (see Figure III: *Anyanwu Shrine at Imilikenu*). Where, as at Umune Ngwa village, the High God is the compound protector, there tends to be more frequent worship, and the prayers themselves are much more like begging requests by dependent children made to a bountiful father than propitiations of a harsh deity. At the Umune Ngwa annual worship, for example, the prayers are as follows:[1]

Ezechitoke, bea   welu oje.
God,   come take kola [i.e., be welcome].
Mmuo nine   di ebea,   bea   welu oje.
Spirits all [who] are to come here, come take kola.
Wetebe   umu   aka,   wetebe   nwanye.
Bring forth children many, bring forth women.
Wetebe   ego   na   ifeoma.

---

1. Prayers cited here and in following passages of this study are not precisely fixed texts as discussed by Vansina, 1961, 56, but are semi-free; the tradition is fixed, but not precisely, and the form of the prayers is fairly stable.

Bring forth money and things good.
Ezechitoke, biko   *zoghede*   *anyi.*
God,   please continue to protect us.
K'etebe   *umu,*   *k'etebe*   *ife,*
May you bring forth children, may you bring forth goods,
ishigi   *dibe.*
head your is sufficient [i.e., you are all we need].
Zogidenu'mu,   *ndi*   *ikenyelu.*
Protect the people, those whom you have given.
Biko   *zogide*   *anyi.*
Please protect us.
Ekwene   *ife*   *obula*
Agree not [that] things unexpected
   ka'ma   *anyi.*
   instead [of good things] happen to us.

The High God is worshipped daily in some areas, although the prayers are normally short. For example, at Aro-uno-Nsukka, the compound headman invokes the High God, here called Eze Chukwu Okuke, every morning and evening. He strikes a tiny *ogene* gong (clapperless bell) four times, then offers kola with the words repeated once:

Eze Chukwuoke, taa oje.
God,   eat kola.
Ka ndu'm dili.
Let life my continue.
Taa   *bo eke* [or *oye, afo, nkwo*].
Today is (name of the day).

Such prayers as these are made at a particular altar dedicated to the High God. At Aro-uno, the altar is a small shrine of stones with a grass-thatched roof supported on three-feet long life-tree sticks. Shrines for the High God are outside in the compound, or in a village square.

The only shrine which a man builds into his house as part of its basic construction aside from the altar to his forefathers is *onuchi* ("mouth" of *chi*, the word *onu* or "mouth" actually meaning "altar" in this context, because sacrifices are made on an altar, which thus serves as the "mouth" by which the spirit eats the sacrifice). When the site of a future house has been determined, the owner comes with friends and, usually, male relatives, and on the spot sacrifices palm wine, vegetable foods—especially yam—a rooster, and kola. During construction of the house, in a corner near or next to the doorway, just inside the entrance, a mud platform about two or three feet high is raised. While the mud is still soft, a stick of the castor bean tree is placed erect in it. This represents the owner's *chi*, and along with the *okuke* suggests the male principle. "*Chi* stands up, and it is strong," as an informant explained. "Even the *chi* for a woman is male." Outside, in the compound, the owner then plants a stick of the life-tree, *ogbu*, which represents or acts as the altar to the High God. Inside once again, the owner makes the *okuke* shrine immediately next to the *onuchi*. This consists of small pots, one placed on the ground mouth upwards, the other used to cover it, the pots symbolizing the roundness of the pregnant belly from which all men come yet also representing the male creative spirit which "brings to life" the infant within the womb and also emerges —as a male human—from such a source.

Upon installing his *chi* altar itself, the owner ordinarily offers a small food and welcome sacrifice to it, with the prayers:

Chi'm,   taa   oje.
Chi my, eat kola [i.e., be welcome].
Chi'm,   laa   mmanya.
Chi my, drink palm wine.
Chi'm,   zo'm.
Chi my, protect me.
Chi'm,   ekwena ka   ife   'memu.
Chi my, let not that things happen [to] me.
Chi'm,   ndu   uwamu,   'nyelu'm   aka.
Chi my, life [of] world my, give to me hand [help].

The next stage of construction, which sometimes is done before the offerings are made, involves the addition of other upright sticks called *nkpulu chi* ("pieces [of] *chi*") which represent the owner's dead male forebears as he wishes to memorialize them. These are not to be confused with the *nna* or forefathers of the lineage, whose symbols are kept in the ancestral shrine house of the lineage (see Map V: *Spatial Relationships—Ameegwu Village, Owele-ezeoba*). The altars to *chi* and *okuke* are thus linked together in the household compound. The annual festival for *chi*, furthermore, is called *agba okuke* (*agba*: "feast"), maintaining the close link between these two aspects of the unitary creative force—it is male insofar as it causes, but in symbols its feminine aspect can be portrayed as a pot (belly-like receptacle). There is no contradiction in this, for the female principle is also depicted as "small male" by reference to the clitoris which is symbolized by the kokoyam and cassava as distinct from the yam symbol for the male principle.

We have seen that the house-owner's *chi* is built only after his father is dead or when he has grown and lives apart, becoming the head of a new household, and that at this time his *onuchi* protects his wives and his children. Above the *onuchi*, moreover, the head of household suspends from the ceiling a net, *anyaka*, which contains a round basket. This is dedicated to his mother, and continues the pot-pregnant belly symbolism, suggesting the householder's gratitude to his mother for having borne him and his desire that his own *chi* help her, whether she is living or dead, otherwise she is protected under the aegis of her husband only, who of course is not a consanguine as the son is.

Variations of the foregoing exist, particularly within lineages of *attama* who descend from Igala. For example, Ugwuoke Attama, *onyishi* of Dimunke clan in Ameegwu village, erected his *onuchi* in the house of the ancestors (*uloarua*), and there also his *okuke* shrine and a *chi* altar for his senior wife. This even more definitely relates *chi*, *okuke*, and the High God to the forces of the ancestors.

Chi is considered separate from the individual, although within him, and is invoked often several times daily in short prayers when one leaves his compound or when one is worried or frightened: *Chi'm, zogide'm* ("My *chi*, protect me.").

As a separate yet intimately associated spirit, and as an aspect also of the supreme High God, *chi* serves especially useful functions in

Nsukkan (and general Igbo) culture. First, and rather obvious, is the fact that God is always "with" the individual, but not God otiose as Chukwu tends often to be when considered in himself as the supreme being. Second, *chi* is a guardian and protector of the specific individual, as distinct from the *alusi* and the ancestors whose tutelary functions serve an extended group of people, so the individual possesses this reassurance that he is never completely divorced from spiritual aid. The *chi* is, finally, that by which the northern Igbo can rationalize many otherwise inexplicable events which personally affect him. Meek has said, in reference to Nsukka Igbo, that "if a man's conduct gets him into trouble he excuses himself by saying (and believing) that his *chi* and not he himself is responsible" (1937:55). This is only partly the case, for Nsukkans realize fully that although *chi* might be responsible for an event, *chi* never suffers, whereas the human does, so the person has the responsibility for protecting himself and for behaving properly despite his *chi*. Ultimately, the cause of suffering is not the action of *chi*, but human failure of some sort—the person has failed to propitiate his *chi*, he has acted irrationally, or he has transgressed the law. Man is considered responsible for his own actions, even though it is agreed that various powerful beings can affect him. On one occasion, during an annual festival for the forefathers while I was accompanying lineage elders of Umu Mkpume, a young man who had neglected his duties to his ancestors was pleading with the elders to make the sacrifices which only they could make to right the wrongs and, excusing his actions, he gave the argument that his *chi* was evil. The senior elder angrily snapped at him: "You are evil! The forefather of *chi* is someone else [i.e., Chukwu], and your *chi* will not do things to your forefathers! You did the evil things!" The *chi*, consequently, can be blamed, but just as a man succeeds by his own efforts and with the help of his *chi*, he fails not only because of his *chi* but also more definitely because of his own actions.

Other Familiar Spirits: Earth

An important god is the deified Earth, *Ane* (*Ani, Ani, Ala*), who is considered to be female and, in the borderland, more or less the equal of the High God in age and practical power. As the saying goes, *Ane na Chukwu ra*, "Earth and God are equal." Ane's equality with Chukwu is thus far accepted, and she is considered his female counterpart, although she cannot do all the things he can. In a perhaps typically feminine manner, she is a recipient, as *Attama* Ngwu Mkpume pointed out: "Even when offerings are made to Chukwu, they are poured on the ground, which is owned by Ale."

Ane is considered to have no parents, although other gods (with but few exceptions) possess *arua* staffs and are said to have descended from something greater or senior or both. The priest of the *alusi* Okwuugwu said that "Okwuugwu is from the earth, where it grew, and then it grew above the earth." Similarly, the priest of Iyi Akpala said, "Iyi Akpala is the daughter of Ane." The priest of Ngwuma-kechi explained that "Ngwumakechi is on the surface of the earth, and so he is related to Ane, but because Earth and Sky touch he is related also to Igwe [Sky]." Although such notions of relationship to or descent from Ane are fairly common, as a rule Earth does not have the usual children-spirits which we will see comprise the spirit-families of most village *alusi*.

Related to Ane, certainly as a supplier of food, is the plant fertility spirit named *Ushuajiokwo* (var., *Mfiajioku*), a female spirit whose shrine is located within each person's compound near the yam barn. This spirit is considered the supplier and protector of crops, and is worshipped before planting time in the dry season, usually in March of the European calendar. All the farm tools are brought inside the yam barn for the ceremony, which is one of the few at which the tortoise—the animal most sacred to Ane herself—can be sacrificed, although only if the goddess demands it. Other familiar spirits include the kitchen spirits mentioned in the preceding chapter, and similar protective medicines. None of these is very prominent though in the hierarchy of spiritual powers in the borderland, where the great conflict occurred between the ancestors and their human control agents and the *alusi* and their mediators.

Man and the Ancestors

Of the familiar spirits, *chi* is closest to the individual; even his ancestors are not so closely related to him, for although he is an ancestor reincarnated his forefathers otherwise are the forefathers of his other living relatives. Their role in Nsukkan life, nonetheless, is extremely important, and the worship of them normally includes at least preliminary worship of the High God and, often, implicit worship of Earth.

How does one become an ancestor? Indeed, what precisely is an ancestor in borderland belief? Meyer Fortes' discussion of "Ancestor Worship" (Fortes, 1965:128–131) includes several points germane to belief in the Nsukka borderland: death alone is not sufficient for becoming an ancestor who is entitled to receive worship. Proper burial and funerary rites conducted by the properly designated persons must be performed. For ancestorhood, the dead person must be brought back home to the lineage and must somehow manifest himself in the life of his descendants and be enshrined.

Some persons die and receive no worship, or virtually none, while others are considered influential in the affairs of the living. Although in rare cases some are women, usually the more important ancestors are men. To the northern Igbo merely being male and old does not make one superior, for like nuclear Igbo emphasis is placed upon seniority combined with individual accumulation and attainment of titled status. A senior woman can become an important ancestor because of the title status and personal powers which she cultivated during her lifetime, or which were accorded her as honors by her respectful children. Far more men than women, however, take titles, or have titles taken for them by their sons, and the Nsukka Igbo inclines to emphasize the male over the female, so the majority of powerful ancestors—including those best remembered—are male, although often of the matriline. Furthermore, village government is controlled by older men, so those forefathers who are represented by statuary or other means (mud pillars or stones) and are considered to be the family's spiritualized governing group are invariably male.

In Nsukka there are two major branches of ancestralism: *arua* worship and the worship of the *nna* ("fathers"), both in charge of familial control persons (headmen). The difference between *arua* and *nna* was explained simply by my informants: "The *nna* are persons [*mmadu*], but not the *arua*." This is often the case, although the explanation requires some clarification: *arua* sometimes are given names which specify them, but in themselves they are representations of the spiritual force of the ancestors rather than the personalities of the ancestors; *nna*, on the other hand, normally are named and remembered ancestors, although in many cases names have been substituted by descriptive words which explain their function in relation to the living. A good example of the latter is the name of one of the forefathers of the village of Umugoji—*Elele*, "Watches-Watches." When I commented to the lineage elder that the name was strange, he replied, "*Elele* had a different name, but we don't know it any more." This is often true for the more senior forefathers in lineages where more than five or six *nna* are worshipped, and suggests the difference between *arua* and *nna*: the *arua* are senior and thus more distant, so they are less remembered than the *nna*. They lived in *mgba ndichie*, the misty "time [of the] ancestors," when things began, whereas many of the lineage forefathers are remembered as persons and are more clearly historical. *Arua* and *nna* also serve different functions: *arua* oversee the entire clan (*ukwaarua*: "great spear") and have spiritual jurisdiction over all the descendants of the originator of the broadest descent group of the Nsukka Igbo; *nna*, however, are the dead elders of a patrilineage (*umunna*) and possess powers restricted to consanguineous members of that lineage only.

Worship of the *nna* consists typically of offerings and prayers made daily and annually by the elder of each *umunna*, and also annually by the *onyishi* of the clan. The following description of the annual festival for the *nna* at Umu Mkpume, when I was a guest of Umu Amoke patrilineage of Eze Owuru clan, furnishes a fairly standard pattern of the annual worship of the forefathers in the borderland. The eleven *nna* of Umu Amoke are the descendants of Eze Owuru ("Chief [who is] of Awulu Market"), a shortened form of the name of the legendary Okpoto founder of many lineages in Nsukka, *Eze Ugwu Eshugwuru*, "Famous King known for his cunning in the forest about Awulu," who was apparently Omeppa, the Okpoto chief of Awulu who allied with the founder of the present Igala dynasty, Ayegba, and became the first *ashadu* (kingmaker) and, in some accounts, the consort of Egbele Ejuona,[2] the Jukun princess of the Ankpa account. This mythical person is sometimes considered to be a foremother in some Nsukkan origin tales.

The eleven *nna* of Umu Amoke are represented by small wooden statues set in an earthern altar; their names, in order of descending age, are:

1. Ezeocha ("white king"), eldest son of Eze Owuru, symbolized by the *ube* or "pear" tree, which is very large, with whitish bark and small dark brown and black fruit.
2. Owego ("way of the companion"), half-brother to Ezeocha.
3. *Origenne* ("Great One of the Mothers"—significance unknown; from *irika*, "to be much"—*origunne*, "big").
4. Name forgotten by informants.
5. Name forgotten by informants.
6. Name forgotten by informants.
7. *Ugwuoke Ngwu Ogwa* ("Great Man, Ngwu, [descended from] Ogwa," who was the legendary first *ashadu*, Omeppa).
8. Name forgotten by informants.
9. *Ukwu Ngwu Owego* ("Great Ngwu, [descended from] Owego").
10. *Okanya* (*okenya*, "Elder"—i.e., "Important Person").
11. *Agidibeoha* ("May You Return Again As Another," an honorific, also intoned as another honorific, *Agidigbwoha*, "Ladder of *Ofo*," "Means of Power.")

Feasting goes on in each household, the worship consisting of food offerings and expressions of gratitude given to the ancestors

---

2. The name means, to Ankpa elders, "maiden who was a proper descendant," from *egbele* ("maiden") and the combined *eju* ("face of") and *ona* ("father"). They also interpreted it to mean "maiden who claimed kingship," from *'jo* ("claimed") and *onu* ("chief"), indicating that it is to be pronounced *Egbele 'jonu* (see Seton, 1928:269–270; Hassan, 1962:3).

for having protected the people during the year. Each member of the household has special duties in relation to this festival. The male head of household buys all the yams, furnishes some *okpa* (ground-pea), and provides the major sacrificial animals, usually goats. The unmarried sons furnish palm wine, and the married sons bring cooked yam (*ji*) or ground-pea or both, as well as cocks and, if they can afford it, goats. Unmarried daughters bring calabashes of palm wine from their prospective husbands (girls are often betrothed as infants), and married daughters bring cooked food and, depending upon their husbands' finances and generous inclinations, sacrificial animals. Junior wives have no particular duties for this festival, but the senior wife (*obonoko*), has several serious obligations which meet needs not merely of the household feast but of the festival itself. First, she must provide all the kola nuts which the head of household will offer to the forefathers. They are therefore made welcome among their own blood relations by this important woman who is only an affine. *Obonoko* must also provide a large cock for blood sacrifice to the forefathers. One informant argued that this was because the cock heralds the day, and giving the ancestors this sacrifice is meant to indicate that they, like the day, should return in the lineage by being reborn in a new child. Other elders, however, considered this fanciful, and said the cock is male (*oke*) and so are the ancestors, and giving them a cock is the *obonoko*'s way of showing that although she is important in the household, the men are more important. Actually the cock is a customary offering which is little more than a token, its value not being as great as a hen's, for example. Its symbolic value, according to one elder *obonoko*, is to suggest that only male foods are sacrificed for the ancestors; other senior women, practical-minded souls, said it helps to provide more meat for the feast and, if the old men had their way, they would probably ask for a goat.

Obonoko is also expected to provide all the palm oil which will be used in the food offerings to the forefathers, she must prepare all the soup for the feasts, must see that all the lamps for guests are made ready, and she personally must cook the food, especially the meat of the sacrificed animals. These preparations by the various members of the household take place over a period of one or two Igbo weeks (4 or 8 days), but the cooking of meat and feasting occurs only after the sacrifices are made to the *nna*, according to the principle whereby the eldest receive their portion first.

The annual festival for the *nna* is held for all lineages of a clan (*ukwaarua*) at the same time, so indirectly the festival also honors the *arua* themselves as well as the lineage forefathers. Certainly the *onyishi* (headman) of the clan—the man in charge of the *arua* staffs— is the person in charge of all the lineage sacrifices. The first sacrifice, accordingly, which takes place about mid-afternoon of the festival day, is made to the *nna* of the *onyishi*'s lineage, who are housed in *uloarua* ("house [of the] *arua*"). Before the elders enter the house of the forefathers, the wooden slit drum, *ekwe* (elsewhere called *ogbonye*), is beaten as a form of announcement to the *nna* that they are about to receive offerings. All sacrifices and prayers directed to the clan or lineage forefathers throughout the festival are made by the *onyishi*, who is the person in closest contact with both the *arua* and the ancestors; assisting him are the elders of the lineages and heads of the more important—in most instances, more senior—households.

On the occasion when I was present, an event occurred which gives some insight into the force of traditional control forces vis-a-vis modernization (usually Europeanization) among the Nsukkans. After the sacrifices of a goat, several chickens, yam fufu, palm oil, kola, and palm wine libations in the *arua* house, a man of perhaps thirty, younger than the elders, appeared in front of the *arua* house and called out to the elders to lift their cruel ban from his shoulders. His father had died the year before, and the son had refused to "feed" them and *onyishi* (i.e., make sacrificial offerings through the *onyishi* to his forefathers); several times during the year he had been warned to perform his proper duty, but he consistently refused or ignored the warnings. As a result of his incalcitrance, at dawn on the morning of the festival day the *onyishi* laid a prohibition upon the man, forbidding him to make any sacrifices whatsoever and forbidding him to kill any animals in his compound for any purpose. The effect of this was to cut the young man off completely from his ancestors and to bring their wrath on him for not having honored them. So the young man appeared to beg the assembled elders to lift the ban upon his making sacrifices, without which his family could not eat. After making his plea, with little apparent remorse (I felt), he retired from the compound.

The elders discussed the situation briefly, agreeing that the culprit should be kept under the prohibition for a while longer because he obviously needed the punishment and, they reminded one another, the "fathers" would not appreciate the elders being too lenient, since they were responsible for seeing that family law be obeyed. So they called the young man back to them and demanded that he make offerings to all the lineage elders as well as the *onyishi*. The young man argued—as I described earlier—that his *chi* was evil, which simply angered the elders further. Then his sister, a grown woman, showed up to plead his case, wailing that all of them would die unless the elders showed mercy. Abruptly the young man was told to bring food and wine offerings or the ban would not be lifted, so he strode away from the *arua* house, appearing dejected.

After this, the party of elders and guests (a shrine priest from another clan and I) moved to Umu Ngwuoke patrilineage, the next in seniority, for the sacrifices there, the *onyishi* having carried the clan *arua* staffs along when we trekked from his own lineage area. The *ekwe* was beaten, we entered, and palm wine libations were poured by the headman over the statues of the forefathers, on the altar itself, and on the *arua* staffs. Odu Asogwa, the lineage elder, recited aloud the prayers for this, his lineage:

> Let all of our fathers eat kola [i.e., be welcome].
> Let [names of forefathers, one by one] drink wine.
> Let [names of forefathers, one by one] eat this animal.
> Let no one who is living die.
> Let no harm come to the rest of your people.

The sacrifice of a goat followed the libations, and the animal's blood was used to wash the statues of the *nna*, the altar, the *arua*, and the *anigo*, a buffalo horn used to supplement the *ekwe* in summoning the spirits from the underworld. Chickens then, one by one, were sacrificed, the first furnished by the *obonoko* of the lineage head to signify her ownership of the palm trees (considered here to be both male and symbols for masculinity), and the others those furnished by Asogwa's daughters. This completed the offerings to the *nna* "who live inside" because they are *ogbuefi* ("he killed cow"), ancestors whose descendants killed a cow in their honor. After this, the *onyishi*, accompanied by Asogwa, moved outside the ancestral shrine house and planted one small green twig of the *ichikeri* life tree. Before this green twig, which represented all the ancestors for whom no cattle had been sacrificed, a small hole was dug for the *arua* staffs, palm wine and kola were offered, and one or two chickens were killed.

Again, as soon as the offerings were made, the young man and his sister reappeared, pleaded (a bit more earnestly, I thought), and retired only to be recalled after a moment to hear the verdict of the elders. This time, *Attama* Iyi Akpala delivered a long oration in which he catalogued the various evils which could descend upon the whole village if such behavior as the culprit's were permitted: flood, fire, famine, epidemics, tornado, lightning, invading enemies, snakes, witches, large animals, unforeseen events, and the like. Afterwards, not to be outdone, although less oratorically, the other *attama* of Umu Mkpume, Ngwu Mkpume, spoke, reminding the supplicant of his obligations not simply to the *nna* but to the *alusi* as well, to Earth, to the god Ngwu, to the goddess Iyi Akpala, and a number of non-familiar deities. The young man and his sister were sent away again while the elders discussed the case, then he was told precisely the goods which he must bring to the elders. He swore that he would abide by their decision, but pleaded that he needed 17 days' time (until his next payday); *Attama* Ngwu swore publicly that he would be responsible for seeing that the man appeared on time. But the elders argued further, demanding that the man appear in four days with palm wine, when they would decide if he might be permitted to have the further extension. The young man agreed, so the problem was solved.

From this lineage the group of elders then moved to the next in descending seniority, the prayers and offerings being the same from place to place, until all the *nna* of the clan had received their rightful first share. Then followed the time for preparing the cooked food, which was consumed that evening, well after dark.

At the evening festivities, each patrilineage feasted in the compound of the lineage elder, the men crowded into the ancestral shrine house, the women and children seated on grass mats and stools just outside the house. Because this is a festival intended to strengthen the bonds of lineage members, married women of the lineage are not present, but go to the lineage of their fathers. If the women are from villages not celebrating the feast of the forefathers at the same time they in most cases share in this feast as well, thereby strengthening affinal ties. More than fifty per cent of all my contact lineages expressed the idea that it was better to marry a woman from a place which made this feast at a different time not only so the woman would not shirk her duties to her husband (an important consideration) but also to keep "secret hatred" and quarrels at a minimum by making the woman feel more at home with her husband's people.

There are many variations of customary activities during *nna* festivals, most of them minor. One important variation, especially in view of its function in strengthening Igbo solidarity, is the *Onunu* ("spirit remaining") Festival, a women's part of the *nna* festival of Ihe-Nsukka. The main feature of the *Onunu* Festival is the *Oromme* ("let it stay for a long time") Ceremony performed by the grown women and young girls at the very old and revered Nkwo Market, which significantly is also the chief gathering place for the *omabe* men's society (one of the major control forces in a large number of Nsukka village groups).

Dressed in their finest, the women gather at Nkwo Market on Nkwo day preceding the *nna* festivals in late January and, to the accompaniment of dancing rattles (*osha*), carry small girls on their shoulders and dance beneath the great *ube* tree (*Pachylobis edulis*). For each festival, there are nine small girls, three from each of Nsukka's "quarters," who are danced about the market and, while dancing with the upper part of their bodies as the women are carrying them, the little girls attempt to snatch a leaf off the *ube*, everyone throughout the ceremony shouting: "Nkwo, oro mme!" ("Nkwo Market and Day, [let Nsukka people] stay for a long time!"). All the little girls are able to tear a leaf off the tree, and it is believed that they thereby have assured the fertility of their respective quarters of Nsukka. The *purpose* of this annual festival is obviously to ensure continued fertility; the festival *functions*, however, to reinforce the union of the many villages comprising the "town" of Nsukka. This union has been maintained through female lines especially since the wide spread of Igala shrine priests throughout the area and the subsequent threats to Igbo social control.

Umuada ("children-daughters") is a women's society parallel to the *omabe* which tends to work as a control force in village affairs and to maintain the bonds between "daughters" (female consanguines) of a clan and their *umunna*, from which they are necessarily separated because of exogamy. Normally the annual *umuada* festival is held at approximately the same time as the annual festival for the *nna*—for example, in the Owele-ezeoba villages, in *Onwano* ("Moon Four") on a *nkwo* day, which is female. At festival time, women of each patri-lineage who are married outside their *umunna* must bring home sacrificial offerings for the worship of the forefathers. Although the eldest woman of the lineage is the main judge and leader of *umuada* meetings (which tend to be frequent, insofar as women are involved in many market squabbles and negotiations), the eldest man of each clan is in charge of the actual sacrifices, which are made at the small-pot shrine of the *umuada* in each clan area. On the following day (*eke*, the only male day in the four day week), the festival for the *nna* takes place in each village of this group.

Arua and Ancestral Force

If the *nna* are relatively identifiable as particular ancestors of specific lineages—despite the apparent mythicization of their personalities and names—the *arua* are considered to be spiritual forces embodied in and symbolized by varying numbers of sacred staffs, although some *arua* staffs in some clans represent actual ancestors.

Arua are, simply, ancestral staffs or spears (see Figure XII: *Arua* —"*At Rest*" *and* "*Upright*"; and Figure XIII: *Ebonyeze and Arua Worship* [*3 Figures*]). Meek called them *aro* or iron staves and said that they "appear sometimes to have been used as a magical means of testing the validity of a decision. For it was stated in one group that in the olden days the holder of the *aro*, when announcing his decision, planted the staff in the ground and said, 'Give ear to what we are about to say, for life is in the ear'. . . . Sometimes, the *aro*-holder took precedence of all other elders, because he was the senior member of a titled society or was the direct descendant of the first person to receive a title" (Meek, 1937:132). *Arua* (var.: *aryo*) probably are of Igbo origin among the Nsukkans, although their interpretation and functions differ somewhat from the sacred spears of central Igbo (see Green, 1947:109–111). They differ also from the *otonshi* of the Umunri, and even from the *okute* ancestral staffs of the Igala. The word might be related to the Bini *Arowa*, meaning "head of compound" (Egharevba, 1949:13; and see Talbot, 1926, II:141) or "master," according to one Igala elder at Ogurugu, although I was not able to confirm this latter interpretation with Nsukka Igbo informants. Ugwu (1958:14) says that the "arua idols" were supposed to be the originators of the families. A northern Nsukka man himself (from Obukpa, due north of Nsukka town), he is speaking symbolically here, for although *arua* are intimately related to ancestors there is consistency in the testimony that the *arua* were brought by family founders or, as the case may be, by *nshie* or Igala chiefs or medicine makers.

Ebonyeze, the headman of Umueze Clan in Ameegwu Village (see Map V: *Spatial Relationships—Ameegwu Village, Oba*) said:

> The first person to make *arua* was *Ezuugwu Esh'ugwuru* ["Famous Chief of the Forest by Awulu"—i.e., Omeppa], in the olden times. I was told this by my father. Eze Awuru was the ancestor of all the people who have this [i.e., *arua*]. That is the way it started.

Informants at Umu Mkpume similarly ascribe to *arua* a source outside their locality:

FIGURE XII. Arua (Number 1)
Arua "at rest" during the night above the doorway to the house of the onyishi.

FIGURE XII. Arua (Number 2)
Arua "upright" in the onu *(altar) during the daytime in the "House of Arua," where the* onyishi *awaits callers.*

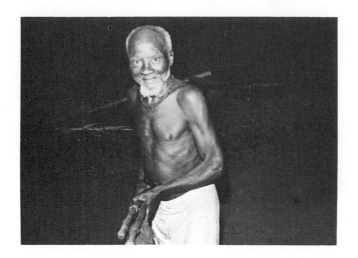

FIGURE XIII. Ebonyeze and Arua Worship (Number 1)
Before dawn, Ebonyeze carrying arua from his sleeping house to the "House of Arua."

FIGURE XIII. Ebonyeze and Arua Worship (Number 2)
Placing arua into the "Mouth of Arua."

FIGURE XIII. Ebonyeze and Arua Worship (Number 3)
Offering kola to arua, after they have been washed.

The *nshie* people originally brought the *arua* to Umu Mkpume, and *arua* worship took rise from them. All *arua* in the whole of Nsukka Division came from the *nshie*, who traveled to different parts of the area and taught *arua* worship to the people.

There are several types of *arua* staffs common in the Nsukka borderland. *Arua* are all kept with the headman of a clan—he carries them with him to his sleeping house at night, where they rest above the only doorway to his house so that their spiritual powers control all who might enter the house; and in the morning when he awakens he carries them with him to his public reception house called *uloarua*, "house of the *arua*," where they are given offerings at dawn and where they remain erect all day, their points (on special sacrifice days) stuck into the earth of the altar or (on non-sacrificial days) their butts set on the earth by the altar. The most important of the *arua* is the "eldest," referred to as *ishi arua* ("head *arua*"). Sometimes it also has a specific name which indicates not only its function as the eldest and most important but identifies it either as an ancestral symbol or as belonging to a given founder. An example of this is found in Umunri-influenced villages (such as Ihe-Nsukka) where it is called *ezeoka* ("the Awka chief"). The chief servant of this main *arua* staff is normally *oziosu arua* ("messenger-slave *arua*"); variants of this are *ojozi arua* ("*arua* who goes with messages") and *ojose*, (Okpoto meaning "iron carried in the hand") as in Owele-ezeoba. *Oshishi-aka*, ("Staff [of the] hand") a brass-encircled iron rod very similar to the *oshishi* staff at Asaba and other Igbo communities west of the Niger, tends to be associated with *arua* particularly in villages having Umunri (*nshie*) lines, such as Ohebe-oba. The *Mpe arua* ("small *arua*") are those staffs which represent the lesser forces among ancestral powers. The last of the shifting *arua* staffs (those which are transferred from one headman to the next) is *okwo* (Igala: "spear"), the short spear associated with the *arua* of *alusi* shrines and which is the spear used in the ceremonial rebirth of the *attah* of Igala from the *ashadu*: the first act of the "newly-born" *attah* is to raise his arm to stab his "mother" (the *ashadu*) with *okwo* (see Seton, 1928:263), suggesting the rejection of the line of the *ashadu* in succession to the throne of Idah. *Okwo* is also similar to the small spears of the Umunri *otonshie*. The non-shifting *arua* staff, finally, is referred to as *okaka* ("it grows old" [i.e., with its holder]). This is a completely iron staff which remains with the *onyishi*; when a new *onyishi* assumes control over the *arua* he must have a smith make his personal *okaka* as his insignia of office.

The actual number of *arua* staffs varies considerably, although in most borderland villages if there is but one staff it will be "head *arua*" (*ishiarua*), sometimes called *Ezeugwu* ("great chief," reference to Omeppa, the first *ashadu*) or *Ezeoka*. In discussing the origins of the *arua* of *Ngwumadeshe*, the *alusi* of Umugoji, *Attama* Ngwu said:

> The forefathers made them a long time ago, so the ceremony must be performed. There were four old men in the time of the ancestors who made the offerings. First there was one, and then he died, so another staff was added, until there were four staffs in this *arua*. After that, there were only four. Ngwumadeshe said: "There are four." So we never had more than four. In some other villages in Oba there are eight staffs in the *arua*, so if our number would ever change, it would change to eight staffs. But in some villages there is still only one staff, because that was the way it was from the time of the forefathers, and men cannot change it.

It is believed that through certain of the *arua*, or through parts of the *arua* shrine, runs the *uzoma* ("path [of the] spirits") by which ancestors are reincarnated among the members of the clan in which they had lived. At Umune Ngwa Village, for example, there are four *arua* staffs: *Okaka; Ojoozi Arua*, the messenger; *Ishiarua*, a thick-shafted lance wrapped in cloth; and *Okaka Eze Nsukka*, the special staff of the chief of Nsukka. From the head *arua* come the descendants of this village. What "descends" is *mmuo*, something of the genetic characteristic of either a specific ancestor or, more often, of a group of ancestors. The *chi* which the newly born child has received from Chukwu comes via a closely related "path of the spirit" in an ancestral altar close to the *arua* altar. This altar is a mud platform (see Figure XIV: *Ancestral Altar at Umune Ngwa*) consisting of a

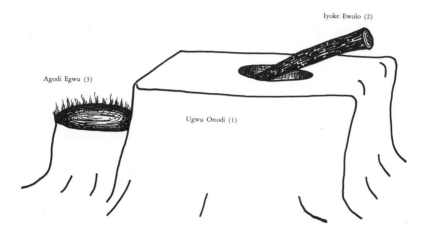

Iyoke Ewolo (2)

Agodi Egwu (3)

Ugwu Onodi (1)

FIGURE XIV. Ancestral Altar at Umune Ngwa
Agodi Egwu (3) Iyoke Ewolo (2) Ugwu Onodi (1)

1. *Ugwu Ono is the present* onyishi *(1962); this title signifies that he is the present "owner" of this altar; when he dies, the new* onyishi *will "own" (i.e., "control")* Umune Ngwa.

2. *Umu Iyoke is the patrilineage* (umunna) *that is senior to the other Igbo lineage, Umu Ara'm, and the non-Igbo lineage, Umakechi. This wooden shaft is the "road" through which persons in the senior lineage are created and given life. The meaning is that Iyoke "did not take back" the people given in the line—that is, this aboriginal or mythical "male mother" gave the lineage people who remained in it.*

3. *Agodi refers to the "younger," "junior," "stranger" section of the village-clan, particularly to Umakechi, the lineage of the* Attama; *the name of this round section of the "pathway of the birth of spirits in people" means "The New People Have the Masquerade." Reference is to the shrine-priest function of the junior lineage.*

large rectangular block called *ugwu onodi* in which is stuck a wooden shaft called *iyoke ewolo* through which come the people of the *onyishi*'s lineage; and a smaller, rounded earthern part called *agodi egwu* through which come the people of the second lineage of the village, the Igala and Umunri-descended line of the *attama*.

Arua worship (*igaarua*: "to give to the *arua*"; *ichaarua*: "to ask from" or "to offer to" the *arua*) follows a similar pattern from village to village in the Nsukka borderland. It takes place daily, is conducted by the headman of the clan, and is completed at dawn or very early in the morning and before the headman has eaten or drunk anything. Protection is needed daily, so the links between the living and the ancestors need constant maintenance. Subjection of the younger to the authority of the elder—the underlying theme of *arua* worship—furthermore, aids in keeping intergenerational conflict to a minimum. *Arua* worship, however, has none of the fear of spiritual contagion which is associated with *alusi* spirits and certain kinds of medicine; this follows the pattern of the *arua*'s relation with the people—they are the forces of the ancestors, the forefathers, and they wish no harm to befall their own people, who after all are the only beings who can properly worship and "feed" them as spirits. It is believed that the forefathers in general, including the *arua*, are as dependent upon the living as the latter are upon them: the living can die off without the aid of the *arua*, but the *arua* cannot "feed" themselves without the living. This is quite different from the case of the *alusi*, who are not related to human beings and who can force people to bring them offerings.

The actual morning worship of the *arua* follows a similar structure from place to place, and consists of the ritual washing of hands, the welcome offering of kola and, often varying, further offerings or requests or both. In each instance the headman arises early, makes his personal ablutions, and carries the *arua* staffs from his sleeping house to the *uloarua*, where he sets them into the altar. A member of his household, often a son or a senior daughter, sweeps the shrine compound while another brings fire from the house to the shrine. The headman washes his hands in front of the altar, then checks the kola nuts in a small wooden case.

Once this is done, the actual offerings can begin. The following are the beings and persons supplicated in the *arua* prayers of the two clans in Ameegwu Village, which has strong Igala-Okpoto influences; and of the combined clan-village of Umune Ngwa, in which an Okpoto patrilineage with *Umunri* overtones has been largely Igbonized and absorbed into the more definitely Igbo clan.

I. Arua at Dimunke Clan, Ameegwu Village, Owele-ezeoba.

The name of this clan, *Dimunke*, means "Master of Their Own People," and has direct reference to the Igala origin of the group, whose chief lineage is Umu Attama, from which come the shrine priests for the *alusi* named Ntiye ("Mother of Destruction"). The headman is Ugwuoke Attama, elder brother of the present shrine priest of Ntiye; he and the other senior men of Dimunke speak and understand Igala as well as Igbo, although they conduct their prayers in Igbo.

1. *Nde nwe ani*:   *kwo aka*   *ututu.*
   Those who own the earth: wash hands [this] morning.
   (*This is a standard formula in such prayers. "Those who own the earth" are the ancestors and gods combined, and in another sense the senior group of dwellers on the land.*)

2. *Eke,*   *kwo aka*   *ututu.*
   Eke market and day, wash hands [this] morning.
   (*Another standard formula, this personification of divisions of time functions to indicate the breadth of the invitation.*)

3. *Afo,*   *kwo aka*   *ututu.*
   Afo market and day, wash hands [this] morning.

4. *Oye,*   *kwo aka*   *ututu.*
   Oye market and day, wash hands [this] morning.

5. *Nkwo,*   *kwo aka*   *ututu.*
   Nkwo market and day, wash hands [this] morning.

6. *Eze Igwe,*   *kwo aka*   *ututu.*
   Chief [of the] Sky . . . wash hands [this] morning.
   (*Reference is to Ezechitoke or Chukwu, the High God, or to whoever rules the sky, in case it may not be the High God.*

7. *Eze Ane,*   *kwo   aka*   *ututu.*
Chief [of the] Earth . . . wash hands [this] morning.
(*Again, reference is to a deity, Earth (Ane), but prudence dictates caution, so it is worded generally in case Ane overnight may have been replaced by some more powerful deity.*)
8. *Taataa bo afo.*
Today is *afo* market day.
(*This stock line is included in most daily prayers to remind all the people of the day, in case they have important business or duties which must be performed particularly on that day.*)
9. *Arua, kwo   aka*   *ututu.*
Arua, wash hands [this] morning.

This completes the washing ceremony, which occurs because all beings supposedly must undergo some cleansing ceremony before eating. "Do spirits really wash their hands?" I asked Ugwuoke, who replied: "Spirits do not have hands. But whatever spirit things they have, before they eat they wash those things."

Following the washing is the offering of kola. This is the actual welcoming of the spiritual forces, which is closely paralleled by the morning offerings of the *Attah* of Idah to his *okute* or of the *Ashadu* to his own (see Seeton, 1928:269).

10. *Ane, oje boo   arua.*
Earth, kola is for [the] *arua.*
(*This statement is explanatory, so that when Earth "senses" the pouring and placing of offerings upon the altar—which is earthen—she will understand that they are not directed to her but to the* arua. *A necessary part of the ritual, this ensures that the offerings go to the ones for whom they are intended; if the ancestors are neglected through carelessness, it will do no good later to claim that offerings were poured out for them but that some other god received the offerings.*)
11. *Arua, taa oje*   *ututu.*
Arua, eat kola [this] morning (i.e., be welcome).
12. *Idenyi Dimunke, taa oje ututu.*

Our female preserver [of] Dimunke Clan, eat kola [this]
morning.
(*Reference here is actually to Ntiye, the* alusi, *according to
Ugwuoke, although his brother, who is the priest of Ntiye, denies
this, claiming that Idenyi is the female spirit of the mothers "of
the olden times." There is a special* arua *staff for her, which is
included with the bundle of staffs only for* afo *day worship.*)

13. *Afo, taa oje ututu.*
    Afo market and day, eat kola this morning.

14. *Eke* . . .

15. *Oye* . . .

16. *Nkwo* . . .

17. *Asogwa* . . .
    (*This is a title in Nsukka, and reflects inheritance of the powers
    of the Okpoto people. It refers to* ashadu ogwa, *"first* ashadu,"
    named Omeppa, *who according to legend was consort of*
    Egbele Ejuona.)

18. *Oriye Attah* . . .
    Slave [of the] Mother [who was a] King . . .
    (*Another reference to Ogwa or Omeppa as consort to Egbele
    Ejuona of Idah.*)

19. *Ngwu Idenyi* . . .
    Ngwu [son of] Female Preserver . . .
    (Ngwu *is the most common name in the borderland for the
    eldest son of Ezuugwu Omeppa of Awulu.*)

20. *Odo nwarua* . . .
    Life [who is] child of the *arua* . . .
    (Odo, *"voice of the chest," meaning heartbeat or life, is
    Igala; in Igala and in Igbo it can also be a man's name, but
    with different vowel sounds or tones—*Ódò, *or* Ọ́dó.)

21. *Egba Ikwunne* . . .
    "Root" or Source of Mother's People . . .
    (*This is explained as reference to a mythical ancestress,
    possibly—although unconfirmed—Egbele Ejuona.*)

22. *Odaba* [often *Odagba*] . . .
    (*Proper name of an ancestor, but here meaning "The Other Side,"*

referring to the arua *powers of Umueze, the other clan at
Ameegwu, who use the word to mean Dimunke is "The
Junior Side.")*

23. *Onyili Edo . . .*
Headman of the Seed [i.e., founding group of Ameegwu] . . .

24. *Ntiye, ngweane . . .*
Ntiye, owner [of] earth . . .
(*Ntiye is the powerful* alusi *of Ameegwu.*)

25. *Ofo . . .*
(Ofo *is a sacred tree from which wood is taken to make title
staffs and staffs of authority of the same name. This reference,
like that to Ntiye, shows that* arua *worship is closely related
to social control, acting as reinforcement of the fact that real
authority is in the "hands" of spirits—the most powerful of
which are mediated by the Igala lineages.*)

26. *Umu Ala . . .*
Children of the Earth [i.e., godlings] . . .

27. *Okwa Ndichie . . .*
Widow [of the] Ancestor . . .
(*Reference possibly to a specific widow closer to the present, but
certainly according to informants another reference to a mythical
foremother.*)

28. *Ofo Eze . . .*
Sacred Staff [of the] Chief . . .
(*The chief here is the chief of Oba, who until quite recently
received confirmation of his title at Idah; again, this reference to a
sacred staff is less a reference to something abstractly spiritual
but to the spiritual supporter of actual political power in the
village-group.*)

29. *Anyanwu . . .*
Sun . . .
(*Reference to the spiritualized Sun which is a source of power,
thus the use of whiteness to symbolize gods and other powers.
Europeans, of course, are not considered to be "white" in this
sense, but yellow or sometimes red; secondary reference to the
High God, Chukwu.*)

30. *Ugwuoke, Ihe Ama . . .*
    Ugwuoke, Arisen Spirit [in the] Family Line . . .
    (*Reference is to the Returner or Ancestor in the family who
    reincarnated in the present* Onyishi, *Ugwuoke Attama.*)

31. *Taa bo afo.*
    Today is *Afo* market day.
    (See I, 8 above.)

32. *Dimodi . . .*
    Master Spirit . . .
    (*Alternate: this is an honorific, meaning "My Master Endures,"
    with reference to the fount or source of power of the* arua—
    Ezeugwu of Awulu.)

33. *Ndi bi   na   igwe . . .*
    Those [who] are in [the] sky . . .
    (*Reference to spirits and powers.*)

34. *Ndi bi   nane . . .*
    Those [who] are in [the] earth . . .
    (*Reference to spiritualized ancestors, whose abode is the
    underworld.*)

35. *Di Iyoke . . .*
    Husband [of the] Powerful Goddess (i.e., Mother) . . .
    (*Reference to mythical foremother's husband.*)

36. *Amooke Ugwu Iye . . .*
    Male Line [of the] Renowned Mother . . . [i.e, the
    important lineage]
    (*Reference probably to unspecified mythical foremother, or to
    Egbele Ejuona—who may be the same—or to both.*)

37. *Ugwu dibe anyi . . .*
    Renowned One, may he remain our own . . .
    (*Reference again is to Ezuugwu Owuru, Omeppa.*)

38. *Ezechitoke . . .*
    High God . . .

39. *Onye n'acho   okuko   nwe   ada . . .*
    Person who wants [the] chicken owned [by the] daughter . . .
    (*Reference here to the* arua *spirit in general, which under the
    circumstances of many Igbo lineages is traced through one's*

mother; from the point of view of the recipient of the sacrifices, therefore, the person making the offering is a descendant of "senior daughter"—ada. *This reference, however, is ambiguous, "daughter" possibly referring to the mythicized foremother, all the Igala-descended persons being her* omu *or "children."*)

40. *Idenyi Dimunke* . . .
Our Female Preserver of Dimunke Clan . . .
(See No. I, 12, above.)

41. *Ishi   gidibe   nwe   ane* . . .
Head you are [i.e., may you be] owner [of] earth . . .
(*The reading here is: "You are the head and owner of the earth."*)

42. *Chukwu,   ginwa   kelu   mmadu nine.*
High God, you yourself created persons all.
(*A stock phrase, this nonetheless reinforces the notion that the sky gods are ascendant.*)

43. *Ndi   ekulu   na   ututu   afo, nguolu mmanya.*
Group greeted on [this] morning afo, drink wine.

The foregoing *arua* prayers support the contention by the Dimunke elders that their clan is descended from Igala and Okpoto forefathers. The parallel clan of this same village, however, claims instead to have been the senior clan and always to have been Igbo. It is interesting, accordingly, to examine the ancestral references—however mythicized they may be—in the Umueze *arua* worship to see whether there is the same sort of consistency between the elders' testimony and the testimony given in the prayers themselves.

II. Arua at Umueze Clan, Ameegwu Village, Owele-ezeoba.

The headman of this clan is Ebonyeze, eldest man of Umueze Clan. He understands a few phrases of Igala, which he claims to have learned over the years by contact with Igala speakers at Oba Market (*Oye Oba*); he does not actually speak the language, and makes no claim whatsoever to Igala or Okpoto descent. His attitudes expressed about use of Igala language suggest strongly that, however belatedly, he and others are using language as a boundary-maintaining mechanism (see Broom, 1954:59). It is no secret in Ameegwu

Village that a great deal of rivalry has always existed between these two clans ever since the original Igbo shrine priest in charge of the Igbo earth-spirit was displaced by the Igala.

The basic pattern of *arua* worship as Ebonyeze conducts it is the same as in Dimunke Clan, although more emphasis is given to Igbo forces. Bracketed numbers are references to the prayers in the Dimunke ceremony, where the prayers refer to identical persons or beings. (See Figure XIII: *Ebonyeze and Arua Worship*.)

1. *Nde nwe ani,*   *kwo   aka*   *ututu.* (I, 1)
   Those [who] own [the] earth, wash hands [this] morning.
   (*This formula, when recited by headmen of Igbo clans, refers specifically to the Igbo ancestral forces who were the original owners of the land; the formula is invariably repeated several times by Igbo headmen, whereas Igala-descended headmen recite it usually as a mere stock phrase.*)

2. *Nde nwe ani,*   *kwo   aka*   *ututu.* (I, 1)
   Those [who] own [the] earth, wash hands [this] morning.

3. *Nde nwe ani,*   *kwo   aka*   *ututu.* (I, 1)
   Those [who] own [the] earth, wash hands [this] morning.

4. *Eze Igwe,*   *kwo   aka*   *ututu.* (I, 6)
   Chief [of the] Sky, wash hands [this] morning.

5. *Eze Ani* . . . (I, 7)
   Chief [of the] Earth (i.e., *Ane*) . . .

6. *One,* . . .
   Free Man . . .
   (One *is Igala for "person" or "free man" as distinct from slave; it is also Nsukka Igbo with the same meaning. The reference appears to be a sarcastic one, the Igbo lineages claiming that the Igala-Okpoto trace descent through a slave, Omeppa, whereas they (Igbo) trace descent from free men.*)

7. *Odagba [Odaba],*   *kwo aka ututu.* (I, 22)
   The junior line (i.e., Dimunke), wash hands [this] morning.

8. *Onyishi Edo* . . .
   Headman of the Seed . . .
   (*Pronunciation here is more distinctly Igbo than* onyili *of* I,23.)

9. *Nche onye* . . .
   Guardian . . .
   (*This is the name of an Nri-installed shrine in Oba—see
   Chart I:* The Household Compound. *It has thus become
   pronounced* nshie one, *"person of Nri." Many Igbo clans
   commonly look southward for ancestry, and several claim actual
   Nri ancestry.*)

10. *Nshie One* . . .
    (See No. 9 above)

11. *Ahoke* . . .
    Strong *ofo* . . .
    (*Reference to a neighboring Igbo clan-village.*)

12. *Idenyi dimodi* . . . (I, 12, 40; I, 32)
    Female Preserver Who Is Our Master . . .
    (*According to Ebonyeze, the reference here is to the Igbo Ane,
    deified Earth.*)

13. *Ufu anyanyi* . . .
    Ofo [which is in front of] our eyes . . .
    (*What is meant here is: "The obvious authority should be that
    of the senior group," namely Umueze.*)

14. *Ugwu Eze Omada* . . .
    Ugwueze, son of the senior daughter . . . (an Igbo ancestor).

15. *Ngwu Eze Eshugwuru* . . . (I, 17, 18, 19, 37)
    (*Reference to Omeppa, legendary chief of Awulu.*)

16. *Egwu* . . .
    Masquerade (i.e., representing the arisen forefathers) . . .

17. *Odonwa Arua* . . . (I, 20)
    Last Child [from *ododunwa*] of the *arua* . . .

18. *Osayi NwEze* . . .
    (*Actual grandfather of the headman, Ebonyeze. Osayi: "our
    foundling; our speaker."*)

19. *Ufu Anyanwu* . . . (I, 29)
    Ofo [of the] Sun . . .
    (*Reference literally is to the Sun's staff of authority, but actually
    this refers to the High God, Ezechitoke, whose mediating priest
    is the* onyishi, *not the* attama. *Because the High God does not*

actually possess a staff of authority, the Headman's staff of
authority is what here is alluded to, so the reference indicates Igbo
emphasis upon Igbo authority and Igbo familial mediation of
spirits as distinct from Igala mediation of hostile spirits.)

20. *Kwo,   unu;   kwosi   okiro.*
    Wash, all of you; wash down upon [all of our] enemies.

21. *Akwo, kwosinamo   na nwunyemu na umumu.*
    Wash, don't wash down upon me or wife my or children my.
    (These references are fairly obvious: who is upstream at a
    washing place is senior or higher than those below.)

22. *Omu,   kwo aka   ututu.*
    Heart of palm, wash hands [this] morning.
    (Heart of palm, the bright green new leaves of the palm, is used
    as a sacred symbol by the Igbo, particularly in the south.)

23. *Nde nwe ane . . .* (I, 1)
    Group [who] own [the] earth . . .

24. *Arua Eze,   kwelu   ekule.*
    Arua [of] Eze Clan, let there be greetings.

25. *Biko,   unu ishi,   unu dibe.*
    Please, all you heads, all you may you be.
    ("Please, may all of you ancestors, spirits, and powers remain
    in charge of all things.")

26. *Nde nwe ane, kwo aka ututu.*
    Group who own the earth, wash your hands this morning.

This ends the washing ceremony. Kola is then offered in turn to all
those beings who have been invited to wash their hands in preparation for the ritual meal, and also to the following beings and forces:

27. *Eze Nweze* (father of the headman, Ebonyeze).
28. *Ntiye* (*alusi* of Ameegwu Village).
29. *Onye umu Ezeoba* ("person gave birth Ezeoba"—the being
    who first began or created the people of this section of Oba).
30. *Aja* [*Eya*] *Owele* ("senior son" of this area—a shrine).
31. *Oho dina ogbodo* (the particular *ofo* tree in the village square).
32. *Nde bi na Igwe* (those who are in the sky—I, 33).
33. *Nde bi na ane* (those who are in the earth—I, 34).

Between the two clans of Ameegwu Village there seems to be, at first glance, a great deal of similarity in *arua* worship, a not unlikely development in view of the close association stretching back a number of generations. The major differences involve the forces to which the two groups make reference. Dimunke Clan makes a great deal of reference to non-human spiritual beings and forces, largely because it has vested interests in furthering the cause of those forces, for which the Dimunke family as Igala were the sole intermediaries in the village. Umueze Clan, on the other hand, emphasizes ancestral forces, specific ancestors, and familiar spirits because it was only these to which the Umueze people could refer for support without having to seek help from the Igala clan. The ancestors mentioned in the prayers of Dimunke are few and of course are referred to as Igala and Idoma, whereas Umueze calls upon some actual ancestors and more ancestral forces and claims that these are Igbo. We will examine other ramifications of this division of familial groups into Igala and Igbo clusters when we look at social control forces in the borderland.

III. Arua at Umune Ngwa Village, Nsukka

Umune Ngwa Village (see Map IV: *Spatial Relationships—Umune Ngwa*) ancestralism, in contrast to that of Ameegwu Village, represents much more casualness in quantity and quality of the prayers and offerings, reflecting the farther removal of this village from the border itself and the stronger maintenance of Igbo control over village affairs.

The village consists of three patrilineages, two of which are typically Igbo in origin—or claim Igbo origin—and the third (Umakechi) possibly Igbo but strongly influenced by both Umunfi from the south and Igala-Okpoto from the north. Village exogamy is generally practiced, although the elders agreed that people of Umakechi—that of the *attama*—in the past had married with people of the other two lineages. When I asked whether people of the senior lineage, Umu Iyoke, could marry persons of Umu Ara'm, several senior men laughed; the headman of the village, Ugwu Ono, explained that this could not be, for they had the same forefathers. Why, then, I asked, was there only one set of *arua* staffs and only one *onyishi* for all three lineages, if Umakechi lineage did not have the same forefathers? *O bonke ndichie* ("It is something [of the] ancestors" —more commonly, *omenala*, "it is customary"), I was informed. The elders explained: "Those people of Umakechi came here a long time ago, before we were on the earth, and our forefathers gave them land and a place to live, and protected them under our own *arua*. They made offerings to Ngwumakechi, and our people made offerings to the *arua*." This means, in short, that Umakechi does not indeed belong to the same actual *arua* group, but for reasons of custom—supported by the fact that their own concerns are less with *arua* than with the *alusi*—feels no need to assert itself as a separate *ukwaarua*. The names of the forefathers who are enshrined in *Umakechi*—indeed, in the shrine house for the *alusi*—give further support to the different origin of this unit:

1. *Ugwu Onenshi* ("Renowned Medicine-Maker"), the founder of the lineage.
2. *Agbo Nwugwu*, "Elder son of Ugwu."
3. *One*, "Free Man" (Igala).
4. *Akpa Mma* ("One Who Displayed the Spirit"), the ancestor who introduced the *Omabe* society to this village.

The actual *arua* offerings in Umune Ngwa differ sharply from those in most of Oba and Imilike to the north and northeast and in Obimo and Nkpologu to the west, where Igala influences were strongest, insofar as they are short, quite general, and make few references to specific ancestors.

1. *Arua, kwo aka   ututu.*
   Arua, wash hands [this] morning.
2. *Kwo aka   ututu   Eke* [or *Oye, Afo, Nkwo*].
   Wash hands [this] morning [of] *eke* market day.
3. *Ezechitoke, bea welu oje.*
   High God, come have kola [i.e., be welcome].
   (*The High God is the household protector in this village and is*

given frequent regular worship, as distinct from villages where
Igala influence is stronger.)

4. *Mmuo nine di ebea   bea   welu oje.*
   Spirits all [who] have come here, come have kola.
   (*Reference is to the more nuclear Igbo group of spirits than to*
   spirits in general, as this reference might be in some other villages
   with stronger Igala lineages.)

5. *Ani,   'na, obu   oje.*
   Earth, look at it, it is kola.

6. *Ani,   'na, obu   oje.*
   Earth, look at it, it is kola.

7. *Ani,   'na, obu   oje.*
   Earth, look at it, it is kola.
   (*The apostrophe to the Earth Goddess, like 3 and 4 above, again*
   is more like nuclear Igbo than borderland Igbo, and is part of
   the Igbo reaction to the presence of alien Igala and Okpoto
   lineages—a subject which we will examine in more detail later.)

8. *Zogide   umu   gi   nine, biko.*
   Protect people your all of, please.

9. *Zogide   umu   gi   nine, biko.*
   Protect people your all of, please.

10. *Zogide   umu   gi   nine, biko.*
    Protect people your all of, please.
    (*Apostrophe still to Ane, the Earth Goddess: "Please protect*
    all of your people.")

11. *Iyi Nsukka, bea   taa oje;   zogide   Umune Ngwa   nine.*
    Iyi Nsukka, come eat kola; protect Umune Ngwa all.
    Zogide   Umu Iyoke   nine ebefa   'jadebelu.
    Protect Umu Iyoke all   from now on to show and to keep
    forever.
    (*Iyi Nsukka is an Igbo-type* alusi, *a sacred stream and deity*
    which is non-alien in origin or because of having fallen into the
    control of Igala. Umu Iyoke is the lineage of the people who
    "own" this alusi, *the senior segment of the village-clan.*)

12. *Bikobiko,   ishi gidibe.*
    Please-please, head you are [i.e., so be it].

This is the common pattern of the Umune Ngwa *arua* prayers; seldom are they more extensive than this, and usually they are briefer. Only rarely are specific ancestors mentioned in the prayers. The High God, Ezechitoke, who is the protector of compounds rather than the *alusi*, Abere, and the Earth Goddess, who controls crop fertility, are emphasized rather than *alusi* or *arua*. This reflects not weakened ancestralism necessarily, but rather the notion held by many people of the village that *arua* are rather distant and abstract, although nonetheless familiar forces. Their ancestralism, indeed, manifests itself most noticeably in the ceremonies and rituals of the *omabe* society (a cross-lineage men's association emphasizing eldership and Igbo unity in the Ihe-Nsukka villages), which we will study in conjunction with control forces. Generally, the power and popularity of *arua* worship (strongest in the borderland areas west, north, and northeast of Nsukka town) vary in inverse ratio with that of the *omabe* society. *Arua* worship was a means of Igbo reaction to Igala presence and control, although it is Igala-type ancestralism, and where Igala were less powerful or infrequent as in Ihe-Nsukka it is quite understandable that such worship would not develop to the same degree as elsewhere.

Variations

Arua, ancestralism, and *alusi* worship in Nkpologu and Obimo-ejuona west of Nsukka Town on the route taken by Onojo Ogboni reveal an interesting variation on these patterns. At Obimo, a hilltop community formed like many others by the Igbo approximately a century ago as defense against stronger and better organized enemies, particularly the slave and tribute seeking Igala invading from the direction of Ogurugu, the Igala-descended *Attama* Adada of Ogwu Ego Village controls both the goddess (*alusi*) Adada and the *arua* for all three clans of the extensive village group. *Arua* in this instance consists less of a set of spears representing spiritual force than of a visible sign of political authority. *Attama* Adada possesses what is called *arua onyishi*, which is his staff of office, virtually the staff of chieftaincy—an obvious Igala institution in this district. This *arua* does not receive daily worship, nor does it have associated with it any mythology. In another large section of Obimo is Umu Ekwa Village, where an Igala-influenced Igbo pattern (as distinct from the clearly Igala pattern of *Attama* Adada's office) appears. In Umu Ugo clan the headman himself is descended from Igala, but has become much more definitely Igbonized than has *Attama* Adada. The Igala components in his name alone indicate his descent: *Ige Attah Elechi* ("Lord Who Watches Over the Spirits"). There are two *arua* staffs here—*okaka* and the large spear, *ishi arua*. The washing and kola ceremonies are conducted each morning, and five specific ancestors are invoked, most of them mythical:

Dimu Aryummuo: ("Master of the People of the *Arua* Spirits"), the founder of the clan.

His "sons":

Alonye di Ngwooke: "Our Spokesman [mouth] who is Ngwooke."

Dimaleke: "Master of the Earth of *Eke* [Python]."

Egbere Ekete: "Maiden of the Round Basket."

Iyooke Ogo: "Mother of the Male In-Law."

Nkpologu-Attah is a large town west of Obimo on the way to the Igala headquarters of Onojo Ogboni at Ogurugu. The pattern there shows the Igala division of authority, with *arua* used as title staffs and, at the same time but on a different level of organization, as ancestral symbols. There are four major *arua* as title staffs in all of Nkpologu-Attah:

Arua Eze, the staff of the Chief, who is Awalawa, of Igala descent.

Arua Onyishi, the staff of the senior Headman, who is Iga Attah Idu, of mixed Igala and Igbo descent.

Arua Asogwa, the staff of the representative of the *Ashadu*, held by Ani Osomanyanwu, of mixed Igala and Igbo descent.

Arua Attama, the staff of the Shrine Priest, who is Oti Idu, of Igala descent, in charge of the combined ancestral and presumed *alusi* spirit named *Ezuugwu Eshugwuru*, the legendary first Ashadu and founder of all of Nsukka.

Ezuugwu indeed is the most important spirit of Nkpologu. Surrounding the central figure representing the ancestor-god (see Figure IX: *Ezuugwu at Nkpologu-attah*) are a number of *arua* spears which, according to the *attama*, indicate his power and do not themselves represent ancestors. Ezuugwu is considered to be the "father" of certain village *alusi* in the area, particularly, but not always, males. Ugwu (1958:34) wrote that

> Ezeugwu Ehuru of Ama Ala was thought to be the reincarnation of a dead Ata of Igala and was believed in certain quarters to be the chief of jujus. This belief in Ezeugwu-Ehuru being the King of all jujus led to the assertion that in certain months of the year all the spirits of our dead ancestors made their way to Ama Ala to pay homage to Ezeugwu-Ehuru and render an account of their stewardship.

This notion that Ezuugwu is ancestral to the entire borderland is supported by the existence of shrines dedicated to some of his supposed spiritual descendants. In the village of Ujobo-obigbo in Ejuona-oba is the shrine called *Okwuugwu*, "the great Ugwu," under the control of the lineage called Umu Attama Ugwu. Okwuugwu is considered to be a male spirit and the son of Ezuugwu. Except for this presumed relationship, the spirit otherwise resembles the usual village *alusi* with Igala or Okpoto *attamas* throughout the borderland.

6. Nsukka Village Religion: Alusi

IN THIS SECTION of the study we will examine the second of the broad categories into which Nsukkan religion is properly separated: the existence, mediation, manipulation, and worship of non-human forces and beings and non-familiar spirits. The control of these non-familiar spirits was the chief method of Igala colonial control over the borderland Igbo.

Alusi: A Problem of Definition

The more important of these non-human spiritual beings are generally referred to as *alusi* or *arusi*, a term which has caused some confusion, largely because it has varying referents in different Igbo districts. Talbot himself (1926:II, 48) exemplifies this confusion:

> Small temples, called Warusi, are put up in honor of Ana [Earth] by the Abadja and Nkanu as also by some of the Onitsha or Awka; they generally contain two to four figures, representing some of the minor spirits belonging to the Earth Goddess.

Then in another place (109, 114–116) he refers to *alose*, which he considered different, saying that the people of Obolo District (i.e., the Nsukka borderland) do not think that the *alose* live in trees or stones, but consider the *alose* to be children of Ezechitoke and Ale (Earth), and believe that *alose* place babies in the womb at conception. He also indicates that *alose* are servants to greater gods, a notion fairly widespread among some northern Igbo (Talbot, 1927: 44). According to my own informants, *warusi* and *alose* are variant pronunciations of the same term, *alusi* or *arusi*, the difference in reference being simply a difference of belief between more or less central Igbo and those Igbo of the Nsukka borderland.

Dr. McWilliams reported that, on 28 August 1841, when the commissioners were in the process of making treaty with Obi Ossai at Aboh, and while Rev. Schön was asking for God's blessing on the treaty, Obi Ossai "started up, and uttering a sudden fearful exclamation, called aloud for his Ju-ju man to bring his protecting 'Arrisi,' or idol, being evidently under the impression that we had performed some incantation to his prejudice, the adverse tendencies of which, it would be necessary to counteract by a sacrifice on his part. The "idol" was "a piece of blackened wood, enveloped in cloth—which the King placed between his feet" (1841 Expedition: 258–261). Jordan (1949:128) also considered the *alusi* to be the images used to represent spirits. Basden (1938:37) used the word *alusi* as synonymous with "figure" or "representation," but elsewhere makes it clear that—at least in the Awka and Onitsha district which he described—*alusi* are "gods" (46, 153). This is less contradictory than it might seem; indeed, in the borderland the word *alusi* refers primarily to the spiritual being which is signified, and secondarily to the figure or altar which is used to symbolize the spirit or to house it.

Northcott Thomas, also describing the Awka-Nri area, classified objects of worship under four heads: Chukwu, alose, personal protective deities, and ancestors.

> Among the alose we find such powers as Aro, the year, various trees, such as Ojuku and Ngu, and various rivers such as Idimili; not only do we have the year, but the equally impersonal Obosinano, four days (i.e., of the week); and we have Agu, who really comes much closer to the evil spirits than to the demi-gods (Thomas, 1913, I: 26–28).

In her study of Umueke Agbaja, Green described *areshe* as "a supernatural symbol of any kind" (1947:185). Boston, concerned with more northerly Igbo, described *alusi* as they are conceived of by the people of Udi Division:

> In ancient Ibo belief, the forests and rivers lying on the fringes of cultivated land are occupied by spirits called *alosi*. . . .
>
> *Alosi* are invisible but are not unlike men, and they are sometimes seen in this form. . . .
>
> In Ibo thought *alosi* are nature spirits which do not strictly need carved effigies or manufactured cult objects to represent them (Boston, 1959:157–158).

Horton too described *alosi* as "spirits": "*Chuku* . . . was the creator of the whole pantheon of *alosi* (spirits), to whom he delegated the power to control the various aspects of nature and the activities of men. In many ways the most important of the *alosi* is *Ani*—the personalized Earth" (Horton, 1956:23). Jeffreys (1954:28) called the *alusi* the "child of the Sun" or of God, thus a "saint."

The term *alusi* or *arusi* appears to be derived from or compounded of *alu*, "prohibited" or "taboo," and *si* from *isi*, "to say," thus meaning "the one who can speak what is otherwise prohibited." The *alusi* is a spiritual being who can make announcements and pronouncements about matters of the spiritual world other than the realm of the ancestors. I once asked Ebonyeze, Headman of Umueze Clan of Ameegwu Village, which was stronger, *arua* or *alusi*. He replied:

> *Arua* was the first brought to us. At the *arua* ceremony, I can call the *alusi* by their names and by the names of their shrines, but at the *alusi* ceremony the *attama* cannot call the *arua* or worship the *arua* at all.

What this means is that the *alusi* can be called upon to support ancestral forces in their overall care for the members of a clan or lineage, but that ancestral forces are not called upon to support the spiritual activities of the *alusi*. This does not indicate, however, that the *alusi* are therefore more powerful or otherwise superior to the *arua*; nor, indeed, does it indicate—as Ebonyeze mistakenly felt—

that the *arua* possess greater power; rather, *arua* function spiritually only for the members of a clan, whereas *alusi* serve no specific kin group at all. They are spirits whose powers range widely and whose limitations come mainly from the will of the *alusi* itself and its relative strength in the territory of another *alusi*. The *alusi* is a spiritual being which is not related as kin to human beings (with the exception of the famous Ezuugwu of Awulu). It is a *different being* altogether from people, and it possesses the powers to speak and do what is forbidden to others. It is oracular, and its powers are extensive.

This extended power typically covers a village consisting of more than one clan (*ukwaarua*). What amounts to the virtual subjection of the *arua*-holders (*ndishi*) to the village *alusi* in the borderland is indicated by the First Fruits Ceremony during the Feast of New Yam. At Owele-ezeoba, for example, each *arua* holder must bring two yams to Ntiye, the village *alusi*. After the men gather, the yam is cooked and then offered to the *alusi*. The *arua* holders and the *attama* are the celebrants and along with the goddess eat the new yam, with no one else permitted to be present. First the goddess is offered yam, then the *attama* eats, and after this the gathered headmen share in the feast. Following the ritual eating by these headmen, the people of the village are informed that they can begin the consumption of the new crop. (Meek, 1937:32–33, describes similar rituals in Eho-Amufu, Nsukka.) The *arua* as ancestral forces are thus revealed to be powerful only within a kin group, whereas the power of the *alusi* extends not only to the limits of the village—including all the kin groups within the village—but in many instances well beyond the confines of the village.

Alusi, then, are independent spiritual beings superior in power to human beings, and only theoretically inferior to the High God and the spiritualized Earth, who are familiar spirits. The most powerful of the *alusi*, and certainly the best known, are village spirits, usually female, who have a shrine and shrine priest (*attama*) to serve them. To understand properly the nature and functions of the particularly important borderland *alusi*, and especially their role in the maintenance of social order (which was a major function in Igala colonization of northern Nsukka) in the face of confused loyalties, it is necessary to examine them according to the relatively loose hierarchy into which they fall.

The functions of the three major non-localized *alusi* are interrelated but distinct, Ekke and Igwe having specialized roles, Ane being a more general god. Ekke appears as the python and is seldom so sacred a being as among more southerly Igbo; as spiritual being he is a forest god to whom sacrifices must be made by those being initiated as shrine priests. Another of his functions is in connection with his role as *Ekke Mmili* ("Ekke of the Rains"): his shrine thus is in the sacred forest forbidden to all except *attama* and, as in Owele-ezeoba, is used in ceremonies to make or to stop rain. *Dibea* or special rainmakers, who are also *attama*, perform the actual sacrifices and rituals. Ekke is thus related to Igwe ("Sky") although he has a closer relationship with Ane ("Earth") insofar as he is always upon her or within her, whereas Sky fertilizes her but does not maintain such constantly intimate contact with her. Ekke is the patron of stream spirits referred to generically as *Idemmili*, which are replenished by rain from the sky. At Umugoji, Ekke Ngwu lives inside the sacred forest of Ngwu, and it is at his shrine that sacrifices are made for the installation of *attama* and for rain-making, during which ceremonies Igwe is called upon by the officiating priest. The rainmaking shrine in *Imilikenu*[1] is closely related to Ekke and Igwe, the rainmaker receiving the salutation, *Igwe*. Igwe and Ekke as deified Sky and deified Python—or as the spiritual beings who manifest themselves respectively in the Sky and in the Python—are related chiefly in their functions as powerful male beings associated with the fertilizing processes including rain-bringing, with overlapping shrine functions and locations in the forests sacred to the *alusi*. Sky gods otherwise, such as the AmadiOha of central Igbo, are largely unknown or unworshipped in the borderland. Earth, as we have seen, is best considered a familiar spirit related to the High God and to ancestral forces rather than to *alusi*.

1. *Idenyi Amoke Oshiga.*

Special Alusi in the Nsukka Borderland

The most important, or the most dreadful (the distinction is uncertain in the northern Nsukka area), of the spiritual beings is the localized *alusi*, who is not a "nature spirit" inhabiting rocks and stones and trees and groves and streams, but is much more. Some *alusi*, one must admit, are nature spirits insofar as they are the owners of natural areas (uncultivated land which is not *okoogboo* fallow land), but the same could be said of God, who owns everything, or of Earth. The Nsukka *alusi* are certainly not animistically-created beings, nor are they so considered (any more than any other gods around the world might be), but are independently existing spiritual beings who own property, have spirit families, and enjoy great power over the lives and property of their human subjects. What gives them their power? Why might one use the word "dreadful" in describing this power, when it has not been employed in connection with such obviously powerful gods as the High God and Earth? Earth, for example, causes *eshiokukwu*, the swelling sickness (anasarca and/or dropsy), so she can be terrible, yet the *alusi* in general are even more dreadful.

The more localized specific *alusi* are indeed powerful and dreadful for one important reason: unlike Earth and God, *they seek offerings*. When they feel neglected, or if the people appear to have become complacent about them—if the people, for example, for too long manifest that easygoing attitude which is generally shown toward the ancestors—or even if they merely want offerings, then the *alusi* will sweep out among the humans, causing disease and accident, misfortune and death. Most important to understand here is that *alusi* are non-human, *different* beings, and potentially hostile, unlike ancestors, Chukwu, or Ane (compare p'Bitek, 1964:32–35).

I will make major reference to the following *alusi*, who together serve as a cross-sectional example of this class of spiritual being in the Nsukka area:

A. FEMALE

    Adada ["Daughter-Senior Daughter"] of Obimo-ejuona
    Shrine Priest: *Attama* Adada Eze Oha. (See Figure X)

Amanye ["Our Spirit"] of Ohebe-oba. Shrine Priest: *Attama* Odo.

Iyi Akpala ["Female Stream Glorifies Earth"] of Umu Mkpume, Ejuona-oba. Shrine Priest: *Attama* Ugwuoke Ugwu Owo. (See Figure VIII)

Iye Owo Uno ["Mother God of the Compounds"] of Imilikenu. Shrine Priest: *Attama* Ugwu Okanye.

Iye Owo Ago ["Mother God of the Farmlands"], junior to above, of Imilikenu. Shrine Priest: *Attama* Udo Eze Mba.

Ntiye ["Mother of Destruction" and circumlocutory "Little Mother"] of Ameegwu Village, Owele-ezeoba. Shrine Priest: Ugwuja *Attama*. (See Figure VI)

Okpo ["Woman," possibly from *Ada okporo*, "strong daughter"] of Umu Egale, Imilikane. Shrine Priest: *Attama* Ugwu Nnadi Eze. (See Figure VII)

B. MALE

Eze Ugwu Eshugwuru ["Famous Chief Known For His Cunning in the Forest"], or *Ezuugwu Ehuru*, or *Eze Owuru*, or *Ezuugwu Owulu*, the spiritualized Omeppa, first *ashadu* and consort of Egbele Ejuona of the Jukuns, ally of Ayegba who founded the present Igala dynasty, and so forth. He is considered to be the parent of all male *alusi* in the northern Nsukka area. His shrine is at Nkpologu-attah. Shrine Priest: *Attama* Oti Idu. (See Figure IX)

Ngwumadeshe ["Ngwu Knows Person of the Forest"], of Umugojioba. Shrine Priest: *Attama* Ngwu Elele.

Ngwumakechi ["Ngwu Knows Which God"—i.e., is powerful] of Umune Ngwa, Nsukka. Shrine Priest: *Attama* Ngwu Nwagbo.

Okwu Ugwu ["Great Ugwu"] of Ujobo-obigbo, Ejuona-oba. Shrine Priest: Ugwu *Attama*.

The borderland *alusi*, although derived from various sources (Igbo, Nri, Igala, and Okpoto), tend to share several characteristics. They are all related at least distantly to God and Earth, some of them referred to as "Child of Chukwu," others as "Child of Ane," but such references seem to suggest the *alusi* are less powerful than those greater gods, rather than any sort of kinship relationship. In general, also, the major Nsukka *alusi* are earth spirits insofar as they possess powers over matters essential to human existence: fertility of persons, especially, and of livestock and crops. Furthermore, the major spirits possess spirit children who are virtually the same throughout the borderland and who are, in some cases, more effective spiritual forces—or more active forces—than the parent spirits. The usual family consists of the following:

1. *Abere, Abele, Obere* ("Maiden"), the senior daughter of the village spirit, from Okpoto.

2. The senior son of the village spirit, with varying names:
   Onumuno ("Chief of the People of the Compound").
   Onumunno ("Chief of Father's People").
   Eya ("Senior Son.")
   Awamu ("Emerged Spirit" or "Prosperous Spirit").

3. *Inyiama* ("Gives People"), a female fertility spirit for whom a women's fertility cult exists, linked with the overall *ama* cult. She is considered alternately the sister of the major *alusi* and the junior daughter.

4. *Ngwu*, a younger son of the spirit, usually inactive except in those villages to which he has migrated and become the main spirit—that is, in Umugoji, Umune Ngwa, and others. In such instances he is considered to be the direct descendant of Ezuugwu Owuru.

5. *Idenyi* ("Friend of Idah" or "Gives Support"—i.e., as a tutelary spirit), a female spirit usually considered junior to the others.

Not all the above children are considered part of the family of every village *alusi*, although most variations are of names rather than of absolutely different beings.

The spirit family as a rule includes an extremely limited range of relationships. Although the parenthood of female *alusi* is ascribed either to Ane or Chukwu or both—perhaps simply as a means of indicating that Earth and God would manifest greater power were they to be compared with these spirits—or in the case of male spirits to Ezuugwu, no grandparenthood of any sort is ascribed to such putative spirit parents in relation to the spirit children of the *alusi*. Furthermore, the line of descent stops with the children unless, of course, one or another of them has become the major spirit of a new shrine, in which case the spirit has children in turn who are usually given the same names as those of their parent's generation: Abere, Onumuno, Eya, Inyiama, Idenyi, etc. What is suggested by this and other matters—e.g., the fact that, in some places like Imilike, the installation of lesser shrines necessitates making offerings to a centralized greater shrine, such as that of Abere—is that the spirit children are in fact generalized in belief and exist spiritually rather than specifically and solely within the shrines dedicated to them. Furthermore, all the *alusi* possess *arua*, which indicates that they have ancestral power, although their specific ancestry is in fact unknown.

The identity of particular spirit children believed to belong to the spirit family in various villages may furnish suggestive clues (never to be considered in isolation, of course) about the tribal origins of the shrine itself, the people owning the shrine, or the family of the shrine priest in particular. For example, the senior daughter, Abere, appears to be limited to the more easterly area and is closely related to the goddess Okpo and other spirits derived from Okpoto in the areas of Obolo, Imilike, and Oba. She is virtually unknown in Nsukka and westward in Ibagwa, Okpuje, and Nkpologu, the areas of strong Idah-Igala penetration, although she is most likely a modification of the Igala *Abule*. Spirits believed to be descended from Ezuugwu, the legendary first *ashadu*, are common to the same area, which is relatively closer to his original homeland near Ankpa in Igala. But the spirit of Ezuugwu is worshipped in Nkpologu itself, symbolizing the much more recent and direct relationship between the administration of that area and the *ashadu* clans of Igala. The presence of Nche onye ("Sentry") and of *Akwari*, protective shrines in Umu Mkpume, may support the origin legends of those people (i.e., claims that their ancestors were Nri), a possibility suggested strongly by the name of the major *alusi* of that village—*Iyi*

Akpala—who is possibly descended from the famous Agbala oracle of the Awka and Umunri area.

The sacred bush common to many, although not all, of the *alusi* shrine complexes is actually the name given to certain important spirits in the Umunri and Awka area: *Agbara* (*Ogbara* in the borderland. It is common for tutelary spirits to own property, of course, including particularly their own compound, but perhaps the most important kind of land held by any *alusi* in the borderland is the sacred grove, referred to by Obi (1963:35) as *ofia alusi*, and called in Nsukka *eshua* ("forest") plus the name of the spirit, as in *eshua Ngwu*, "forest [of] Ngwu." This grove might be quite extensive and is usually taboo to all villagers save the *attama* except upon rare occasions such as the installation of a new priest, when the village elders are permitted to enter the grove to witness that the ceremony has been actually and properly performed under the guidance of senior *attamas*. But this sacred forest is never the same as the *ogbara*, the latter being a sacred bush shrine usually located close by the main shrine compound. A shrine slave (*osu*) daily sweeps the *ogbara* in some shrine compounds (e.g., those in Imilike), although in others (e.g., in Oba) the bush is permitted to grow wild for an entire year, then is cleared and cleaned, the sacrificial area prepared only for the night ceremonies honoring the village *alusi* during the annual festival. Basden (1938:78) said that a generic word for shrines is *agbala*, but in another place described *Agbala* as the daughter spirit of the important central Igbo shrine, Igwe ka Ala. Jeffreys (1946:89), citing Meek (1931:5), argued that the Agbala cult was brought to Nsukka directly from Nri. This point is repeated by Ugwu (1958:3) who said that the Nri man, Dimaleke, was the specific importer of the Ogbala cult to Nibo, Nsukka; and Uchendu (1965:98) identified *agbara* as spirits which occupy forests and rivers on the fringe of occupied lands. These functions and roles of *agbara* or *agbala* seem to have been lost in the transition to the Nsukka borderland, where the spirit or shrine has simply been absorbed in a greater and more powerful group of spirits.

Alusi Powers and Activities

Alusi function as tutelary yet independent spirits, the source of their attitudes and activities lying in the power ascribed to them. This power is essentially spiritual, but its results can be both spiritual or material or both. Among some of my informants it is considered derived power whereas among others it is spiritual power in itself and shared by all spirits.

Attama Okpo:
> Okpo came from Idah, in Igala, during the time of the fore-fathers. The First Man, Omowo Atta Idah, brought the shrine from Igala.
> Okpo can do what she pleases. She has strong medicine. She is not related to Earth, but to the Children of the Spirits [*umogbaro*]. We do not know where her power comes from: that is a secret Okpo keeps for herself.

To consolidate this last point as well as the notions of Okpo's powers, the *attama* recited the following proverbs:

> *Ngi   ka   Okpo   aro   oma.*
> Your good is Okpo's fortune good.

This means that a human being is never so fortunate as Okpo, for what is a small bit of good luck for a person can be the goddess' extremely good fortune, insofar as she can exact the greatest amount of anything which a person owns or receives. Without asking people to come to her, she receives gifts all the time. The other proverb is:

> *Ya gbamanu,   Okpo ya gbamanu   efia.*
> He runs away, Okpo she runs away [with] cow his.

This means simply that Okpo always wins, and will demand and take what she desires.

Attama Okwuugwu:
> Okwuugwu is from the earth. It came up from the inside of the earth, where it grew strong [i.e., like an ancestor], and then it grew above the earth.

Attama Iye Owo Uno:

Iye Owo did not come from anywhere else. It originated in Imilike. Inyere was the first person to worship Iye Owo. He was the First Man of Imilikenu. A very long time ago, Iye Owo had a child because her people were becoming very numerous, so that child was called *Iye Owo Ago* because it lives by the people of the farmland, away from the homesteads.

Attama Ngwumadeshe:

Ngwu is male. I cannot tell where he came from. When I was born, after the death of my grandfather, who was the last *attama*, they said that I must be the *attama*, and I made the sacrifices. Ngwumadeshe was made [? first worshipped] in the days of the ancestors. It has power, because it will kill me if I do not make offerings to it, but I do not think it was made by men. I think only the shrine building was made by men, but the spirit was not made by men. It was with the Returners from the beginning of the world. Ngwu gets power from Chukwu, so it is especially a follower of Chukwu, not Ane [emphasis here upon the sky god rather than the typically Igbo earth god].

Attama Amanye:

Amanye was made by Chukwu, who gave her the power to save people who are dying of sickness. She is invisible, and no man can see her, because she is one of the *alusi*. She lives in the earth, and her stream is in the ground, too.

Activation of Alusi Power

Ugwu Nnadi Eze, *Attama* Okpo, explained that "Okpo is very powerful. She kills thieves, people who swear falsely, poisoners, witches, and enemies of the people. She can heal the sick and make women bear children when they had no children before." To a certain extent this summarizes the retributive functions of many village *alusi*, although it is useful to look at these functions in greater detail.

1. *Disobedience and Oath-Breaking.* "If anyone disobeys Adada," explained Eze Oha, *Attama* of Adada, "she will hurt him. That is when a person is told he must do a thing, but he refuses to do it." This is the case of direct disobedience of a command made by the *alusi*, which is normally communicated by means of the *afa*, the form of divination common in this district, to the *attama* and through him or his messenger to the person or persons concerned. The incidence of this sort of disobedience is naturally rare among Nsukka Igbo, largely because most rural peasants are either firm believers in the powers of the *alusi* or are sensibly prudent even when slightly agnostic. "Disobedience" broadly considered, however, is another matter, and includes the failure to be truthful in one's dealings with others particularly of any traceable kin group: that is, the *ukwaarua* or even the *ogbodo* village consisting of more than one such clan and having putative ancestral or associational ties. Truth in itself is not considered a necessary virtue, but rather truthfulness applied to the serious interpersonal dealings which make up the bulk of northern Igbo village affairs. When a problem arises, consequently, which is serious enough to cause doubts about the truthfulness of the individuals concerned, the litigants or discussants (as the case may be) resort to the oath, which is spiritually observed by a cluster of powers including Chukwu, the ancestors, Ane, and the *alusi*.

A common oath involves palm oil and kola nut. Oil is poured on the bare earth, and kola is broken, after which the oath-taker's finger is cut and blood is dripped on the oily spot of earth. A piece of the kola is then dipped into the mixture of earth, oil, and blood, is put into the mouth, and the person makes his statement. Breaking this sort of oath arouses the anger of Ane because it clearly is an insult to Earth, and she punishes the offender with *eshiokukwu* ("body swells up": anasarca, dropsy and ?). Because the ailment is punishment for such an abomination, no person is permitted to touch the body, which is carried with raffia hoops and is "buried" by being cast into the "bad bush." If a person who has not taken such an oath, or any other sacred oath, develops the ailment, it is assumed that he has somehow committed an abomination and is being punished by Earth. Another common sort of oath in the borderland is more directly observed by the *alusi*. On sacrifice day at the *alusi* shrine, after blood sacrifices have been made, any person wishing to make a public oath or declaration will receive a small bit of sacrificed kola from the priest, place it with a drop of the sacrificial blood in his mouth, and state his case. Should he violate this, the *alusi* will pursue him relentlessly to his death, which normally is in the form of blood sacrifice or accident, although it can be by means of disease.

2. *Violation of Sanctioned Relationships.* Proscribed acts falling under this category include incest, which is the marriage between two members of the same *ukwaarua* or between a person and a member of his *umune*, but not necessarily coition between two such persons, although this is normally avoided also; direct acts of disrespect toward one's ancestors, which are punishable by the *ndichie* themselves through the agency of the living elders but which also arouse the wrath of Chukwu and the *alusi*; murder, the killing of a person from one's own *ogbodo* village or sometimes village-group; and adultery, which is related to theft. Nsukka Igbo tend to differ from central Igbo insofar as girls before bethrothal are permitted sexual freedom, although after marriage they are expected to have no sexual relations save with their husbands or, in special cases, with his designated proxy or with an *attama* in charge of an *inyiama* cult. Adultery accordingly is considered a violation of the husband's right to assign his wife's duties and loyalties, for it is believed that an adulterous woman could develop loyalty to her lover as distinct from her husband, which in turn could cause extra friction between husband and lover and, perhaps, break down Igbo associational loyalty and increase the power of resident Igala or Okpoto lineages. This restriction seems to have grown in part out of Igbo opposition to *inyiama* fertility cults, in which *attama* were the sexual partners of some of the women and were likely to lay claim to the children so produced by arguing that the goddess Inyiama had the right to cancel marriage rights by restitution of bridewealth.

Ugwu Okanye, *Attama* Iye Owo Uno, explained:
If one man takes another man's woman, the family must solve the problem about bridewealth and such matters. But if she

is taken away and does not want to go with the man who takes her, the kidnapper is a thief, and Iye Owo will kill him unless he brings many offerings to the husband and to Iye Owo. When women were more plentiful, and even in those places nowadays where they are more plentiful, if one of them goes to the house of a different man, the *attama* carries the *ofo* [sacred staff of authority] of the *alusi* to her and warns her to go back to her husband. If she refuses, she becomes the property of the *attama*, who can get bridewealth on her head or can make her *igbele* ["maiden"—here meaning "slave" or *osu*] and keep her in his own compound.

3. *Witchcraft.* As a group and as individuals the *alusi* are strongly opposed to witchcraft, which I use here to mean that sort of disease in which one is "infected" with aggressive and malevolent spiritual power[2] enabling him or her to transform lycanthropically (usually into bats or owls but also into other night creatures such as the hyena or civet) and to visit normal people and to consume parts of their bodies, usually spiritually but even at times physically. "*Amozu* [witches] give the people of Imilike very much trouble," explained *Attama* Iye Owo Uno. "Evil spirits go inside a man and make him *amozu*, and then he travels at night like a vulture, but he is very small and has a red mouth. He kills livestock and makes women lose their children."

The *alusi* punish or destroy all witches whom they can discover. *Attama* Ngwumadeshe: "The spirit will not permit witches to come close to Umugoji, for it will kill them. They all know this, so they do not come here at all." If a person is suspected of witchcraft—actually, *of being bewitched* is a better way to express this—because he seeks too often to be alone, he requests privacy, he wanders at night without company, he manifests special interests in such organs (human or animal) as the heart, liver, or kidneys, or other odd

2. Malevolent, aggressive behavior is manifested by the witch after having become "bewitched" by another witch; witchcraft is not usually sought by persons, for the individual who wishes to use antagonistic force against another will get aggressive medicine from a sorcerer.

behavior, he is captured and is taken before the *alusi*. *Ofo* divination, the casting of *afa*, and oath-taking will be combined to determine his guilt; if these fail, he is given poison as ordeal. If he is found guilty, the spirit may kill him unless he undergoes elaborate (and often costly) cleansing ceremonies. As a rule, trials for witchcraft do not take place in the borderland, although witches are occasionally smelled out and disposed of, usually through the agency of the *attama* masked as Onumuno, the *alusi* senior son. The senior son of the *alusi* is considered to be a strong spiritual antagonist of witches:

Attama Okwuugwu:

> If one man says another is a witch or is using sorcery against him, the *afa* is consulted and the victim will be told to make an offering to Onumuno. If it is not so serious that Onumuno is required, the victim will go to a *dibea* and get some medicine to ward off the sorcery used against him.

4. *Theft.* In most of the borderland theft is defined as the stealing of another person's goods, although in some places "other person" means only someone from one's own village, not necessarily strangers unless they are under the protection of one's village or of one's in-laws. Usually, however, strangers are either invited guests, are members of a neighboring community related through affinity, or are expected to enjoy the protection of kola hospitality, so stealing from them is forbidden.

As one might expect, *alusi* are particularly concerned about their own property and, related to this, their own reputation.

Attama Ngwumakechi:

> Ngwu will seek out all thieves and kill them. Any person who steals the things owned by the spirit, or things that ordinary people have placed under his protection, will be killed. The person who has had things stolen will come to the *attama* with an offering, and the spirit will be asked to seek out the thief, within four or seven weeks [16 or 28 days]. After that, the thief will die unless he comes forth to return the stolen goods. The thief can make a secret offering to Ngwu, and the *attama* will tell him to return the stolen goods, so at night

the thief will bring the things to the shrine, and the *attama* will then tell the man whose things were stolen that his things were brought back and they are waiting for him.

Ochege ("She Guards Continually"), the great independent Abere of Oye Oba, the important central market of the Oba village complex, on May 19, 1964, killed a renowned professional thief. This thief had offended the *alusi* by having stolen from Oba people and by having murdered an Oba man, so his throat was cut—presumably by the *attama* and his attendants—and all his worldly goods, his children, wives, cattle, goats, foodstuffs, farmlands, and all other property, after divination decreed it were taken by the *attama* in the name of the *alusi*.

Petty thievery is usually less severely punished. Generally restitution of the stolen goods must be made, and the thief must make special offerings to the *alusi* of his village, which ends the affair. Extreme wrath, however, is apparently rather natural to the senior spirit daughter, Abere. *Attama* Okwuugwu: "Abere kills if somebody steals her own property, or any property placed in her safekeeping." But this is because such theft is a challenge to the power of the spirit, and she—like most other *alusi*—is aggressive enough that she accepts any challenge.

Continuing Positive Functions of Alusi

"Positive" here is used as distinct from "retributive," and is the more accurate method of viewing the nature and operations of these village spirits. *Alusi* exist for their own ends, to satisfy themselves, for they possess powers greater than those of humans. Because power enables one to do as one pleases, the *alusi* can do as they please, and are believed to exist not for humans at all: they oppose murder and thievery because these are socially disruptive forces which could affect the *alusi* themselves—the god's property might be stolen were thievery tolerated, or the god's priest might be harmed were murder permitted. Witchcraft is opposed because it is intolerable for humans to be carrying with them—whether intentionally or not—spiritual power. Contact with such power might lead to the ability to manipulate it, and practice in the elimination of spiritual power could lead to the development of dangerous human rivals to the fear and prestige of the *alusi* itself. To maintain orderliness so that human beings remain dutiful subjects who do not overreach themselves, therefore, the *alusi* function continually as guardians and restorers.

1. The Alusi as Guardian

Although theoretically all the *alusi* in a village protect the people against misfortunes (except those brought upon the people by the *alusi* themselves), the one most important protector and guardian in a large section of the borderland is Abere, who is usually considered to be the senior daughter of the village spirit, although independent "big" Abere exist, most often as protectors of markets. Although Abere's function as a protecting spirit is assumed chiefly by the High God, Ezechitoke, in most of the villages of the central Nsukka complex (Ihe-owele, Nru, and Nkpunano), in the village groups northeast of these Abere guards almost every compound, a larger Abere shrine protects every *otobo* or village square, and each market possesses a protective Abere shrine. Ochege is the market Abere of Oye Oba. Imilike, divided into two huge sections, has a very powerful Abere guarding the main market for each section. The principal shrine (called *Abere ime Oye*, "Abere inside Oye Market") is the northernmost, in the "lower" or junior section of the town, Imilikane, which is the more Okpoto and Idoma. The smaller shrine, located in the senior and somewhat more Igbo section of Imilikenu, is *Abere ime Nkwo*, "Abere inside Nkwo Market."

Ugwu (1958:35) said: "In Orba, Obukpa, Ofoko, Imilike, 'Abere' (woman juju who carries all good luck and curses in her market pan) is still believed in with unmitigated credulity." Ugwu Okanye, *Attama* Iye Owo Uno of Imilikenu, explained that

> Abere is a collection of dead women. When the women of the village die, they go to join her, and become part of her. It is

nkpuluobi [fig., "soul"] that joins Abere, and these are called *nd'Abere* ["group of Abere"]. Married men worship Abere so they can make children. Women cannot worship Abere. That would not be the right thing, so it is not done. Only the people of the village can worship Abere, and the women are strangers, so they cannot worship her.

This interpretation of Abere's role was not supported by any other informants even in Imilike, most of whom pointed out that Inyiama instead was more interested in matters of fertility than Abere. Ugwuja *Attama* of the shrine of Ntiye:

Abere is not a collection of women or the souls of women. She is like Idenyi and others—a child of a bigger *alusi*, who has many children. The reason Abere is in so many compounds is that if a person goes to the diviner he will say to that person, "Ntiye wants you to have a shrine to Abere where you will make offerings." The people then collect pots, maybe only one pot, and build a small thatched roof to cover it, and this they put at the path leading into their compound. No sacrifice is made to Abere in the daytime: she is a night spirit [*mmuo anyashe*].[3] Abere protects people and their property. The people say: "Abere, look at this little chicken. I am raising it for you." Sometimes a chicken will have many chicks, which will be raised up and sold, and then a goat will be brought for Abere. She likes these things, and she protects the people then.

Attama Amanye: "Abere is *mmo anyashe* ["night spirit"].[3] She is at the entrance to the compound to wait for bad things to arrive and then to drive them away or to destroy them." *Attama* Okpo: "Abere is a protector against sickness and especially sudden death or things that the people do not know will happen, like accidents. Abere also kills thieves." *Attama* Iyi Akpala:

Abere is the messenger for Iyi Akpala, and her servant. She

3. The variation here results from differing emphases: at Ameegwu Village she is most important as a spiritual being; at Ohebe she is most important as the mask embodying her power.

goes to a person and tells him whenever Iyi Akpala wants a sacrifice, and the person has to bring some things to the shrine. When Abere visits the person, she goes at night, and as a spirit. No one can see her, but the person knows she has visited him, and he can tell it. After she has visited the person during the night, he will go the next day to a diviner to find out all the things he must do.

This happens to a person sometimes because the *alusi* wants an offering. But it happens also to thieves and other rogues. A man might steal something, like a goat or something else. The man who has lost this tells me. I tell the man what offerings he must make—money, chickens, yam, oil, and other things, and all these things are given to Iyi Akpala. The good things wake her up [i.e., activate the spirit]. Then she takes her son, Onumuno, and Abere with her, or sometimes she just sends Abere alone, and they visit the guilty person. After this visit during the night, I will carry the *oho* [sacred authority staff] of Iyi Akpala to the guilty man, along with a kneeling mat. The man must kneel on the mat and touch the *oho* and swear that he is innocent, or else tell the truth. If he lies, he will die the next night, and the *alusi* will eat all his things. If he tells the truth, he must return the things he stole, and then he must give good things to Iyi Akpala and to Abere.

Among the Igala, Abule is a masquerade[4] controlled by the land chief, and is used in maintenance of the wellbeing of the people, ritual cursing, and social control. A noisy night-spirit, it symbolizes the collective authority of the dead, and is used in cleansing the earth of abomination. As Boston has said (1968:155–156), "This association of the collectivity of ancestors with the land is one of the basic notions of Igala religion, and the *abule* masquerade is one of the few forms in which this notion is translated into a form of social control." In the Nsukka borderland, similarly, Abere, who is probably derived from Abule, acts as an important social control agent. Through the mediation of the attama, her range of activities

4. That is, a masked and costumed figure embodying the spiritual being.

is, if anything, wider than her Igala counterpart (or original), and she is considered a spirit who is not seen, rather than a mask.

Abere in particular, plays an important role as the chief guardian and visiting spirit who is dreamed of, fantasied and envisioned, always during the night, usually but not necessarily by a guilty person. Combined fear of sudden death at the hands of the masked *attama* and his assistants late at night, or the worry over public exposure and resultant shame, or both, help to bring the guilty party to justice. In such public societies as those of the northern Nsukka borderland (as, indeed, in many other West African communities) it is virtually impossible for a person to go unsuspected for long after he has stolen anything or committed other crime. Should his family discover his wrongs, they will advise, urge, even insist that he make restitution; his wife or wives, who of course are not members of his family, may very well have awaited a chance to express righteous indignation or other hostilities by exposing him, not directly, perhaps, but through innuendo which will lead immediately to village gossip. Furthermore, knowing he is a thief, the culprit is likely to anticipate and expect a visit from Abere during the night. He will try to put the notion out of his mind, but it will persist, and he will experience brief daytime fantasies of some awful-looking monstrosity floating in the dark skies above his house and in the darkness about his bed while he is lying there helpless and weak. His appetite will be affected; people will notice he consumes much kola and stays up late at night. His wives will wonder at him, and at times he may lose his potency and excuse it by claiming he is sick but he will go to no diviner or *dibea*. To avoid being accused of possibly worse deeds than that of which he may be guilty, he will attempt to busy himself, grinding tobacco, repairing farm tools, visiting friends, who will importune him to go home and sleep. But he will fear sleep, knowing what might transpire. Anticipating more and more, working so diligently to rid his mind of the notion of the nocturnal visit, his nervous agitation increasing, when he finally does fall into exhausted sleep he might, during that first night, experience pure restful slumber because of the very weariness, but then, irony of ironies, feeling more easy the next day, the fantasies seeming to be less a threat, his spirits lifting, when he sleeps again it is only to dream. The dynamism was there all along. In his dreams, sooner or later, Abere appears. I spoke to a woman who had dreamed of Abere. In her case the goddess was merely seeking offerings; the woman reported that the spirit appeared in the form of a great flying creature with huge teeth and powerful horns. Was it a bat made large in fantasy, or a mask? An indignant no: everyone knows what bats and masks look like—this was like nothing else in the world save all the great frights rolled into one.

The visited person will not wait long, as a rule, to visit the village *attama* to seek help in keeping the aggressive night spirit at bay. He has undergone trial by psychological ordeal and he has lost. This is normal and usual, although now and then the rare cynic or the hardened criminal scoffs successfully at the idea of spiritual visitations. In such an instance, he will be warned by the *attama* that if he is engaged in any evil behavior he must come to the shrine and make amends with the *alusi*. Only the extremely rare person ignores these warnings, for when all other techniques fail, force remains-through poison or the knife, again at night and during one's sleep. There is public warning well ahead of time that the *alusi* will be searching for a culprit, for the priest on successive days will publicly request the spirit to help such and such a person to recover his stolen goods.

The first warning by the *attama* might well be a general warning to the village rather than a specific warning to an individual singled out from the others, even though many might suspect a given person is guilty. Should thievery or murders continue, one of two sorts of swearing might be resorted to by the priest. He might, in discussion with the lineage elders and *onyishi* of the clan, decide upon public oath-taking by all persons who could conceivably be suspects. Or, accompanied by the elders, he might pay a visit to the most likely suspect and request that person to swear his innocence upon the *ofo*. If the individual is innocent, neither public nor semi-private swearing will worry him. If he is guilty, however, either method can be equally effective in creating the proper mood for his psychological ordeal, for the *ofo* oath introduces authority even beyond the often capricious power of the *alusi*—Ane will not tolerate false oaths, and the spiritualized ancestors of the person will be offended at his sacrilege so they, too, will work to punish him, especially through the agency of the clan elders. With such a combination of spiritual authorities working against him, particularly as they are supported by living authorities—shrine priest and elders—who observe his actions ever more closely, the guilty party almost invariably confesses and makes restitution.

The borderland villager guards against witchcraft by two particular methods, aside from the general antagonism of the parental village *alusi* toward witches: either he installs an Abere shrine, or has a medicine-maker install anti-witchcraft medicine (*ogwu*) in his compound or house. In the northeastern border sector particularly both methods are often combined: one will install a small Abere shrine at the head of the entrance path to one's compound, and *ogwu* at the doorway of the sleeping house or above the entrance in the case of a walled compound.

2. The Alusi as Restorer

Alusi not only guard villagers against murderers, thieves, and witches, but help to protect the people from disease or are the only means of restoring health to the sick when the disease has been caused by the spirits themselves (the more common situation). Certain *alusi* are also important in the maintenance or restoration of fertility and potency in humans.

Attama Amanye: "Chukwu gave power to Amanye-oba even to save those who are dying of sickness. If people are sick, they go to the diviner and they learn that they must bring a sacrifice to Amanye."

Attama Ngwumadeshe: "If someone has fever, he will tell his people to go to the diviner. Or if he has very strong sickness and cannot talk, the people will go to the diviner to see which spirit is worrying the man, or if he has an ordinary illness. If Ngwu does not appear in the divination, then the people will go to a herbalist for a cure. The invisible sickness that people cannot see is the kind Ngwumadeshe takes care of."

Attama Ngwumakechi: "Ngwu protects people from sickness, and he helps to cure them if they become sick. He can help barren women to have babies, too."

Attama Okpo: "Okpo and her children can heal sick people, and make women bear children when they had no children before."

Attama Okwuugwu: "If somebody gets sick, and he learns from the diviner that it is Okwuugwu who caused the sickness, he will bring offerings to make the sickness go away."

Yet there are definite limitations among some *alusi*, according to certain informants. *Attama* Iyi Akpala: "The kind of sickness that makes a man go to Iyi Akpala is belly trouble, headache, sores that do not heal, when a woman cannot have children, and smallpox. She doesn't know much about healing leprosy. A lot of people used to come to her when they had leprosy, but they rotted away and died."

The junior spirit daughter named *Inyiama* ("Gives People") is usually a specialist in matters of fertility, although like the other spirit children she can perform most of the actions requiring spirit power. *Attama* Okpo: "Inyiama helps barren women to become fertile. She protects people from sudden death, and cures them when they have disease. She can also kill thieves, or help to kill thieves. But she is strong in helping to make babies. She is stronger at that than *Ugwu-ebo Igbele* ["Ugwu increases maidens," an *alusi*] at Umugoji." *Attama* Iyi Akpala: "Inyiama is female. She saves people from dying. People are born, and then they die. Inyiama can make them [i.e., infants] remain with their family."

The incidence of infertility and impotency appears to be rather high among Northern Nsukka villagers: in a small sample of 169 supplicants taken from a brief ethno-medical survey of ten consecutive sacrifice days at the shrines of Iye Owo, Okpo, Ntiye, Amanye, Iyi Akpala, and Ngwumadeshe, thirty-six (21.3%) of the cases directly involved problems of infertility or impotency. The consensus among my own informants who included shrine priests and other elder men and women was that the *alusi*—particularly Inyiama —"cure" more than half of the cases, which strongly suggests a functional basis for the problems.

The importance of Inyiama in this regard is also suggested by the existence of a cult named after her. *Attama* Amanye: "Inyiama are also women. The diviner determines if the woman is wanted by Inyiama. This is when a woman might be sick, and she goes to the diviner and the *afa* [divination seeds] say that Inyiama must have an offering."

Attama Okpo:

> Okpo has many *inyiama*. These are people who have become special worshippers of Inyiama for the sake of having children, and sometimes because they were sick and were cured.
>
> It is only an *attama* who installs a person as *inyiama*. Usually it is a woman. She might be barren or have some sickness, so the diviner tells her that she must become *inyiama*. This woman then sends for me, with a message that she has been told to join the *inyiama* people [i.e., *ndinyiama*]. I have my people gather together the *inyiama* people, and we go to visit that woman, who furnishes a payment fee to the *inyiama* people. Sometimes this is £1, sometimes as much as £5. When these people visit the woman, she feeds all of us with palm wine, fowls, and food [i.e., *okpa*, yam fufu, palm oil and peppers]. After we make the sacrifices, the woman has a small shrine to Inyiama in her house. From this time onward, she will start to get well, or she will become pregnant and start to have children.

Question: "What makes her have children now, if she could not have children in the past?"

> It is the power of *Inyiama* inside every *attama*, who is always leader of the *inyiama* people, and leader of the *inyiama* women. All women have children in their bellies, but the children can be given life sometimes only by Inyiama, not by the ordinary means with the woman's husband.
>
> When the woman gets well or has a child, she will go to Inyiama Okpo and make a major sacrifice, and from this time on she will be called "Inyiama" as her title.

Inyiama members of the borderland must observe several behavioral regulations:

1. They are forbidden to eat millet, as are *attama*. This prohibition applies generally to holders of the *ama* title in the borderland, and to most Igala and Okpoto descent groups there.

2. Any fowl which should perch on the head of an *inyiama* woman must be killed as a sacrifice to Inyiama. I inquired among several informants whether they knew of any cases of this having happened, and all of them replied in the negative. This ruling, they explained, had been handed down and needed to be observed even if no one knew exactly why it should be.

3. No person, including her husband, can knock on the door of an *inyiama* woman's house; the caller must clap his hands outside the house, and call out to the *inyiama*. The reason for this lies in the nature of *inyiama* membership itself: insofar as the institution resembles polyandry, the *attama* becoming an additional sex partner of a married woman and often the genitor of her children, this regulation helps prevent rivalry from developing between men (who might already be of divided loyalties—e.g., Igala and Igbo) and ensures that the woman shall decide who may enter and who must remain outside. The symbolic aspect of the situation was explained by several *attama*, including the priest of Okpo, where the *inyiama* cult is very strong: the *inyiama* woman cannot be treated like an ordinary wife by her husband, whose sexual access to her is definitely limited. He must give up some of his access to the woman for the sake of having children, who become members of his patrilineage (*umunna*) and, even more important, members of his wife's *umunna*; as his children to whom he is pater if not genitor, they owe him numerous duties and will give him some support as an ancestor as well as furnishing him with a persuasive link with the influential lineage of the *attama*. One result of this practice—whether it was originally intended or not—was that, along with other factors, it increased the widespread shift to uterine descent.

4. *Inyiama* women must not touch a dead body. The reason given for this was that the woman has been dedicated to the spirit who gives life, and to touch a dead body is to endanger or weaken the effect of the feminine power because of the essential aggressiveness of the dead.

5. If an *inyiama* woman is inside a house one is not allowed to hand her any sort of open flame, which is essentially aggressive and thus symbolically antagonistic medicine as opposed to the female and cooling medicine derived from Inyiama. This prohibition is related to number three above, suggesting again the restriction placed upon male access to the woman and masculine activities directed toward her.

3. The Alusi as Controller of Land Rights

Related to the function of the *alusi* as protector and restorer is the role of the spirit in relation to land rights, allocation and use, and disputes over land. Because of the ethnic division in who controls different sorts of spiritual beings—Igbo lineages control their own ancestors and furnish *onyishi*, who control Earth and High God worship, although not exclusively, whereas Igala lineages control *alusi*—the *alusi* are perhaps more important in border land matters than they are farther south among more nuclear Igbo peoples. According to oral traditions in the borderland, the "original" owners of the land (probably the earlier arrivals) were the Igbo, and the Okpoto and Igala came later either as refugees or, more impor- tant, as conquerors. One can hypothesize then that in the pre-Igala period Igbo controlled the land exclusively, and therefore allocation and use of land were in the hands of Igbo headmen and possibly title societies and some age groups as well. With the arrival of the outsiders, however, a certain amount of land for dwellings and farms had to be alienated for the strangers' use. Certain lands and properties not already owned by Igbo *alusi* were taken over by the Igala. Such lands also had to be assigned to the Igala-introduced spirits, such as the goddess Okpo at Imilikane, or the god Ezuugwu at Nkpologu. Once any land was alienated, the "ancestral" rights to that land became Igala, not Igbo, and of course where that land was owned by *alusi*, it was even further removed from Igbo con- trol.

The Igala shrine priests were important persons in the communi- ties in which they settled, for they usually controlled both divination and the capricious and unpredictable *alusi*, whose punishment for actual or alleged wrongs often consisted of sacrificing property, even certain lineage lands known as "fallow lands" (*okoogboo*). Once the *attama* were settled and their powers fairly well secured, the settlement of further land disputes tended to fall under their control whenever those disputes affected extra-clan matters. Disputes between lineages within an Igbo clan, for example, were settled, and still are, by the gathered *onyishi* of the clan and the headmen of lineages, as well as titled men and the particular litigants. But disputes between different clans affect the village itself, and such disorder is not tolerated by the *alusi*, who in the person of the shrine priest intervenes and very often is the final arbiter. The common first fruits ceremonies in which the village *alusi* receive sacrificial offerings before any of the clans can harvest and consume their crops are constant reminders of the importance of the *alusi* in relation to the land and livelihood of the people.

Worship of Alusi

The worship of *alusi* is determined largely by their nature, and therefore contrasts somewhat with the worship of *arua* and the forefathers, the High God, or Earth. Although the ancestors are given offerings daily (mainly extensions of family hospitality to the dead forefathers along with expressions of family respect for and dependence upon them) and are given annual festivals which function to draw together all members of the patrilines, there is seldom any sense of urgency in the offerings or prayers, never any noticeable anxiety expressed by the celebrants, but rather an easygoing attitude of communion between the living and the spiritualized dead "fathers" (*nna*). This is because the ancestors are indeed members of the family, and although they are dead and very powerful they also depend upon the living to "feed" them, and as "returners" (*ndichie*) they reincarnate among the newly born, so they are certainly familiar and essentially friendly and sympathetic spirits.

But the *alusi* are not related to any family of man—with the exception of the "sons" of Ezuugwu of Owulu. They are independent spirits, powerful in themselves, and as the very common saying goes, "they can do as they please." Jealous guardians of their own power and reputation, the *alusi* commonly strive to force people to bring offerings to them and to make public submission to them. Typically they seek offerings through the implements of divination —when anything inexplicable occurs in the village or to any person, he has recourse to the *afa*, and in most instances the *attama* (who is the diviner, usually) notifies the people that the village *alusi* is looking for sacrifices.

Alusi become offended at the least slight to their power, no matter how "unintentional" the slight may be. For example, at the Okpo shrine one sacrifice day, a woman appeared with a headload of objects which the *afa* at Obollo Eke had advised her to offer to Eya Okpo in order to obtain a cure for her son, who had come down with an unfamiliar disease. The young man had traveled to Benin some six weeks (twenty-four days) earlier, and while in Benin he had become ill and immediately returned to Obollo. His condition worsened, so his mother—his closest living relative—went to the diviner, who indicated that Eya Okpo had brought on the illness because he was angry. When the young man was asked about the nature of his behavior toward Okpo and her spirit family, he confessed that he had not informed either Okpo or Eya that he had planned to travel away from the village area (he had been living in Imilikane). This carelessness on his part was construed by the gods as a slight to their powers, so they used him to give the entire area an object lesson in submission. Another example of arbitrary exercise of power as distinct from an offense given an *alusi* is the case of the goddess Iye Owo of Imilikenu which was described in an explanation of village layout by *Attama* Iye Owo Uno:

> Iye Owo is "owned" [i.e., owns and belongs to] by Umu Inyere. About thirty years ago she forced the people to move to the present part of Imilike where they now live. The people had lived along the stream itself [i.e., owned by the goddess],

but a pestilence descended upon them, and full grown men were dying off, and grown women, so the diviner was consulted, and the *afa* said that Iye Owo had descended upon them because of her power rather than because of evil wishes on her part or because of particular evil behavior on the part of the clan. There was a narrow path through the village, and leading to the stream, and Iye Owo was so powerful that she moved along the path and killed people who seemed to be crowding her way to her stream. So when people moved to their present location, they built their houses with very broad paths and large areas between them, so that when Iye Owo goes through the village she has plenty of room.

The *alusi* are conscious of their power and jealous of their reputation as well. *Attama* Ngwumadeshe: "If a person does not look after Abere properly, she will punish him by bringing sickness upon him." *Attama* Ngwumakechi: "Diigbo Ugolodu [a male spirit, 'Old One—Person of the Night'] kills people who commit crimes or fail to make offerings in the way they should be done. Onumuno is like that, too. If he wants an offering, a chicken will be offered him when he asks for a chicken; if he asks for a goat, then he will be given a goat."

Such powerful spirits must be regularly "fed" with sacrifices, and they must be obeyed whenever they demand extra sacrifices. If they are not fed properly, if they are neglected or given niggardly sacrifices, their retaliation is swift and definite. The gods are, of course, appeased by gifts, and the more serious the god's manifestation of power the more important the offering ought to be. "In the olden days," explained *Attama* Okpo in response to my question about the large number of shrine slaves (*osu*) owned by that *alusi*, "the *igbere* [Igala: 'maidens'] would be brought when Okpo was killing the people of a clan and when Okpo said that a human being must be brought and given to the shrine." The villagers thus manifest submission through such obedience when the *alusi* demands, and especially through strict observance of certain customary offerings: daily "*arua*" offerings to the spiritual ancestral power of the *alusi*,

first fruits offerings to *alusi* at harvest festivals, and the annual
festival offered each *alusi*.

1. *Daily Arua Offerings to Alusi.* The shrine priest daily makes
some sort of offering to the *arua alusi*, which consist of *arua* staves
outwardly identical to those representing the spiritual power of the
human ancestors. In the northeastern borderland area the offerings
are made at dawn, before the *attama* has eaten. In the western sector
and central area of the Igbo-Omabe villages, offerings are made
three times each day. For example, offerings are made to Adada at
Obimo at dawn, about noon, and at night after sunset. The shrine
priest washes his hands and offers kola in the morning, yam or
kokoyam at the noon ceremony, and yam or kokoyam with a palm
wine libation at night, along with any blood if there happens to
have been an animal sacrifice. The purpose of the daily offering is
very like the offerings made to human ancestral *arua*: to remind
those spiritual forces that they are relied upon by the living and are
welcome each day among the people whom they ostensibly protect.

2. *Special Weekly Prayer and Sacrifice Days.* There is no prayer day
common to all village *alusi*, and no apparent patterning of or reason
for the assignment of particular sacrifice days. Nor could I ascertain
the reason why some *alusi* had two sacrifice days per four-day week
while others had only one such day. Such minor differences not-
withstanding, the actual ceremonies and prayers during the weekly
sacrificial day are remarkably similar. In this section I will describe
the standard prayer ceremony at Umugoji, and selected offerings
during a typical sacrifice day at Imilikane. These illustrate particularly the emphasis made by the Igala shrine priests upon the non-
Igbo ancestry of their *alusi*, whose powers support the Igala in their
control over the Igbo villages.

1. Ngwumadeshe Shrine, Umugoji: Oye Day

The shrine priest washes *arua* Ngwu with water.

The shrine priest washes his own hands with water.

Kola is prepared (peeled and split), then is offered with the following prayers:

1. *Ngwu, taa oje   ututu.*
   Ngwu, eat kola [this] morning [i.e., be welcome].
2. *Ishi bu   Ohebe . . .*
   Head [who] is [of] Ohebe [i.e., Amanye] . . .
   (*This reference to the goddess Amanye at Ohebe-oba is fairly
   common and standard in such prayers, for many of the* attama
   claim that their particular alusi *are related to or allied with
   certain other* alusi. *Sometimes this reflects a desire of a less
   prestigious priest to link himself with one better-known or
   wealthier; on other occasions there are legends linking the Igala—
   more usually, Okpoto—forefathers of the* attama *together as
   fellow travelers who founded* alusi *cults or took over existing Igbo
   cults "in the olden times" in separated Igbo villages.*)
3. *Ngwu Ocha . . .*
   Ngwu White . . .
   (*"White Ngwu" in this context does not refer to skin color or to
   Europeans, who are "yellow" or "red" to the borderland Nsukkans.
   "White" instead is the characteristic of the sun, which is the
   great source of heat and light and is in the sky, so it is associated
   with sky gods who are ascendant over earth gods. Ngwu, then, is
   here referred to as extremely powerful in his divinity and
   superior—by implication— to Igbo earth gods.*)
4. *Nde nnona   afifa . . .*
   Group living [in the] small forest . . .
   (*This has reference to a particular group of* alusi *who dwell in
   the sacred forest owned by Ngwu—eshuangwu—which is
   restricted to all but* attama. *These* alusi *include Ekke and
   Igwe, among others.*)
5. *Ane Ugoji . . .*
   Earth [of] Ugoji . . .
   (*This refers to both the land of the village, and to Ane.*)
6. *Oye . . .*
   Oye market day (sacrifice day for Ngwu) . . .
7. *Oha Oba . . .*
   People of Oba . . .
   (*Reference is to the gathered personal powers and spirits of the*

people native to the entire complex.)

8. *Ntiye* . . .
   (*Ntiye is the powerful* alusi *of Ameegwu Village.*)
9. *Biko, unu* . . .
   Please, all of you [i.e., who are addressed] . . .
10. *Ugwuoke*   *Oheegba* . . .
    "Prestigious Male" [i.e, Ngwu] of the dancing ground . . .
11. Ngwu, ekene . . .
    Ngwu, greetings.
12. *Onye nwane,*   *ekene.*
    Person who owns earth, greetings.
    (*This last reference is to Ngwu, who is considered to be the "real"*
    owner of the earth, insofar as his power is more greatly feared
    than that of the familiar spirits and his priest—although in
    latter days perhaps not so much as hitherto—possesses more
    political and social control than do the elders and other titled men.)

After this service in the shrine house of Ngwu, the *attama* moves
to the smaller *Onumuno* shrine, where he offers kola and repeats the
short opening prayers, after which he returns to the Ngwu shrine.
At the entrance path to the shrine the *attama*'s iron staff of office is
stood upright in the ground. This is called *ngbulu*, an Igbo term
designating an iron staff or even, in some contexts, a walking stick.
Near this symbol on sacrifice day is a small, very ancient spear with
a five-feet long wooden shaft and an iron head. This is called *okwo*,
an Igala term for "spear," and is considered to be the specific
weapon of Ngwumadeshe.

2. Okpo Shrine, Imilikane: Afo and Eke Sacrificial Days

On sacrifice days at the Okpo shrine the usual religious objects are
exposed: the caparisoned-horse-shaped figure representing Onumuno, the buffalo horn (*anigo*), the small double gong or clapperless
bell called *oluebo*, the small single gong (*Ivom ogene*), and the very
large ceremonial *ogene* called *olu mminyi*. (See Figure XV: *Sacrifice Day*
at Okpo Shrine.)

FIGURE XV. Sacrifice Day at Okpo Shrine (Number 1)
Attama *Okpo carrying major shrine implements,* arua *and* ogene *bell, to* House of Okpo *in the morning.*

FIGURE XV. Sacrifice Day at Okpo Shrine (Number 2)
Dog and yams intended for sacrifice.

FIGURE XV. Sacrifice Day at Okpo Shrine (Number 3)
Offering of cloth to Onumuno.

FIGURE XV. Sacrifice Day at Okpo Shrine (Number 4)
Dog being bled for Onumumo.

FIGURE XV. Sacrifice Day at Okpo Shrine (Number 5)
Chicken being offered to Onumuno.

Early in the morning on each *afo* and *eke* day the *attama* brings out the various sacred objects immediately after he carries the *arua* staffs of the goddess Okpo to her altar and offers the initial morning kola welcome to the spirit and her family. By the time he has finished this offering and is placing the other sacred objects in front of the shrine, vultures are gathering in two great leafless trees nearby. The birds appear only on sacrifice days, knowing well that blood will be shed, and they boldly attempt to snatch away carcasses of sacrificed animals. People begin to arrive at the shrine in the early morning, bearing the usual assortment of offerings: chickens, *okpa* (ground-pea) flour, red feathers (*awo*), yams, yellow *odo* clay, kola, palm oil, the special black salt (*unu, nnu*) used in offerings to the *alusi*, netting, cloth strips, eggs, dogs, goats, and the like.

With the supplicants who are present, the *attama* enters the Okpo shrine and takes his place before the earthern altar while the visitors squat on the floor of the larger room. The priest beats the large *ogene* gong to indicate that sacrifices are about to be offered. Then he blows several very loud blasts on the buffalo horn (*anigo*), which is also a war horn, to summon the aggressive spirits, the *alusi*. This is believed to awaken or to activate the spirits. Slowly pouring a palm wine libation, the *attama* in a loud voice invites Okpo and her children spirits to come forth and to be welcome among the people; perhaps half a buffalo horn of wine is poured on the altar, the *attama* sips a bit of it, and he then passes it about to the supplicants, each person taking some of the wine.

Case No. 1: A man has been sent by the diviner because his infant daughter is sick with "cough" (*ukwara*), and will probably die unless Okpo helps somehow. The man passes his offerings to the *attama*, who remains by the altar; then the supplicant goes outside the shrine house and kneels on the ground, addressing Okpo in a loud voice, explaining his need for help, and promising that if his daughter survives he will bring a female goat to Okpo. The priest repeats the prayers and promise to Okpo at the altar, pours another libation, offers kola nut, and hands the food offerings to his *obonoko* (senior wife), who does all the cooking of sacrificial foods after they have been inspected by the ceremonial supervisor of animal offerings, *Oga*, whose task it is to make certain that blood sacrifices have been properly bled. After prayers and offerings are made, the supplicant walks over to the *ulonna* ("house [of the] forefathers"—see Figure V: *Forefathers at Imilikane*) to wait while other supplicants make their offerings. All will then have to wait until the foods are prepared, after which they will eat together with the *attama* and his people.

Case No. 2: A man and his wife have been sent by a diviner, and are present with their three-year-old daughter to make offerings to Eya (Onumuno), Okpo's senior son. The problem concerns whether this child will remain with her parents or is possibly a trickster spirit (*ogbanje* or, more commonly in the Nsukka borderland, *ikpakachi*), for the woman's previous children all died either shortly after birth or before the age of three. Divination indicated that Eya Okpo wanted a yam, palm wine, a young cock, a young black male dog, and one kola nut. The offerings are carried into the Onumuno shrine, where the priest again beats the large gong and blows the buffalo horn. The dog is sacrificed first, its throat cut and its blood drained into a pot and then wiped over the top of the horse-like Onumuno figure and the *ofo* of Okpo, which is kept in the Onumuno shrine because it is a male symbol. The chicken is then sacrified, and the *attama* prays to Onumuno, requesting him to heed the suppli-cants' plea. After palm wine libations, the supplicants and their child retire to the house of the forefathers to await preparation of the sacrificial foods. They will share in eating the meat of the dog and chicken because the sacrifices were not made directly atop the Onumuno figure; had the priest killed the animals on the figure, only he could have eaten the meat, for Onumuno is especially sacred to these borderland shrine priests insofar as he is male and is one of the most significant of the several symbols of male Okpoto and Igala occupation personnel in Igbo villages. He is the horseman, the warrior, the power figure.

Case No. 3: A young woman is plagued by the death of her children; although she becomes pregnant regularly, none of her children survives (i.e., "chooses to remain among the living"). Divination indicated that there was possible *ikpakachi* trickster activity involved and advised her to seek help from Eya Okpo and from Okpo herself. The supplicant gives her sacrificial items to Onumuno, and then with the *attama* returns to the Okpo shrine building, where she promises aloud that if Okpo will help her to have four children who remain she will afterwards become *inyiama* and for the rest of her life will be *ada* ("daughter") to the *alusi*.

Case No. 4: A bond-servant (*ohu* slave) arrives carrying a great load of offerings, and explains that his master was sending the things to Okpo because divination indicated that the man must appeal to the *alusi* to have his potency restored. Replying to the *attama*'s questions, the servant explained that his master was a rich man and very busy and could not come to the shrine. The priest indignantly sent the servant packing, with the message that Okpo was powerful enough to have her own way in all things, so the servant's master was to appear at the shrine next sacrifice day or suffer the consequences of having insulted the goddess. (The master came as he was ordered, and in an automobile; after a brief status-oriented quarrel, he submitted to the shrine priest.)

Case No. 5: A trussed-up dog and other sacrificial items arrive at the shrine, the carrier explaining that an old woman was coming all the way from Obollo-Eke but she had sent the things ahead so that the *attama* would know she was coming. A while later she arrives and explains that ever since her only child died, his *oyima* ("child of spirits"—i.e., ghost) bothers her every night in her dreams, telling her that he doesn't want to be dead but wishes to return among the living. The loss of sleep and the anxiety caused by the nightly visitations have made the old woman ill, so the divination indicated that she must sacrifice to the *arua* ("ancestral powers") of Okpo and to Okpo herself. In fact, she was advised to spend at least one entire day at the Okpo shrine, inside the main building and close to the *alusi*, so that when the ghost of her son would reappear Okpo would instruct him to remain among the dead and not continue to bother his mother. In this case, the *attama* counsels the woman at the Okpo shrine for over an hour, then assigns one of his slave-wives (*igbele*) to make her comfortable and see to her wants for the remainder of her visit.

3. First Fruits Offerings to Alusi

Typically, the *alusi* are "fed" first fruits at harvest festivals in the borderland, as at Owele-ezeoba (described earlier), in the feast of *Nkpuru Nkashi Ntiye* ("Ntiye's heap of kokoyams"). Similar is the case of the *Isiji* ("head yam") Festival referred to as *Agba Ugwu* ("feast of Ugwu") at Eholumona. Here, before yams may be consumed by the ordinary people, the headmen (*ndishi*) must ceremonially carry selected yams to the shrine of Ezuugwu [Ehuru] Di Agbamere where they are first presented and consumed. Such first fruits offerings are linked, among other things, with the functions of *alusi* as fertility spirits, and at first glance thus appear to be simple expressions of village gratitude that the spirits have helped to furnish another year's crop. But the meaning of the festivals is rather the subjection of the ancestral spirits and even Earth to the *alusi*, or at least the subjection of the "priests" of the ancestors, the High God, and the Earth—i.e., the kin-group elders—to the once politically more important shrine priests of the *alusi*.

4. Annual Festivals Honoring Alusi

The village *alusi* in the borderland are given annual festivals which are major regular celebrations of their powers.[5] Most commonly, annual festivals for *alusi* are moon festivals by name, the festival

5. These have different names: "The Feast of . . ." as in *Agba Ugwu* above; or terms designating the method of worshipping the spirit, such as *ochakata Abere*, *ichaka* referring to the wickerwork basket rattle in some districts and, more often, the hollow calabash covered with a network of cowries forming a rattling instrument used to accompany some dances, and *ata* ("father"), thus a celebration using the older method of the fathers which is also employed in *omabe* secret society festivals.

being designated by the number of the moon during which it is held. Certain *alusi* are given festivals quarterly, rather than annually. This is particularly the case with the Maiden, Abere. For example, at Ama Ala, Oba, the household Abere shrines are called *Ite Abere* ("Pot[for] Abere"), are usually very small, and like such shrines everywhere in the district receive no regular daily prayers but are sacrificed to upon the advice of a diviner. Because Abere is such an important spirit, however, it is felt important that she be made welcome more than once per year, so every four months the people of the village gather at *Onu Abere* in the village square and hold a festival honoring the goddess. These festivals occur on the third, sixth, and tenth moons. Once every four years, furthermore, on a moonlit night, a major festival for Abere as Night Spirit is held, and masks come forth from the *Omabe* bush and dance and worship at the larger shrine of Abere in the village square. The main purpose of this festival is to demonstrate the subjection of the members of the *omabe* society to the Maiden.

The Moon Festival for Ntiye

The festival of *Onwaano* ("Moon Four") held annually for Ntiye, the *alusi* of Ameegwu Village, Owele-ezeoba, is a typical example of this form of worship. The festival is held in the fourth moon (the weekly sacrificial day at the shrine of Ntiye is *Afo*, the fourth day). Ugwuja *Attama* and others: "The custom for Ntiye began long ago. It came from Enugu-Ezike and places north of there. Ntiye's day was always *afo*, and her moon was *Onwaano*."

On the morning of the festival day, adult men of the village begin early to clear out the small sacred grove just southeast of the Ntiye shrine area referred to as *Ogbara Ntiye*, where the Night Ceremony repeating the Day Ceremony will be conducted, although directed to Abere instead of to Onumuno. About nine in the morning, "announcements" are made throughout the village area. The "Herald for Ntiye" (*Onyenakwulu Ntiye opi*: "Person who calls to Ntiye [with a] flute") walks about the shrine area and village with the horn of a water buffalo with which he frequently blows melodious messages intended as invitations to the festival (see Figure XVI: *Festival for Ntiye*). At the same time a number of small boys are beginning to play the *echi*, a wooden xylophone made of banana stalks and pieces of palm wood, announcing that the festival is soon to begin. For the night ceremony the *echi* will be carried to Ogbara Ntiye along with *Ogbonye*, the slit log drum,[6] which is also sacred and is kept with *echi* in the house of Ntiye, being taken out only for the annual festival, although *Ogbonye* is brought out for the Second Burial Ceremony of a grown man, it being understood that every man is a member of *omabe*, the secret society.

The highly decorative figure representing Onumuno, which suggests the trappings used in caparisoning a horse, is placed just outside the house of Ntiye, close to the life-tree, the *ejulosi*, and the musicians assemble and begin to play. The small boys who had been playing the *echi* are replaced by grown men. Other men play the large wooden gong-drum called *ogbonye*, the *anigo* or buffalo horn, the metal flute called *igwe*, wooden flutes called *osu*, and the small double *ogene* clapperless bell called *oluebo*.

The ceremonies begin inside the house of Ntiye, the *attama* seated before the altar of the goddess, partly separated from other cele-brants inside the shrine house by hanging cloths. (See Chart VII: *Inside Ulo Ntiye.*) He is prompted in his prayers by an elder assistant who is titled *orie* ("he eats"—i.e., food of the spirits offered in sacrifice). The first prayers consist of the standard invitation to the goddess and to the sacred bell used to summon her to have their "hands" washed on this festival morning:

Ntiye ane,   kwo   aka   ututu.
Ntiye [of the] earth, wash hands [this] morning.
Oti, kwo   aka   ututu.
Bell, wash hands [this] morning.

Accompanied by the ringing of a small clappered bell, the *attama* washes the *arua Ntiye*, then leans forward and touches his forehead on the earth in front of the altar from which protrude the large number of staffs designating the "ancestral" powers of the goddess.

6. Central Igbo: *ekwe*; Western Igbo: *obene*.

FIGURE XVI. Festival for Ntiye (Number 1)
"Herald of Ntiye" (*left*) *with flautist, signalling the goddess and inviting her to the festival.*

FIGURE XVI. Festival for Ntiye (Number 2)
Washing of sacred bell by attama *inside the House of Ntiye.*

FIGURE XVI. Festival for Ntiye (Number 3)
Onumuno worshipping Ntiye in front of her house as musicians play.

FIGURE XVI. Festival for Ntiye (Number 4)
Onumuno worshipping Anyanwu and High God.

FIGURE XVI. Festival for Ntiye (Number 5)
Musicians playing at Ogbara *Ntiye for the "Night Spirit" during Night Ceremony.*

FIGURE XVI. Festival for Ntiye (Number 6)
Shrine priest inside Ogbara *Ntiye sacrificing to Night Spirit; Onumuno, in foreground, is inactive, subject to his senior sister, Abere, the Night Spirit.*

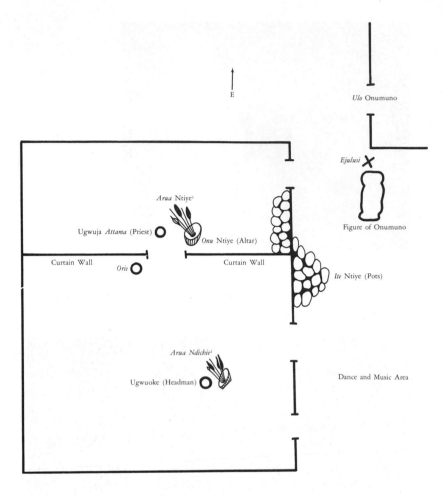

E

Ulo Onumuno

Ejulusi ✗

Figure of Onumuno

Arua Ntiye[1]

Ugwuja *Attama* (Priest) ○

Onu Ntiye (Altar)

Curtain Wall

Orie ○

Curtain Wall

Ite Ntiye (Pots)

Arua Ndichie[2]

Ugwuoke (Headman) ○

Dance and Music Area

Notes

1. "Ancestral" power staffs of Ntiye, kept and worshipped only by the *Attama*, Ugwuja.
2. Ancestral staffs of the Dimunke Clan, headed by Ugwuoke.

CHART VII. *Inside Ulo Ntiye*

Outside meanwhile the *echi* and *ogbonye* are being played feverishly.

Following this washing ceremony are the kola offerings beginning with invocation of the *ofo*, the symbol of authority. These prayers the *attama*, prompted by the *orie*, chants in a rapid voice amidst constant bell-ringing and very loud music from outside the building.

1. *Ofo, kwo aka   ututu.*
   Ofo, wash hands [this] morning.
2. *Welu oje   taa.*
   Take kola [to] eat.
3. *Taa oje   na tata   bu   afo.*
   Eat kola for today is *afo* market day.
   (*These prayers and invocations are all directed to the* ofo, *the symbol of political authority—but not* ofo *in general, rather the* ofo *of Ntiye, which is therefore the support of the political ascendancy of the Igala lineage of the shrine priest in Ameegwu Village, despite the seniority of Umueze as the original Igbo "owners of the land."*)
4. *Onumuno,   taa oje.*
   Onumuno, eat kola [i.e., be welcome].
   (*The senior son is addressed first among the spirits because the daylight ceremony is focused upon his powers as the chief daylight supporter of his mother, Ntiye; he is the spiritualized male warrior and horseman, analogous to some of the mounted northern warriors who originally supported the Igala lineages in the Nsukka villages.*)
5. *Anyanwu . . .*
   Sun [i.e., High God] . . .
   (*This is the manifestation of daylight, in which Onumuno is active.*)
6. *Onye nwe   ane . . .*
   Person [who] owns [the] land . . . [i.e., Ntiye].
7. *Ane Owele . . .*
   Earth [of] Owele . . .
   (*Reference to the collected spiritual power of the area of Owele-ezeoba and its shrines and people.*)

8. *Mmuo nine   di   na Owele . . .*
   Spirits all [who] are in Owele . . .
   (*A more specific reference and invitation than above, and including ancestral spirits and ghosts as well, so that no forces may be offended.*)

9. *Onye nwe   ane . . .*
   Person [who] owns [the] earth [i.e., Ntiye] . . .

10. *Onye nwe   ane . . .*
    Person [who] owns [the] earth [i.e., Ntiye] . . .

11. *Onye nwe ane . . .*
    Person [who] owns [the] earth [i.e., Ntiye] . . .

12. *Onye nwe   ane . . .*
    Person [who] owns [the] earth [i.e., Ntiye] . . .

13. *Onye nwe ane . . .*
    Person [who] owns [the] earth [i.e., Ntiye] . . .

14. *Onye nwe   ane . . .*
    Person [who] owns [the] earth [i.e., Ntiye] . . .

15. *Nalumu,   mmonu,   oje   taa.*
    Take from me, spirits all of you, kola [and] eat [it].

16. *Ngwumadeshe,   taa'nooje.*
    Ngwumadeshe, eat four kola [as a special offering].
    (*Reference to the major* alusi *of Umugoji.*)

17. *Iyi Akpane-Owele,*
    Goddess [Who Displays the Earth of Owele-ezeoba],
      taa ano   oje.
      eat four kola.
    (*The reference here is probably to Ntiye, although Iyi Akpane is a very minor stream-owning* alusi *with a shrine about two miles away—too minor, in fact, to be singled out for this very special four-kola offering.*)
    Biko, biko!
    Biko, biko!
    Please, please! Please, please!
    (*These supplications further increase the likelihood that No. 17 refers to a very powerful rather than a relatively weak spirit.*)

18. *Amanye Ezooba,   taa oje.*
    Amanye chief of Oba, eat kola.
    (*This is the* alusi *at Ohebe.*)

19. *Onye nwe ane . . .*
    Person [who] owns [the] land . . . [i.e., Ntiye].

20. *Idenyi Ome . . .*
    Idenyi Who Does [i.e., as she promises] . . .
    (*Reference to the junior daughter of Ntiye.*)

21. *Ishi bu   Ohebe . . .*
    Head of Ohebe-oba [i.e., Amanye] . . .

22. *Idenyi Amanye . . .*
    Junior Daughter [of] Amanye . . .

23. *Ugwu n'egbu   Oba   egbu Eha . . .*
    Ugwu who owns Oba [also] owns Eholumonna . . .
    (Ugwu, *here—"Honor" or "Prestige"—refers to Ezuugwu
    Ehuru, the legendary founder of all lineages of* attama *in the
    borderland.*)

24. *Ugwu   di Eho . . .*
    [Ez]Ugwu [Ehuru] Master of Eholumonna . . .

25. *Eze Mkpume di Agbamere . . .*
    Chief of Mkpume who began festival worship . . .
    (*This is actually a reference to Ngwu Mkpume, thus another
    reference to the great First Man and founder of the lines of*
    ashadu, *Ezuugwu Ehuru.*)

26. *Ugwu, ojome ome Nsukka . . .*
    Ugwu, god who does [what he promises] of Nsukka . . .
    (*The shrine for this manifestation of Ugwu is at Ishi Akpo,
    Nsukka.*)

27. *Ohe Nsukka . . .*
    (*Reference to a water shrine, in a swamp.*)

28. *Iye Ago Nsukka . . .*
    Female Water God of the Farm [in] Nsukka . . .
    (*Reference to the goddess controlling a well.*)

29. *Ugwu Ihe   Obukpa . . .*
    Ugwu controlling Obukpa . . .
    (*Reference again to Ezuugwu.*)

30. *Ntiye Ogbodu* . . .
    Ntiye of the village . . .
31. *Oye Ugwu* . . .
    Market and Sacrifice Day for Ezuugwu Ehuru . . .
32. *Ogele mmili* . . .
    Water Gong [clapperless bell] . . .
    (*Reference to the bell used in alusi worship.*)
33. *Ezuugwu Ehuru, taa oje.*
    (*This is the final offering to the greatest of spirits, according to
    the Igala-descended* attama *and the elders of his lineage, and it
    focuses attention upon the forefather of the* ashadu *lines, who
    spiritually supports the* alusi *priests and their consanguines
    scattered throughout the borderland.*)

The great *ogene* is pounded slowly, and the *orie* distributes kola given
him by the *attama*.

The celebrants and observers inside the house of Ntiye now move
outside. Instrumental music increases in quantity and variety, women
dancing as men play the instruments. After the wives of the *attama*
dance, he dances with the great *ofo* staff of Ntiye in his right hand.
In front of his dancing feet, the women make marks in the sand with
their hands, indicating that attempts to hold him back are as mean-
ingless as mere lines drawn on the ground. Yellow clay (*odo*) as a
sign of submission to Ntiye is daubed about the right eye of the
women and some men present. Meantime the *attama* has disappeared,
and attendants shield the Onumuno figure as he gets under it and it
is strapped to his bent back. Thus masked in the Onumuno figure,
the *attama* carries a large, sharp matchet and dances, first saluting his
mother, Ntiye, in front of her house. As the music continues, he
moves outward from the house of Ntiye, then returns to the main
entrance area as if he is unable to be separated from his powerful
mother; here he is surrounded by the elders and attendants, and
women dance again as the music increases in pitch and speed.
Onumuno dances about the area again, ringing a bell constantly as
the sacred rattle-iron spear, *oje*, is rattled against the earth to summon
the spirits. Then suddenly all movement stops, and the group led by

the masked figure moves away from the house of Ntiye. Onumuno leads the way, stopping first at the shrine of Anyanwu where he "bows," resting his "head" on the earthen mound while women dance and music again increases to a frenzied pitch. (See Chart VIII: *Procession and Recession of Onumuno*.) Although Onumuno remains motionless in this worship of Anyanwu, the elder carrying the *oje* occasionally rattles it against the earth. Again the music stops, everyone present cries out, "Oooh!" and Onumuno sets out for the now cleared *Ogbara* Ntiye, where the night sacrifices will be made, pauses there briefly, and moves to the village square where he bows for a long while before the *ofo* tree while women dance and music is played. From this point the group moves to the sun shrine in front of the *omabe* secret society house; a quick bow to this shrine, then another before the shrine to Idenyi, then straight back to the central shrine complex with but a short stop once more at Ogbara, a short stop at Anyanwu again, a final stop in front of the house of Ntiye, and then Onumuno returns to his resting place near the *ejulusi* tree. It is important to note that in the "traveling" of Onumuno he completely bypassed Abere, because she is the night spirit while he is the guardian of the daylight, so their functions are parallel; more important than this, however, is the daylight emphasis upon the warlike male spirit who need not even bother to acknowledge what to him is both junior and female.

After the Onumuno figure is replaced on its stand, there is further music, concluding with special war music played by flutes, drums, wooden gongs, and the buffalo horn. In the past only men who had killed enemies in battle were permitted to dance to this music, which is played only at the annual festival for Ntiye (and other *alusi*) and at certain Second Burial ceremonies—of titled men out of Igala lineages. After three or four minutes the flutes drop out of the music, which then changes into music used traditionally to send warriors out of the village to fight. Following this, animal sacrifices are made for Onumuno and especially for Ntiye, and the morning festivities are completed.

During the night following this day's festivities, the *Onwaano* festival very definitely comes alive. The ceremonies of the daylight,

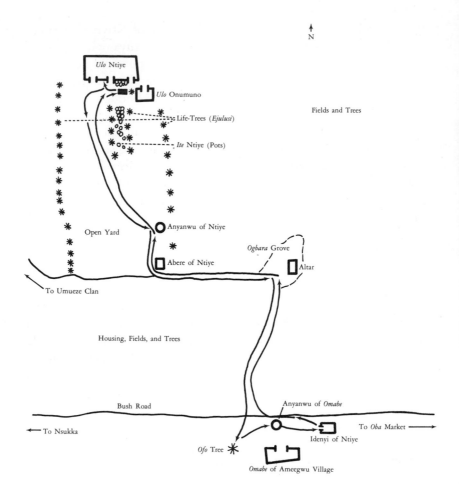

CHART VIII. *Procession and Recession of Onumuno*

with the prayers and prayerful respect manifested by Onumuno toward Anyanwu, the Sun and symbol of the power of the Creator God, are but a prelude to the night ceremonies. Once darkness has settled upon the wooded area of Ameegwu Village, Onumuno is again activated and is moved to the sacred grove of Ogbara Ntiye. The shrine itself by now has been roofed with fresh-cut palm fronds, and all weeds and underbrush have been cleared away. Upon his arrival at Ogbara, Onumuno is placed on the ground beside the altar, and the carriers of the *arua* of Ntiye hand the staffs and spears to Ugwuja *Attama*, the priest, who briefly inspects and identifies each one, gathers them in his arm, and carries them inside the Ogbara shrine, where he sets them in the softened earth of the small circular pit or "mouth" (*onu*) prepared earlier during the day for this purpose. While this is going on, the village people arrive and are assigned seats in several concentric arcs about the shrine.

The drummers and other musicians soon begin to perform, although throughout the early stages of the evening gathering of people the *echi* had been played. There is much talk about arrangements for the sacrifices, discussion among some of the gathered worshippers about the proper conduct of the ceremony, and the final settling down of people and participants. Several small boys gather close to the shrine, each of them holding a chicken in his arms as sacrifices for the evening.

The music from the *ogbonye* and *echi*, preceded by the herald's calling by means of the buffalo horn, rises in pitch, flutes are played for a while, and the *attama*, seated before the altar of the Ogbara shrine, begins the night prayers. All the various spirits are welcomed and invited to enjoy the hospitality of the people; these introductory prayers are identical to the morning prayers; when they are completed, the *attama* begins the sacrifices.

1. He pours palm wine libations and welcomes Ntiye:
   Ntiye, nwulu [nuolu] mmanya.
   Ntiye, drink   wine.
2. He offers a split kola nut and says:
   Ntiye, taa oje.
   Ntiye, eat kola [i.e., be welcome].

Then, one item after another he offers to the goddess, with the prayers:

3. *Anye ji   unu   ge okuku.*
   We   hold [for] worship your chicken.
   (*That is, we offer you chickens as our means of honoring you.*)

4. *Anye jinu   genli   nkashi.*
   We hold [for] worshipping you food-kokoyam.
   (*"food-kokoyam" here refers to "cooked kokoyam."*)

5. *Anye jinuge   okpa.*
   We hold [for] worshipping you ground-pea.

6. *Anye jinuge   utaba [utara].*
   We hold [for] worshipping you fufu [pounded yam].

7. *Anye jinuge   nlijii.*
   We hold [for] worshipping you food-yam [i.e., cooked yam.]

8. *Afo   nine   anye wete   ife   etuawe*
   [This] year all [of] us   brought things [that] are piled up
   ekene ge.
   to greet you.

After this the remainder of the foods are cooked, although many foods have already been prepared and are ready to be eaten; those which are prepared, including the animal sacrifices from earlier in the day, are now eaten by the people. Afterwards, there is more music and a special dance is performed by the *attama* and his senior wife. A few closing prayers follow, and Onumuno is returned to the display stand by his house in the Ntiye shrine area, the other religious objects are returned to their respective places, and the festival day has ended.

The purpose of the night festival, according to the *attama* and the gathered elders who are the major participants in the ceremony, is to gain protection from the *alusi* during the nighttime as well as during the daytime, Abere being particularly potent as a guardian against witches, who operate at night. Abere is not called upon specifically during the night because the entire night ceremony is directed toward her, for she is the most important spirit of the darkness; yet to call her by name under the circumstances of the shedding of blood is deemed not advisable because of the danger of exciting her by direct address. During the night ceremony she, rather than Ntiye, her mother, is considered to be the one referred to by the words *onye nwe ane*, "person who owns the land."

Commentary

Several further points arise in connection with *alusi* which bear discussion. First, the *alusi* are most clearly distinguishable from familiar spirits in their behavior, particularly from the viewpoint of borderland Igbo villagers as distinct from members of Igala lineages: familiar spirits can be trusted and relied upon, whereas the *alusi* is always unpredictable. This very unpredictability makes them more dangerous to human beings, and because they are not controlled by Igbo but rather by the shrine priests of Igala lineages, they are the more powerful spirits in borderland communities. Indeed, they are the key to Igala colonialization and control of the northern Igbo. We will look at this more closely in the following chapter.

Also important in relation to *alusi* and to Igala and Okpoto control of the borderland is the constant reference to the First Man, Ezuugwu Eshugwuru, not only in ancestral rituals but especially in ceremonies honoring *alusi*. When his name is called in the extension of invitations to spirits, it is believed, no other spirits are to be called, for he is said to be the greatest of spirits and is not to be insulted by being placed second. As we have seen, he was the Okpoto chief and first *ashadu*, Omeppa, also called *Ogwa* ("First"), who in several legends is associated with Ayegba, the founder of the present Igala dynasty, and in other legends even with Egbele Ejuona, the mythical foremother of Igala and some Nsukka groups. He is definitely considered to be the father spirit of certain male *alusi*, and at least one source of power for certain medicine shrines—*ogwu*—which have neither ancestral nor *alusi* personalities otherwise associated with them.

At first glance, it might seem that such relationship of so-called *alusi* with a reputedly human forefather contradicts the usually clear distinction made between *alusi* as alien spirits and other more familiar or humanly-related spirits such as ancestors, Earth, and God. Actually the borderland villager maintains the distinction insofar as Ezuugwu Ehuru, despite having been human, was indeed alien as an Igala (or Okpoto), and certainly does not represent familiar Igbo spirits or Igbo ancestors. Where the ruling line all claim Igala descent, however, as at Nkpologu-Attah, Ezuugwu takes on a double aspect: to the Igbo lineages he or, more commonly, his *alusi* children or representatives (e.g., Ngwumadeshe, Ngwumakechi, Okwuugwu, Ugwu Ohoro of Imilikane, and so forth) are *alusi* and alien and dangerous; but to the Igala or Okpoto lineages from whom come the shrine priests he and his children are largely ancestral and to that extent controllable.

As an "Igala"—actually Okpoto—Ezuugwu possessed special powers related particularly to the creation of war medicine, for he is considered to be especially powerful as a conqueror, and his highly figurative and descriptive name (which is not at all a name but rather a description of him) indicates that much of this power derived from his ability to manipulate spiritual forces. His "cunning in the forest" (*esh'ugwuru*) suggests immediately his ability to make war medicine, for such medicine is associated with sacred forests (as he always is) and also with hunters' rituals by which the latter are said to increase their ability to succeed against animals and the myriad spirits known to inhabit forests. *Eshua Ngwu* ("The Forest of Ngwu"), for example, is typically the area in which *attama* are installed, where they receive their powers, and where in the past war medicine, including arrow poison, was made.

The descent of the various Ngwu *alusi* in the Nsukka borderland from Ezuugwu Owuru emphasizes male spiritual descent and, indeed, male shrine control by Igala and Okpoto priests. Female *alusi* remain because the Igala found them in the borderland villages when they conquered/migrated to the area, but the male spirits were brought from the north or were converted in the belief system from the more commonly Igbo Ngwu to an Igalicized Ngwu controlled by a lineage of Igala shrine priests. This is even more clearly the case with such a spirit as Okwuugwu of Ujobo-obigbo, a male *alusi* descended from Ezuugwu. Many of the Igala and Okpoto shrines in the borderland are also dedicated to war medicine and to spiritual power in general. For example, there is *ogwugwu* (Igala: "war medicine") with several shrines north of Enugu-Ezike; and the *Oshuoru* or *Oshioru*, a poisonous bush related to plants used to make war medicine and arrow poison usually enclosed in a mud wall.[7] Such shrines are considered "male" even when they are not particularly personified, largely because their powers are aggressive, and they are said to have been introduced by the Igala; where they are personified, of course, one usually finds that they are considered to be directly descended from Ezuugwu.

This emphasis upon the role of the male spirit is carried out also in the important functions of Onumuno, the senior son of the village *alusi*, whose figure is like a saddle with fringes and decorations, sometimes including bells, creating an unmistakable resemblance to a caparisoned horse—definitely a northern power symbol. It is not a symbol for a horse as such, though; according to *Attama* Iyi Akpala it was medicine that some soldiers of the north carried on their horses when they went to war, while *Attama* Ngwumadeshe explained that it was the "iron" power which the northerners carried on their horses, enabling them to conquer everyone. I felt that he was referring to Fulani, but when I asked him about this he said, "I think they were Igala, not Fulani."

Although lip service is given to the belief that the village *alusi* is indeed more powerful than her children, in truth Abere as the Maiden and Night Spirit and Onumuno as the Chief and Day Spirit are emphasized most. For example, the Onumuno figure is exposed during most annual festivals, regardless of whomever the festivals are meant to celebrate. In Umu Mkpume, Onumuno is exposed during *Onwaano*, a forefather festival; *Onwa Ishiji*, a harvest festival; and on *Onwa Mbu Ezeoba*, a festival celebrating the *eze* or chief of Oba, whose title in the past was confirmed at Idah. Thus, although not every festival exists for the sake of the *alusi*, Onumuno's presence —and the authority of his sole human intermediary, the *attama*—is constantly felt.

7. The masquerade made with parts of this plant and used in the annual festival is called Obo Oshioru ("it clears bushplant").

The ascendancy of the male principle in the belief and ritual activity of many clans—especially Igala-descended ones—in the borderland is, I believe, closely related to the situation in which the Igala and Okpoto descent groups of shrine priests found themselves. They had come as priest-chiefs, as colonializing aliens among a population not always completely willing to receive them, yet not hostile to the point of maintaining armed opposition—which of course could have been suppressed. These men, furthermore, carried a cultural tendency to accept matrilateral descent, yet their own origin legends told of the male ascendancy of Agenapoje over Egbele Ejuona because of his ability to make war medicine— apparent support for their actual emphasis upon agnatic descent whenever possible. Like Agenapoje, the *attama* were medicine makers and manipulators of spiritual power and as aliens they needed to maintain their own lineage positions. Thus they emphasized their patrilines. Yet in most instances they had inherited control of female Igbo gods, so what was more natural than that they would give greater emphasis to the male offspring of those gods—Ngwu and Onumuno—to independent medicine shrines very like their own farther north, and to the Night Spirit, the Maiden, Abere, reminiscent of Egbele Ejuona of legend, and of their own Abule who supported the powers of the land chief?

To understand better these emphases upon the male offspring or what are considered to have been the peculiarly Igala-originated spirits (such as Abere, Okpo, and Ezuugwu Ehuru) we need to look more closely at the role of the *attama* himself as priest and diviner. For the *attama* was and still is extremely important as an agent of social control in most of the borderland villages. To what extent he holds ascendancy over the indigenous Igbo lineages, and to what extent he is subject to them, of course, varies from individual to individual and depends upon many factors, including chance. How the shrine priests came to consider themselves Igbo men descended from Igala or Okpoto, furthermore, might be clarified by a closer look at their various roles in their villages.

PART THREE

Control &
Adaptation

7. Forces of Social Control

THERE ARE four clusters of social control agents in the Nsukka borderland: (1) those of the families and households, or the familial political control agents, particularly the *ndishi* ("group [of] heads") as holders of kin group *ofo* and as "priests" of the ancestors, Earth, and the High God; (2) those consisting of general political and social titles, in most instances Okpoto or Igala in origin; (3) those consisting of associations, including age-groups which tend to be less important than secret societies, especially the *omabe* which is controlled by combined elders and *attama*; and (4) those essential for the protection of the people from unknown dangers, the diviners, or equally essential for the neutralization of hostile spirits, the shrine priests.

Lineage Control Agents

The most important forces of social control defined by family groups are the groups of headmen (*ndishi*) of each village or village-group, who are the holders of the *ofo* staffs which are the concrete symbols of political authority. The political structure of the borderland Igbo communities in part parallels the extension and limitation of spiritual powers of the different sorts of ancestral forces. Unlike nuclear Igbo, who indicate political supremacy by the size (extension of authority) of the *ofo* staff held by a given kindred head, the northern Nsukkans determine supremacy by the class of ancestral forces a given individual has responsibility for worshipping. The elder who serves the *arua* for the entire clan (*ukwaarua*) is the *onyishi* ("head person"); his council consists of those elders who are in charge of worshipping the *nna* ("fathers") of each patrilineage; together these elders constitute the ruling group of the familial village or of the clan. Moreover, the early hour of daily *arua* worship and the *onyishi*'s being the celebrant are related to the principle of seniority upon which familial control depends: the forces represented by the *arua* are the most senior and powerful of the entire "family," so they deserve first share in the goods of the people, and their importance is thus pointed up by the headman's early offering. The position of elders and the institution of eldership in Nsukkan villages is thereby maintained: if the headman can subject himself to the family spirits, then surely the living "children" can subject themselves to the authority of the headman and their other elders (see Shelton, 1969, 1969b).

The *ofo* nevertheless is important in the borderland. In his "Ethnographic Report" on Nsukka (1931), Meek wrote that

> The authority possessed by virtue of seniority by descent or by priesthood has a material embodiment among the Ibo. This institution is that of the *ofo*. It is a stick, sometimes roughly shaped to represent a human figure. . . . Each senior householder holds the family *ofo*, which he assumes at a special ceremony. . . . The priests of cults also have *ofo*s representing their religious authority, and such an *ofo* might have precedence over one based on patrilineal seniority.

Onyishi Ugwu Ono of Umune Ngwa:

> "The *onyishi* always carries *oho*: it shows people that he is the eldest man. Anyone who holds it cannot tell lies to people. *Oho* is related to the old dead people, the *ndichie*."

In the Nsukka region it is simply the staff of authority, then, unlike the same symbol farther south in Igboland. Jeffreys has written that

> In towns away from direct Umundri influence, the *ofo* appears

to become confused with ancestral stakes, and possibly, at times, identified with the ancestors. In Umundri use, the *ofo* is a sacred bundle and, as such, it remains throughout the ritual for gaining immortality by taking title. Amongst the Umundri it never becomes either an ancestral stake, or identified with the ancestors (1956:130).

The title of *onyishi* (if it can be called this in much of the borderland, where it is largely a descriptive label) is usually assumed informally, its determination resting upon seniority. *Onyishi* Eleje NwAsogwa of Amuukwa, Nsukka:

"Any man whose turn comes up, when the *onyishi* dies, will become the new headman. On that day when he makes offering to the *arua* he will gather the other elders together and he will feast them. He will cook a goat and have palm wine, and he will tell the elders that he is the eldest man and is the one who must keep the *arua*, so the staffs will be moved to his lineage house where he keeps his forefathers."

The headman is the person with final control over land owned by his own patrilineage, this control depending, again, simply upon his being the eldest man; his control of land owned in common by the clan (*ukwaarua*), however, as distinct from patrilineage lands, requires special efforts on his own part. The feast called *iruma* ("to sacrifice [to the] lineage") must be given by every head of household in order to gain the right to possess the common land or *okoobho* ("fallow farm") when his turn—determined by his rank in seniority —occurs. In this feast, all males of the clan are fed with palm wine, chickens, goats, sheep, dogs, at least one cow, as well as plant food. First to be feted are the living elders, then each age-group in turn: *ndegale, okolobia,* and even the young boys, *ndezukwu.* This feast is most common in the areas of the northeastern borderland where Okpoto influence is strongest, and very likely derived from those aboriginal "Igala," for the man giving the feast must dress his hair in the peculiar style of the Okpoto chiefs: the entire head is shaved except for a one-inch circle at the mid-forehead hairline, especially if he is a relatively young man (i.e., not yet one of the *ndishi*). As he

FIGURE XVII. Okpoto Hair Styles (Number 1)
Okpoto child, Ankpa.

FIGURE XVII. Okpoto Hair Styles (Number 2)
Ugwuoke, of Ameegwu Village.

grows older, like the elder Okpoto man he will wear the hair knot at the back of his head, in the style of *attama* and of chiefs among the Okpoto (see Figure XVII: *Okpoto Children's and Adults' Hair Style*).

Land not included in that peculiar classification of "common land," however, and even cases involving control of *okoobho* land, fall under the jurisdiction—largely ritual—of the *onyishi* in his role as symbolic "owner" of the people (*onye nwezi*; compare Uchendu, 1965:40), and because of his function as the priest of both the High God and, more important, of Earth. Chubb has written that

> Individualistic as the people are, the usage regarding land has favoured common ownership by a group rather than by individuals and the reason for this is to be found in the Ibo religion. The conception of an earth goddess is common to all Ibo and it would, in the not distant past, have been natural for a group to control land—since in the ultimate analysis every group must act through some individual if it is to get anything done—through the individual who had access to the deity and whose religious duties brought with them the right or the obligation of controlling the land associated with the deity (Chubb, 1947:8; compare Boston, 1967:29–31).

As the intermediary between the living and the dead, furthermore, and, perhaps equally or more important, as the intermediary between the clan and both Earth and the High God, the *onyishi* is in an important position. In all cases of offence given to the ancestors or of abominations committed against Earth—and this makes up virtually the whole system of ordinary morality in northern Igbo villages—the *onyishi* is the only person with the power to cleanse the offender and thus to restore right order to the family community. He can withhold from an individual the right to harvest crops, and if necessary he can enforce his injunction by calling upon the gathered elders and heads of households to give him physical support; and he can curse offenders in the name of the forefathers and *arua* powers whom he represents, thus for all practical purposes guaranteeing to the offenders that their wives will bear no children, their crops will die, and they will experience dreadful "accidents" or will come down with incurable diseases.

Modifying the foregoing description of powers, though, is the fact that certain controls exist over the *onyishi*'s actions, so that he is by no means an absolute ruler of the family. He is limited, first, by his councillors, the group of *ndishi* who are the heads of the patrilineages within the clan; without their support he cannot have his orders enforced, and as a rule he will not oppose them but will through persuasion, connivance, and often bribery, work hard to gain their consensus. Secondly, he is limited in his actions by rivalry, by the desires of his juniors to take his place, coupled with the elders' definition of his practical ability to maintain control over the clan and lineage groups. If his behavior becomes too consistently erratic the gathered elders can quite easily depose him and replace him with an elder from among them who satisfies the needs of seniority and at the same time is somewhat more amenable to their suggestions and to what they define as "good thinking." Thirdly, the *onyishi* control of his kingroup is limited by the interest spiritual beings and forces have in the misdeeds of his people. What I mean here is that so-called abominations against Earth or offences against the High God or ancestors are seldom interpreted simply by the diviners, who usually indicate that the village *alusi* or, perhaps more commonly, one of that being's spirit children has taken serious interest in the offences committed by a particular wrongdoer, so that an *attama* is introduced as mediator and the *onyishi* does not possess full power to exculpate the individual. Finally, the *onyishi*'s influence as a social control agent is limited by the influence of titled persons.

Titled Persons

Most titles in the Nsukka borderland are, in fact, Igala or Okpoto titles or modifications of these. *Onyishi* itself is a formalized title in certain parts of the borderland, particularly where the Idah-Igala influence is strongest—in the westerly areas of Nkpologu and

Obimo. In Nkpologu, for example, only two clan groups can possess the title of *onyishi*, which rotates on the basis of seniority: Ama Ikwerre, the patrilineage (?) or clan (*ukwaarua*) of the present *onyishi*, and Ugwu Onyishi, a clan believed to be descended directly from Ezuugwu Ehuru. The present *onyishi*, Igaattah Idu, keeps the *arua* staffs in his own house, for upon succession to the title the headman does not move to a special *arua* house as in other parts of Nsukka. *Ichi* medicine is said to be *ogwu* closely related to the Igala war (and Igbo funerary) medicine called *mmanwuofia*, and is considered to be the medicine most sacred to the headman aside from *arua*, so sacrifice is made to it as well as to *arua* by every *onyishi*. The salutation for the *onyishi* at Nkpologu is *edoga*, "one settles strength" ("one is a lord"), a common salutation for *attama* in many other parts of the borderland (compare Meek, 1937:154).

Closely related to the formally titled *onyishi* is his messenger-servant with the title *eri* in Nkpologu, which is the same name as First Man among the Umunri. *Attama*, too, have such a messenger: *Attama* Ntiye, for example, is served by his *orie* especially during the annual festival for the *alusi*. The *eri* at Nkpologu has the duty to bring supplicants from the diviner to the headman. Whenever kola is presented to the headman, *eri* breaks it, after receiving it for the headman. Similar to *eri* is *ozhioko* ("message-youth"), "messenger," who performs similar tasks for headmen in Oba and Imilike. Another titled man with somewhat more power than *eri*, *orie* or *ozhioko* is *osaye ezeoba* ("our speaker [for] chief of Oba"), who carries messages between the Igala-appointed *eze* ("chief") of greater Oba and the people of that district.

Aside from *attama*, which I will deal with separately, there are three other politico-religious titles of varying importance in the borderland: *eze* ("chief"), adapted from Igbo for "important person," a descriptive term; *ashadu* (Igala: "slave," from *osho*, "wandering child," and *adu*, "slave"), a title of persons of Igala administrative clans controlling most of the borderland; *asogwa* (Igala: "descendant [of] Ogwa," from *osho*, "child," and *ogwa*, "first," a name of the aboriginal *ashadu* in certain Igala legends), a fairly common title carrying more social prestige, by linking the person with the Igala and Okpoto, than political power. There are several lesser titles such as *ishiiwu*, "head of law," largely honorific, and *igwe*, "iron," also somewhat honorific (see Ugwu, 1958:29), although originally it had been the title of the head of the Igala community, as in Urho (see Bradbury, 1957:67).

Chiefship, as I indicated earlier, was not a typical institution among the Igbo, although it occurred commonly among the Umunri and, of course, among the Igala and Okpoto. Ugwu (1958:29) argues that the Umunri of Awka Division introduced the *eze* title in many areas particularly in southern Nsukka, but that by and large the *eze* title as a political title came from Igala. Many *eze* were undoubtedly Igbo, who had to have their titles confirmed at Idah by the *attah* or the *ashadu*, but others were just as certainly Okpoto and Igala men. In Umune Ngwa Village, for example, are large earthen symbols identical to those Igala shrines due north of Enugu-Ezike referred to as *ogwugwu*. These, my informants explained, are "related to the old people, and are signs of the *eze* of the olden times." The mounds are called *ogo*, "relative-in-law," and are given offerings by the lineage of the *attama*, indicating the probably non-Igbo origin of the *eze* for whom they were dedicated. At Nkpologu the institution of *eze* is still most clearly political and under Igala lineage control. *Arua eze* there, which is the highest political office, is held by Awalawa, who claims direct descent from Idah Igala. *Eze*ship there is hereditary and is limited to the members of only the one patrilineage (see Meek, 1937:154).

The *eze* held a rather loosely defined role as political leader among people not accustomed, nor very strongly inclined, to centralized government. He was, to all intents and purposes, the representative of the *attah* or *ashadu* in the district over which he had nominal control, and he presided over high-level conferences among the headmen, shrine priests, and holders of the *asogwa* title, but apparently all he could do was act as a sort of master of ceremonies or president of such gatherings. He was a receiver of first fruits, but only *after* the *attama*-mediated *alusi* had received the actual first fruits of any harvest; he was deferred to in a token manner in cases of land disputes, which were usually settled by the headmen, sometimes with the help of shrine priests. He was a leader, although not the most important, in the secret societies, particularly *omabe*, and he was an important consultant in any plans which a community might make for warfare against neighbors. Beyond these functions, until the onset of British administration, when many *eze* were made warrant chiefs, he had little real power in the borderland.

The Idoma title, *agu*, "leopard," took precedence over *eze* in the farther northeasterly areas of the borderland: for example, at Ohebe, both the *onyishi* and the *attama* Amanye carry the title, *agu*, as a title and as a salutation, although of late (and perhaps in the past, also) it has become more of an honorific salutation suggesting the supposed greatness of these individuals than an actual title with strong political or religious significance. More important, however, is the use of the same title in the extreme westerly part of the Division, at Ogurugu. The actual chief at Ogurugu bears the title, *attah ago*, "father leopard," designating his presumed (probably putative) links with the Idah royal line.

Ashadu is an Igala title used frequently in Nsukka, although not associated directly with Nsukka persons but rather with Okpoto on the northern side of the border. Boston has pointed out the importance of understanding the role of the *ashadu* and *Igala mela* (the nine Igala) whose headmen form the group of kingmakers in the Igala nation. The major branches of the *ashadu* group

> are localized along the Ibo border in the southeast corner of Igala. From both Igala and Ibo sources it is known that formerly Igala loosely controlled the adjacent part of the Ibo country to the south of the present border in this area and that the Ata's influence extended south of Nsukka. The Ashadu acted as one of the Ata's chief political agents, and in exercising this control is said to have collected tribute from a number of Ibo villages (Boston, 1964:118; 1967:23).

This is further substantiated by Omusa Oni's account. After the conquest by Onojo Ogbone, he said,

> Nsukka was called *Ashado*, and Ibagwa was called *Att'Igala*.

Some of the old names of places in Igboland were *Enugu Ezike Amuushu, Nsukka Amuushu, Ogurugu Amuushu, Opi Amuushu,* meaning that all of them belonged to the Igala.

The significance of this is that Nsukka, being farther inland and away from Igala, was therefore under more direct jurisdiction of the *ashadu*; all the areas, though, whether deep inland in Igbo country or close to the original Igala border, were under control of the Igala, which is the meaning of *ama ushu,* "people following."

In the Igbo towns of Nsukka, Obukpa, and Okpuje, furthermore, there is a common saying:

Nsukka Ashado Idah.

This consists of the name of the town plus the title plus *Idah,* designating that the town is controlled directly by an *ashadu* who is responsible to the *attah* at Idah. Ugwu (1958:12) includes the town of Eholumonna and cites variant titles linking these areas to Idah and *ashadu* control: "Nsukka-Asadu-Atta, Okpuje-Asadu-Atta, Obukpa and Eha-Alumona Asadu-Atta. This suggests that some villages in Nsukka had some political connection with the Ashadu who was and still is one of the chief lieutenants of the Atta of Igala."

Boston has argued that "in Igala tradition concerning the Nsukka Ibo villages, the part played by Onoja Oboni in their conquest is recognised, but overshadowed in interest by the role of the Ashadu as the Ata's chief representative in the area" (1960: 57–58. See also Seton, 1928:259). Actually the *attama*—who in most cases was also the diviner—was to most ordinary rural Igbo much more important than the rather distant administrative officials such as *ashadu* or *eze*.

The importance of the *ashadu* in traditional Igala government and in control of the borderland areas is further stressed by informants among some of my own contact clans. For example, we saw references to the legendary first *ashadu*, *Ogwa* ("first," "earliest"), whose name was Omeppa and who was presumably Igbo but more likely Okpoto (see Seton, 1928:269–270), among the *nna* of Umu Mkpume and the *arua* of Dimunke Clan of Ameegwu Village although not in its sister clan, Umueze, which claims to be mainly Igbo in origin. Similar references occur elsewhere among groups claiming close ties with Igala, as in Nkpologu and even in Ihe-Nsukka. In the latter, in Umuozhi Clan of Amuukwa Village, which owns the site of an old Igala defensive fort, the forefathers are named as follows:

Ocho Ogwa: Grandfather Ogwa.

Asogwa Owo NwOcho: Descendant of the aboriginal First Igala, thus "Titled Man Who is Son of the Grandfather."

Ugwu Anye Asogwa Ihe: "Our Renowned *Asogwa* of Ihe."

Asogwa Ihe Attah: "*Asogwa*, Father of Ihe."

Ozhi: "Messenger"—the one who first carried the news that the Igala were coming to Nsukka.

Asogwa is a title generally without much political importance, although it is otherwise significant in that it deliberately links the individual holding it with the *ashadu* clan of the Okpoto. The *arua asogwa* at Nkpologu-Attah is the staff of the representative of the *ashadu* in that large town, and is theoretically subservient to the staffs of authority of the *eze*, who derives his power from Idah, and from that of the *attama*, who is supported by the great *alusi* and father-figure, Ezuugwu Ehuru. Actually, its line of authority derives directly from the *ashadu*, who is represented by the *asogwa*. Among the Etsako, across the Niger from the Igala—and especially the Ukpila subtribe—*asogwa* is a senior title; and Meek (1937:145, 151–152, 167) has pointed out that the *asogwa* is in direct charge of the *omabe es'atho* ("*omabe* mask-wearers") in Nsukka Division, which is still indeed the case.

A final title of this general class of titles, according to some writers, is the *ama* title, which generically includes political titles, but is represented most importantly in the priestly title of *attama*. Ugwu (1958:29, 30) has said that

the "Ama" titles were political mostly. "Ama" titlemen were also great social figures. When an animal was slaughtered for "Second Burial" or for some juju worship, parts of the meat went to the titlemen. A titleman with an "Odu-Atu" staff of office [*oduatu*: "Bell Which Orders"—i.e., people to move aside from its carrier] was respected anywhere he went. He was free from the molestation of people and even juju masks.

In the Ayamelemu area of Uzo-Uwani there are various title holdings which mark out the holders from the rank and file of the community. One of the greatest of these titles is "Amawulu." [See Thomas, 1913, II:3, 13—*amaunwulu*.] This involves complicated ceremonies, some of which are secret and require only a few people whose parents distinguished themselves fighting in one of the ancient wars; or who themselves claim to possess some extraordinary magical powers.

In no wise does Ugwu indicate how such *ama* titles are political, however; nor was I able to elicit from any of my own informants any evidence that such titles were in fact political, with the exception of the title *attama*, which is not a title from *within* the *ama* title system: *attama* have inherited titles, and indeed are the "lords" in charge of *ama* title groups, which are chiefly potlatch-type title societies by means of which non-Igbo *attama* were able to develop a relatively loyal Igbo group in the villages which they controlled. Thus ordinary *ama* societies parallel the specialty fertility *ama* cults already described as *inyiama*, with largely Igbo membership under the control of a shrine priest usually descended from non-Igbo lineages and clans.

The Omabe Association

The most important cross-lineage association in the borderland is the *omabe* society, which itself is strongly although not completely controlled by *attama*, such titled persons as *asogwa*, and even some *ndishi* of more than usual personal prestige. *Omabe* is variously interpreted by different informants, the following meanings having been given it: "it is spirit," from *o* (it), *mma* (spirit), and *be* (is); "it strikes people," from *o* (it), *'ma* (strikes), and *ibe* (people), which is less likely. Among shrine priests and *asogwa* in charge of maskers of this cult it was argued that the words mean "sons of the village," from *oma* (sons) and *ogbe* (village). Thus it means "the male side," and has reference to the ability of the group of men to make war medicine, among other things. It also means "sons of the earth-mask," from *om'* (sons) and *abule* (the land-chief's mask) indicating the relationship between this society and the *alusi* Abere. Although this latter meaning derivation is the one I believe is correct, the most common Nsukka pronunciation today is *omabe*, so I will use it.

Meek (1937:78) wrote that "the cult of Omabe is of a similar character [to that of *odo*]," and

> at Nsukka the deity appears annually in one or other of the villages or quarters, each of which has a cult of its own. On his reappearance he mourns for those of his devotees who had died since his last appearance, and when he departs, three days before the rising of the new moon, a wooden gong is beaten.

Omabe is a men's secret society which is ancestral insofar as the maskers represent the risen dead ancestors who originally controlled the making of male, aggressive war medicine in the forest (as was the case of the mythical Agenapoje and, especially, Ezuugwu of Awulu Market), although it is not associated with any one descent group. Elders are clearly in charge of much of the ritual and ceremony involved in the appearance of maskers, their dancing and worship of the spirit of the *omabe*, but the actual performer of sacrifices is the *attama* and, as I mentioned earlier, the person in direct charge of the maskers is one with the title *asogwa*.

Although the *omabe* society has one or two apparent social control functions—for example, notorious offenders against public morality are whipped mercilessly by the maskers, and maskers sometimes enforce rulings by the council of village elders which have until their appearance been scoffed at—in general *omabe* is like the *alusi* insofar as its effect is largely to disturb, to frighten by a display of uncontrolled or barely controlled power. Thus it resembles the power released by war medicine, which leaves devastation in its wake and which requires cleansing ceremonies so that the earth and the spiritual forces are satisfied and "cooled down." It is also like the *alusi* (particularly Abere, who is influential in social control and to whom the *omabe* maskers once each four years ritually subject themselves) in the unpredictability of its actions, although it is obviously not nearly so terrible, for it is visible and material rather than invisible and spiritual. Both "beings" seek offerings and are known to act capriciously. "What is the difference between *omabe* and *alusi*?" I inquired of the gathered *omabe* society elders at Ihe Owele, Nsukka, by whom I had been invited for the society's celebration in 1964. Their answer:

> You can see the *omabe*. You have seen it yourself. It can be seen with the eyes. If the *omabe* wants an offering, it will come in the daylight, directly to the person, and it will tell him that it wants an offering. But the *alusi* are invisible, and only the diviner can tell what kind of offering they want. The *omabe* is bringer of evil [*ekwensu*]. All of its things, the things it does, are against the law of the people.

Why does it bring evil? Why do the people tolerate it?

> It does as it pleases, but it does not kill. It began in the olden times, so once a year it returns, and we remember those times.

The annual appearance of the *omabe* follows a set pattern. Four days before the opening ceremonies, during the night on *afo* market day the society members have the ceremony of *onye kulunye* ("person called us"), which is a secret and relatively quiet erection of lines crisscrossing the village square, to which are tied small humanoid figures made of grass, interlocking Kano-type knots of woven grass, and the like. On the main opening day (*oye*) of festivities the village men trek to the wooded grove known as *Iyi Nsukka*, "Mother [of] Nsukka," where they attire themselves in their cloth costumes and masks. Once ready, they leave the grove and follow special paths known as *uzoma*, "path of the spirits," to a sacred grove known as *Nkwo Nsukka*, which is the site of a very old traditional market, thus the name. Here gather the men, approximately 2000 of them, heavily armed and highly decorated and/or masked. Obeisance is made by maskers and dancers to the major *arua* figure of the *omabe*, *onyishima*, "head person [of the] spirits," dances are performed to demonstrate the prowess of the society's members, and after sacrifices are made to the spirit of the *omabe*, the maskers disperse to their own villages.

Preceding the arrival of the *omabe* maskers in the village are heralds, calling out:

> *Nde one nwe eze?* ("Which freeborn people have the chief?")

Response by ordinary members of the society already in the village:

> *Anyi nwe eze!* ("We have the chief!")
> *Nde one nwe mmo?* ("Which freeborn people have the spirit?")

Response: *Anyi nwe mmo!*

The maskers first go to the compound of the village *alusi*, where they salute the altar dedicated to them, return to the village square, dance, and now and then chase away onlookers.

On the following day (*afo*) the members of each village society gather in the *omabe* house, which is located in the village square, and celebrate the coming of the *omabe* with music and sacrifices of male foods. This ends the period of the first visitation. The next period occurs two weeks (eight days) later, when the maskers gather at *Oye Nsukka*, another traditional market, offer sacrifices and dance; this is repeated four days later; finally, four days after this, and a total of four weeks (four times four days) after the first visitation, the *omabe* come forth into their individual village squares, the maskers speaking the so-called *omabe* language which is produced by the masker's blowing through strands of spider egg-sac silk as among the *mmo* society maskers at Onitsha. During this time, certain special "secret" words are spoken, often by a masker addressing someone.

Masker, to titled or elderly man:

> *Ogbu* ["It kills"—signifying *ato*, "buffalo"].
> Response:
> *Ata, ngwane* ["Father-lord, owner of the land"].
> Masker:
> *Ndidi okooko* ["Patience cultivates wealth"].
> Response:
> *Ata* [or Igbo *Nna'm*, "My father"], *ngwane*.

To untitled yet grown men the masker speaks the person's name, and receives the above response. To youths the masker makes a hiss-moan threat, to which the youth, if intelligent, replies:

Nni oko   n'egbu   nw'esi.
"Food hot that kills son of pig."

This means that the "hot" or aggressive actions of the *omabe* can kill the speaker, who called himself "son of a pig" to indicate that he is helplessly subject to the masker and that he is a despised person and essentially distinct from those to whom pig meat is forbidden. After a morning of this, the men retire to the *omabe* meeting house, dress in their ordinary clothes, and return to their compounds, where the remainder of the day is given up to more or less potlatch-type feasting. Thus the visitation is finished for another year.

What degree of social control does *omabe* exert? The chief function of this society appears to consist in creating a certain degree of social disorganization, if we consider ordinary and typical organization to derive from a combination of descent-group structures and general control of the unexpected. The borderland village does keep the "unexpected" or "chance" relatively under control, save for the sometimes erratic behavior of the *alusi* and this ritualized disorganization (or, rather, temporary rearrangement of powers, accompanied by anxieties on the part of some individuals that the *omabe* may punish them) caused by the secret society once each year. The powers of the *omabe* are well known, and only little children and fools think the maskers are anything but quite real men who during this season are behaving as enforcers of the law regardless of lineage or clan affiliations. But the disorganization and anxieties aroused by the annual visitation of the *omabe* are controlled at least in time and are not so truly erratic and unpredictable as the *alusi*. Accordingly, those persons in the villages who are guilty of behavior that would stimulate the *omabe* to punish them certainly know of their guilt and, aware that the society will be activated at a specific time of the year —the time of war and masculine assertiveness after *ishiji*, when the foods are male foods and the men are no longer eating the female foods of the period of famine—they have ample time to make amends and to correct their ways. For *omabe* is a disorganizer only symbolically insofar as its behavior imitates warfare. It actually contributes to social organization in its secondary role as a policing force. "Where did *omabe* come from?" I inquired in numerous places. "From the time of the ancestors," was the stock reply. Altering the question, however, to "in the olden days, when people went to war, what did *omabe* do?" elicited the response:

> It was the *omabe* who went to war. But there is no war these days. That is of the olden times. Then, the leaders of the *omabe* made the medicine; they were *attama* and older men, and the *omabe* carried the medicine on them.

It is clear that the society functions differently today from what it— or its antecedent war society or head-hunting society—did in the past. Its apparently disruptive nature nowadays is thus a symbolic reflection of the disturbance to Earth resulting from actual war: the wildness of aggression which is released by war causes everyone to fear, for the powers can strike out in all directions. So these days it is at least partly controlled; the arrival of the maskers is predictable annually; their behavior is limited to beating, and not beating just anyone, but normally the guilty. And only hints of the original disruptive and dangerous character of the war-season of the year remain. For example, in the prayers to *omabe*, the *onyishi*, after telling the *omabe* to be welcome and pointing out to the spirit that the society's members have all the sacrifices which were promised during the last visitation, asks,

> *Biko   ekwene ife   obuna'me   anyi.*
> Please let not things whatsoever [unexpected] happen to us.

So *omabe* is a social control force, of sorts, controlling otherwise uncontrolled human behavior and, by striking people with the fear of potentially uncontrollably disruptive forces it reminds them annually of the virtues of peace and of ordinariness in life, politics, and the normal means of social control. The grown daughter of *attama* Ngwumakechi, Oyima Agbo, commented to me on this particular point, when none of the lineage men were present:

> They are wild with the *omabe* every three years [i.e, when each

quarter of Nsukka receives a major visitation; maskers join the celebration annually, however], and that is enough. They frighten people, and many people behave themselves just because they are frightened of what *omabe* will do to them. But all it does is to make us happy it is not here more often.

Attama and Diviner

While the disruptive influence of *omabe* occurs periodically, the much more powerful, and less predictable force of the *alusi* is present always, day and night, forever hovering about the village. At any time it pleases, the *alusi* can roam about to seek sacrifices, which it need only demand to receive. To exist peacefully with the violent *alusi*, the village needs two people: one who can "read" the unreadable, who can interpret the will of the spirits—the diviner; and one who can mediate between humans and those spirits—the priest. In Nsukka borderland villages these persons, often the same man, are the most important agents of social control.

(1) The Diviner
I have written elsewhere on divination in the Nsukka borderland (Shelton, 1965c), so there is no need to repeat those materials here, but some further discussion of the diviner as an agent of social control is in order. Because in societies such as that of the Nsukka borderland many empirical explanations for the various vicissitudes of life are either less satisfying than the people wish, or are not able to answer fully questions dealing with intentional causality and the unforeseen, and because Nsukkans—in perhaps an overemphasized rationalism—demand an explanation for virtually every attention-rousing event, matters arise almost daily which can not be logically or mnemonically handled, so people consult the diviner to determine which unseen force may be the causal agent. The shrine priest, in most cases, combines his priestly duties and divination, as distinct

from the situation in much of central Igboland, so that the Igala and Okpoto were able—initially, at least—to maintain general control over the occupied Igbo villages, for no Igbo villager in the colonialized areas could discover the causal and intentional agents behind his troubles, nor make the regular propitiations to avoid such troubles, without recourse to the Igala diviner and shrine priest.

The diviner is referred to by several descriptive labels. Once in a while someone may use the term *dibea* or *dibea afa* (compare Basden, 1938:54–55), but this is not common Nsukka dialectal use; in the borderland, *dibea* refers to a "native healer" or herbalist, or to a sorcerer (one who can manipulate *ogwu*, "medicine"). "To divine" is *igba afa* (pronounced *igbaafa*), meaning "to join the *afa*" or divination implements together in such patterns that the will or intention of the otherwise unknowable can be "read" and understood. The diviner, therefore, is *onye n'agbaafa*, "person who divines," or more commonly, *ogbaafa* ("he divines"). Another common term in the borderland is *ikwa ojuju* ("to spread out to ask"—i.e., "to cast out questions"). So the diviner is also called *okwojuju*, not to be confused with *akwa ojuju* ("cloth-question"), the cloth which is wrapped around an ancestral spear and is used by Igala for certain oaths. The third term for diviner is *ogbaagbo* ("he divines") from Igala (see Seton, 1929:44, 50).

The method of divination is the casting of strings of *afa* or half shells of wild almond and the interpretation of meanings in the patterns of concave or convex shells which turn up. Although some persons of diffusionist persuasion who have studied divination elsewhere might suggest that divination and other cultural influences flow solely from monarchies to segmentary societies, *afa*—the method of divination common in Nsukka—"may have derived from the Yoruba *ifa* or vice versa" (Talbot, 1926, II:187), or both systems may have derived from an aboriginal method. Like *eba* divination among the Nupe, as Nadel has argued, the method is far from uniform, and differs from locality to locality (see Nadel, 1954:38; and for the Yoruba viewpoint, Bascom, 1966). Regardless of the origins of the method, it is a form of divination that is an extremely significant element in the lives of the people it serves and enables them to satisfy their need to understand that which otherwise would remain forever unknown. And what is unknown, in Nsukkan belief, is uncontrollable.

What has meaning among the borderland people is (1) that which is or which occurs because of mechanical or "natural" (not "logical") action and the meaning of which can be understood by observation, (2) that which occurs because of non-observable yet logically determinable causation, and (3) that which occurs because of non-observable and non-logically determinable actions and the meaning of which can be determined only by divination. These categories are not utterly separable: they are merely different kinds of cause-effect situations distinguished less often by Nsukkans than by outsiders. Their separability becomes apparent when problems arise; as Horton (1967:59–60) has pointed out, sometimes in the confrontation with the unusual or uncanny, in the face of anxiety-provoking situations, and in certain types of crises theatening the society. Then the Nsukkan in effect asks: Should this event be judged by divination, or is it a matter of common knowledge or common sense which can be rationally determined without recourse to magical or mysterious methods? Divination thus deals with the mysterious which eludes human experience or reason. A man can interpret another human's reaction to an event; but he cannot foretell the reaction of an *alusi*, for human beings are less whimsical than are the gods, particularly the *alusi*, who have the power to do as they please.

The prayer to gods and ancestors, and even to the *omabe*, "let not unexpected things happen to us," is a prayer that the world be, as much as possible, logical, ordered and sane, and humanly understandable. The implication is not that the world is somehow chaotic in itself and that the activities of gods are required to maintain it in some orderly fashion, but rather that the gods themselves are forces of potential disorder. The *alusi* are particularly unpredictable so they are especially solicited to restrain themselves and to avoid too whimsical exercises of their powers, thereby assuring men the luxury of a relatively orderly life. This restraint helps to give man an immediate future which he can trust, stabilizing his life, relieving some of his anxiety, and carrying with it a built-in reason for its breakdown whenever "chance" occurrences do happen. Since the *alusi* have the power to demand attentions over and over again it is wise to propitiate them as regularly as possible, and when trouble occurs, one must "cool" them down once again so that order may be restored.

In what sense, one might ask, is the diviner an agent of social control rather than simply one who functions in the village communications network, albeit in rather specialized communications? The Nsukkan proverb common among diviners suggests the answer:

Eha 'noona   mbekwu   onigi agba   onwoya.
Afa staying in tortoise shell does not cast itself.

This means several things. Generally, it means that what one has in mind, but does not speak, will not speak itself, for human will and intention as well as voice mechanics are required. The divination implements are stored inside a tortoise shell, but without the human agent they will tell nothing. In short, a person is required to cast and to "read" the *afa*, and that person—the diviner—possesses a great deal of power, for there is no one to gainsay his reading of the *afa* save one of his colleagues. As Horton has said, if the divination doesn't succeed, the client might have the diviner try again, or he might go to another diviner—although this is rare in the Nsukka borderland; but the client never really doubts the efficacy of divination, for there is no other means of determining the intentional cause of important events (such as "accidents" or serious illness or related catastrophe) and therefore no other means of alleviating the problem (see Horton, 1967:167; and Shelton, 1968b). The diviner is the one person who possesses this specialized ability, and only through his agency can the ordinary people—which include persons of all ranks, even the titled—maintain some safe margin of activity, some neutrality, in relation to the capricious and often hostile *alusi*. Add to this point the fact that in most of the borderland the diviner is also the priest of the local *alusi*, and his role as a control agent becomes even clearer, for he not only contacts the people to communicate the wishes of the gods to them but also must be contacted by the ordinary people whenever they wish to "speak" to the gods. Thus we turn to the final agent of social control, (and) the most important on a village [level] and on a person-to-person level, the shrine priest.

(2) The attama

The common Igbo word for shrine priest is *eze* plus the name of the particular spirit to whom the priest is linked, such as *ezaala, eziigwe,* and the like. In the Onitsha-Awka area, priests of *alusi* are generally given such a title, the plural being *ndezalose* (see Thomas, 1913, II: 269), and in central Igbo such terms as *onyishi agbara* or *onyishi arusi* ("headman [of] spirit") are common, as is *onyeji ishiagbara* ("person [who] holds head spirit"), applied to both *alusi* and ancestral priests. But in Nsukka there is a sharp distinction made between priests of *alusi* and the *ndishi* (headmen) who act as priests of ancestral spirits, the High God, and Earth. The *alusi* priest invariably has the title *attama,* an Igala title for shrine priest, and is descended from Igala and Okpoto forefathers.

The title *attama* requires some explanation. In an early paper Horton suggested that the title "appears to be of Igala origin (*Ata* = chief, lord; *Ma* = spirits)" (1954:319). This is correct, although it might be amplified. *Atta* in Igala means, first, "father," and thus "king" or "lord"; *ma* can be from the Igbo-Okpoto *mmo* ("spirits") but is probably secondarily this, having the primary meaning of "many" as *ama,* indicating a unit of people and in this context particularly the members of the Igala-controlled *ama* title society (this is supported by Seton, 1929:45, quoting the Igala *Attama,* Omachi, at Ifaku). The title is sometimes confused, furthermore, with others. For example, the Igala *attebo,* "father [of] magic," has been described as a priest who takes part in numerous ceremonials —some of them religious—among the Igala (see Seton, 1928:272). My own Ankpa informants, however, argued that *attanebo* is actually the *attama* involved in the special making of medicine called *ojuju,* or divination, *ebo* referring to the spirit of the *arua* staff which he carries. The *attebo*, further, as Boston has explained, was responsible for worship of early royal ancestors (1967:25), and according to Clifford (1936:418) is the chief priest, the first of whom was said to be Ape, the priest in the household of Ayegba.

Most commonly, however, the title has been confused with the Umunri title, *adama* (*ada* = "he speaks with"; *mwa* = "spirits"). Meek has said that the office of *attama* was "introduced as part of the religio-titular system disseminated throughout Iboland from Nri," and

> It is instructive to note the recurrence of this belief that the real rulers of the town are the ancestors or spirits, and that living persons who act as rulers are merely the agents of the ancestors. This doctrine is the basis of priestly-chieftainship, and the divine kingship which is found among the Jukun, Igala, Yoruba, and Bini tribes.

Yet, in somewhat contradictory fashion, in the same work:

> It is believed that when an Atama dies he becomes reincarnated as the Ata of Ida, and when an Ata dies he becomes reincarnated as the Atama of Amala. It was the custom for a new Ata of Ida to send a goat and chicken to the Atama of Amala for sacrifice to Ezugu, the Atama in return sending to the Ata some of the magical chalk of Ezugu (Meek, 1937:159–161).

Jeffreys (1935:346–354) described the Adama of Nri as a priestly group who were the custodians of regalia in coronation and king-making ceremonies. In a later paper (1956:129) he described the Adama as the servants of the Umunri divine king yet equal sharers with the king in tribute. Thomas (1913, I:50–52) said that Adama men performed the burial rites for Umunri kings and "are said to eat the property of Nri because they are bigger than the King" (supported by the fact that when Ndrinamoke came from the sky he found Adama already on the earth), and he cited an origin tale stating that the Umunri people "put alose and ajana [earth sacrifices] everywhere." This last point agrees with some origin tales in the Nsukka borderland, which are part of the lore of a few particular villages, which I have described elsewhere (see Shelton, 1965). In

Ohebe-Oba, for example, *Attama* Amanye explained: "Eze Ikpoke, Eze Nshie, brought Amanye to Ohebe, and he was the first *attama*, the first person to worship Amanye and the first to worship the *arua* here." But even in such places which claim Umunri ancestry, including Umu Mkpume, the *attama* are ignorant of the Umunri title, *adama*, as I have already pointed out (above, p. 14).

The Igala title, *attama*, on the other hand, is the title of shrine priests in the Nsukka borderland, who with few exceptions claim Igala ancestry. The title itself is hereditary usually within a male line. *Attama* Okwuugwu: "I became *attama* ten years ago. I was chosen by Okwuugwu, but the grown men of my people taught me the things I must know. Before I was *attama*, my grandfather, Arugwu, was *Attama*, and before him, his great-grandfather Ezuugwu, was the *attama*." *Attama* Iye Owo Ago, Udeeze Mba: "When I became *attama*, I had to make special sacrifices to Iye Owo and to Anyanwu Ezechitoke. My father taught me the things I must know, because only our people have *attama*."

ATTAMA NGWUMADESHE OF UMUGOJI:
A new *attama* makes prayers in a shrine in the bush of Umugoji, and sacrifices there to Ekke [Python] and to Onumuno. The place is called *eshua Ngwu* [Ngwu's Forest]. While he was still alive, the former *attama* told me that an *attama* must never go into *eshuangwu* until after he has made those sacrifices, so it took me four years before I could make all those offerings, and then I could enter the forest. I could go out of the village during that time, but the forest was forbidden to me, and I could not go inside it.

The Ekke shrine there consists of very large pots and many brass rods—the things we used for money in the olden times before pennies and shillings were brought to us.

All those four years it took me to accumulate those goods, offerings were made regularly to Ngwumadeshe, but until I made my special sacrifices to Ekke I received no part of the sacrifices. Only if somebody would offer a cow to Onumuno, I would have a share in that, but I received no share in offerings to Ngwu. The person who made the prayers and offerings once each week [every four days] to Ngwu before I had made my special sacrifices was *Attama* Ngwu Ashua'm of Amaala-oba. The very day I entered the sacred bush for my sacrifices, he received a whole leg of the cow I killed, but this was the last of his share in things. He then went back to his own place permanently, and after that I was *Attama* Ngwumadeshe.

We began to make the sacrifices at the time when the chickens were going inside, at night, and we finished them by the time of the first cockcrow. I was dressed in a black *agbada*, which was tied around my waist with a different cloth. This was the dress of a strong person. Black is the customary cloth for this ceremony [borne out by Egbele Ejuona's having given a black robe to Omeppa as a mark of his title as original *ashadu*; customary also in the installation of *inyiama* women].

On that first day we began the ceremony by killing a cow. *Attama* Ngwu Ashua'm directed me to the very place where I had to kill the cow for Ekke. I did not use a pot to catch the blood of the cow, but I had to let it go down into the ground in that exact place so it would go down to Ekke, who lives in the earth under that shrine. When I killed the cow, I called the name of Ekke and told him that I had the things required for the offerings, and I asked him to protect my life and protect my family, because I did not steal those goods or rob any person, but I worked hard to accumulate them. So I said: let Ekke help me and beg Chukwu to multiply my goods.

Then I sacrificed more than sixty chickens, forty kola nuts, four huge pots of palm wine, a large basket of yam fufu and cocoyam, and a whole pot of palm oil. My own *itarigba* [patri-clan] offered one female chicken [an important sacrifice as female, symbolizing the killing off of a "lineage" of chickens]. In the Forest of Ngwu we first took the liver from the cow and cooked it with a chicken there. Then we brought the meat home out of the forest and it was shared by the entire village.

One year later, I went again to the bush of Ngwu and I offered a ram to Ngwu, thanking him for making me *attama* and for keeping me well and keeping my family well. Once when I was very sick, Ngwu demanded that I sacrifice another ram in that bush, so I did it. After I made that offering, I became well, and I have been well ever since then.

UGWUJA *Attama* OF AMEEGWU VILLAGE:

The *attama* is the person who makes offerings to *alusi*, as I make offerings to Ntiye. We wear certain things: the tooth I wear on this chain about my neck is *iziago* ["tooth of leopard"]. It is one sign of the head of a shrine, along with the brass bracelet and anklets. The *attama* shaves his head except for this small knot of hair, which marks a titled man. Someone in the family of a dead *attama* has dreams, and others have dreams, too; then another *attama* is brought in and he is given sticks. Each stick is for one person, but the diviner doesn't know which stick is for which person, and the *afa* selects the new *attama*. Then this person shaves his head and wears these things and makes the offerings to the *alusi*. (See Figure XVII: *Okpoto Children's and Adults' Hair Style*.)

The items of attire and costume, including *akwebi* (*akwa ugbi*), "cloth-feathers," which is the red cap with the circle of red feathers worn by the *attah* and the *onojo*, are fairly standard throughout the borderland, *attama* having the same formal ceremonial costume as the *onojo* (traditional Okpoto chief) of Ankpa and the chief of Eteh as described by Sieber (1965). Many of them, as I have already pointed out, refer to themselves as "leopard" and compare their titles to that of the *attah*, although this is clearly exaggeration if it is considered politically. As Boston has indicated, the leopard is a major symbol of kingship in Benin culture and is the totem of the Igala royal clan (1962:376). The title of the traditional Igala ruler of Ogurugu includes *ago*, "leopard," and Meek (1937:158, 162–163) describes the use of this praise-name by *attama* in other parts of the Division. Related to this is the use of the talking drum, which is called *idah*, the name of the Igala capital, for recitation of the praise-name of the *attama* during festivals and especially when the *attama* eats or drinks in public.

In what respects might the *attama* be considered a powerful agent of social control? Were the Igala correct in establishing these men in their particular posts? Actually, the technique used by the Igala tended to be based upon their astute recognition that, among the Igbo,

> common interests in mythical values, common sacred places and so forth were more important unifying factors than the secular sanction of force—which is invariably the prerequisite of large-scale political consolidation (Anene, 1966:15).

The Igala furthermore realized that such a pervasive influence of religion provided a basis, as Anene says, "for the important role of priests who mediated between god and man." Years earlier Talbot correctly remarked that "in the north the most important man in a town is often the Atama or juju priest" (1926, III:601). The importance of the *attama* lies in the fact that he is the only person who can neutralize or cool down an activated *alusi* and, moreover, he is usually the diviner at the same time, so that he is virtually in total control of the unknown. First fruits offerings have to be brought to him, as the spokesman for the *alusi*, and only afterwards can the *ofo* holders, the heads of patrilineages, permit their people to complete the harvests and consume the fresh crop of food. Because the *alusi*, unless it is "fed" quite regularly and generously, will seek offerings most voraciously, the *attama* as master of the shrine area is the recipient—in the name of the god—of a great amount of tribute. The tribute, the inherited lands, and special gifts enable him to practise polygyny and to help his own clansmen to purchase non-inherited titles, though most of these are not of extremely high order in the borderland. His prestige and social status caused many Igbo clans to seek affinal alliances while at the same time there was resistance to Igalicization. During the 1918 war between the British colonial government and the village-group of Imilike, the *Attama* Iye Owo saved the district officer, Arthur Robert Whitman, from the people, an act which demonstrates the power of the *attama* and indicates something of the relationships between Igala and Igbo lines.

While it can be understood that as priest of a village-wide and potentially hostile god the *attama* would possess considerable social and even economic influence (social control of an important sort), what of his role in such areas as political decision-making, law enforcement, community reorganization, and the like? We have seen how interlocked in the Nsukka borderland are religion and other matters of human society, so one must repeat that there is no nice separation of the *attama*'s role as priest from his other social roles. This would not necessarily guarantee him widespread importance, yet most *attama* in the borderland—although not farther south in Nsukka, where Igala and Okpoto influence are much slighter—are very important in community control.

Political decision-making in the borderland did not generally involve any unit larger than a village-group, Nkpologu-Attah perhaps being the largest group having political unity. There, for example, decisions were arrived at through consultation of the *eze*, *onyishi*, *attama*, and *asogwa*, after each—with the exception of the *attama*—had consulted with his own group of advisers. More typical, perhaps, is a village-group such as Imilikenu, or even a smaller unit such as Ameegwu Village in Owele-ezeoba. In Imilikenu, a very heavily populated village-group, decisions are arrived at by the gathered holders of *ofo*—that is to say, by the various clan and patrilineage *ndishi* (headmen)—along with the two *attama* of Iye Owo, the senior and the junior. Issues are placed before the group by whichever smaller contingent has introduced the meeting, by the senior *onyishi*, or by *Attama* Iye Owo Uno, the senior of the two priests, and usually after much argument consensus is reached. What in particular increases the *attama*'s political influence, aside from everyone's awareness that they represent something larger and more powerful than a descent group, and aside from personal oratorical and related talents (which are normally although not always developed in a shrine priest as a matter of course) are the personal debts and obligations toward the *alusi* which over a period of time the *attama* are able to impose upon heads of households. These obligations are often debts of gratitude for the *alusi*'s having lifted the curse of illness off members of a lineage, having enabled the infertile to bear children, and the like. "What stands behind one gives one power," say the Igbo. In Imilike, Iye Owo stands behind the two *attama*; behind each *onyishi* stands his own patrilineage or clan; when one asks which is the stronger, there is but one answer. So the *attama* are listened to and are heard, not slavishly, of course, but with the reasonable attention which sensible elders devote to those supported by powerful beings.

At the village level, at Ameegwu Village, where there are two clans, each with an *onyishi*, and one *attama*, political decisions are matters of consensus always, although sometimes (as everywhere) with some grumbling. One clan is the line of the *attama*, and its headman is the *attama*'s elder brother, while the other clan is a traditionally Igbo line. The residential areas of the village are patri-localized according to clans, Umueze being located on one side of the Ntiye shrine area, and Dimunke located on the opposite side. Such a village is so small that there is hardly a "council" of elders, but rather a group of household heads who advise each of the *ndishi* on political matters. When such decisions are made virtually everyone in the village is aware of the decisions from the beginning of arguments. Because the number and proportion of Igbo and Igala families are relatively equal, the *attama* need not rely so strongly upon created obligations, indebtedness, and personal charisma as in, say, Imilikenu. Suffice it to say that no serious political decision can be made without the concurrence of the *attama*, but that most of the time the *attama* easily concurs with the decisions of the gathered elders.

Law enforcement in Nsukkan communities is not truly separable from religious sanction, and invariably involves more than one person or group. Offences against ancestors, the High God, and Earth invariably arouse the interest of the village *alusi*, although not always to the point of activating its powers. Activation probably results from the opportunities seen by *attama*—and not so cynically perhaps as it sounds at first—to increase the influence of the being whom they serve, and thus to enhance their own prestige and influence. Offences against the *alusi* itself, of course, arouse the interest of the clan elders for the simple reason that this powerful spiritual force must be pacified as soon as possible, lest the entire community suffer. In both sorts of offence against the public good, therefore, the *attama* is important as a social control agent, direct or indirect. Even in cases handled by associations such as *omabe* he is consulted, for he is in ultimate charge of that society. Thus, although "law enforcement" is a matter of public action and is certainly shared by a large number of village persons, the *attama* is always somehow involved, whereas other community leaders—*ndishi*, titled persons, leaders of associations—are involved in only some cases.

"Community reorganization" is a term which I am using to denote several more or less related events in many northern Igbo agricultural communities. There are two major kinds of community reorganization. One occurs when the population of a village has grown too large for all to remain centrally located, and a section will migrate, the resultant settlements or "farm areas," being designated by the suffix *ago*, meaning "apart" or "farm." The second is the shifting of an entire population from one area to another, usually because of events interpreted by divination, as in the case of Imili-kenu described earlier (p. 151). Other sorts of changes have occurred in the past, including the alienation of persons as *ohu* slaves in exchange for arable land, the development of hilltop communities for better defense against enemies, the creation of new lineages within clans by means of adoption, and the accommodation of non-customary industries such as Dane-gun factories. A major latter-day example, for that matter, was the University of Nigeria, Nsukka, which caused some displacement and necessary reorganization of certain communities. Community reorganization, like political procedure, involves decision-making by the *ofo*-holding *ndishi*, the important titled men (who are all *ndishi* or holders of political titles or both), and the *attama*. The decision to move a segment of population is not lightly taken, but is determined by common sense and supported by the consensus of elders. Those who move are accompanied by a "child" of the village *alusi* ostensibly to "protect" them, but also rather obviously to observe them and to maintain sacrifices from them. Such is the case of Iye Owo Ago, the "daughter" Iye Owo "of the farmland," who accompanied the Imilikenu settlers when that large group moved out from the central village several generations ago and cleared new bush. With the establishment of the new shrine there is, of course, a naming of a new *attama* to serve the god, thus an extension of the power of the shrine priests of an area.

In village-wide conflicts over land (an area of constant conflict among Igbo as with many other agrarian peoples), the *attama* is especially influential, and his role as a social control agent is clearly demonstrated. The *attama* is constantly concerned with the land and its produce for several reasons, important among which are that his *alusi* in many cases was an earth spirit when its worship was taken over by his Igala forefathers. The presence of the spirit-daughter, Abere, in the borderland indicates this close link between the *alusi* and all matters of the earth and lands: as the Igala say, *Abule fane nwochi* (Boston, 1968:156), "Abule cleansed the land," reminding one of the role not only of this *alusi* but of the *attama*. The *attama* in the borderland is very much like the land chief (*onu ane*) among the Igala and Okpoto: he is the ritual guardian of the land, and his ritual duties cannot be delegated to another; as the priest of the village *alusi* he is able to exercise much social control, for no other person can control the spirit whom he serves.

We have seen already that first fruits offerings are given to the *alusi* by the lineage and clan headmen, who thereby ritually acknowledge the supremacy of the *alusi* in village affairs. Ultimate control of the influential *omabe* society, too, is held by the *attama*, and during that society's annual festival maskers make obeisance first to the *alusi* shrines before engaging in their various other activities. The *attama* also is normally the diagnostician—as diviner—of personal and social ailments: when individuals are brought down with serious illness, of course, they go to the diviner to determine the intentional cause of the ailment; but when ills befall an entire village—such as a loss of the water supply, a failure of crops to grow, epidemic, and the like,—the diviner becomes even more important, and since he is the *attama* as well he is in a very powerful control position over the people.

The *attama*'s power as a ritual guardian of the land is also illustrated in land distribution, particularly when the problem involves more than an Igbo clan. When the dispute occurs between lineages of a clan, the headmen of the various segments form a council to try the dispute. On certain occasions one side or the other might call in a shrine priest to act as an outside witness or even to give third-party advice, although this is not common. These disputes do not as a rule involve the village *alusi* and therefore provide no opportunity for the *attama* to become involved. But when the dispute is between two or more clans, then it becomes a village affair in which both the *alusi* and its priest are concerned. Why? In more typically segmentary Igbo villages elsewhere, such a case would be tried by the gathered group of headmen and litigants, discussed and argued out until it was settled in one way or another. But such conditions no longer exist in the borderland villages precisely because of the Igala and Okpoto migrations and conquests and because of the presence of the stranger lineages in those villages. This presence of the Igala priest's lineage and its traditional notions of village government have changed the Nsukkan system somewhat, so that at the village level land disputes are not merely the affair of gathered heads of kingroups. Those individuals are no longer the sole rulers of the village as they may have been in the aboriginal past and are elsewhere in Igboland. The *attama* becomes directly involved in the land dispute in the borderland, but less in his own person than as the agent of his god, and his role is that of a mediator, an arbitrator, and to a certain extent—depending also upon his personal persuasive abilities—as a judge. "Owner of the land" has differing meanings, as we have seen, when the phrase is used by Igbo *ndishi* in the *arua* ceremony or when it is used by Igala shrine priests in the worship of the *alusi*: in the former case *ngwane* refers to the Igbo lineages and clans and to their ancestral land; in the latter case *ngwane* refers to not only those lands owned by the *alusi* as specific properties and by the priest's Igala lineage and clan, but also to the entire village, which is "owned" by the *alusi* as the protector of all things on the surface of the village earth and the master of the priest who is the ritual land chief.

As an involved and important participant of cases involving land disputes, what does the *attama* actually do? First, of course, he meets with the gathered litigants and the council formed of clan heads, major titled persons including the heads of maskers and secret societies, and the *eze* (chief) if the community possesses someone with this title, which is not too likely insofar as *eze* were appointed over larger political units. When the case is being heard, the *attama* makes public the concern of the *alusi* over the potentially disruptive affair, or the spirit's concern over what may be an injustice about the land and a departure from tradition in the behavior of some of the involved individuals. If in the course of hearing the case the council of gathered elders and titled persons agrees upon a decision which is satisfactory to the priest—and if the conflict itself is resolved, this will often be sufficient—he informs the litigants, or the guilty party if the case involved guilt, of the offerings which they must make to "cool down" the *alusi*. If such offerings are made and the people do not renew the conflict, the entire matter is thus settled. On the other hand, if the council cannot agree upon a course of action which is satisfactory to the litigants, the shrine priest himself will attempt to decide the issue; if even this is unsatisfactory to the litigants, divination is resorted to, and here the cause of the *alusi* and of the *attama* will be favored, if only because the priest himself is usually the diviner. One can hypothesize that in an earlier period the word of the *attama* was probably more influential, because the direct threat of armed enforcement of Igala rule existed. As time passed, though the Igala lineages remained, furnishing shrine priests for the *alusi*, the *attama*'s role tended to be more important ritually than politically, but the priest nevertheless retained wide power in land disputes because of his control of divination and the *alusi* itself.

Social control in the borderland operates through a network of interacting agents, including human and divine persons, forces which can be manipulated and those which cannot. Social control of course depends heavily upon individual personalities, some people being infinitely more capable of leadership than others, regardless of social role, rank, or title, whether acquired or inherited. In earlier periods, according to all my elder informants, the relationships between Igbo and Igala descent groups and their leaders were clearer: the Okpoto and the Igala were the definable "strangers," and their god—although often originally Igbo—had turned into a "strange" god, more easily provoked than before and controllable now only by the stranger priest. But after generations of exogamous marriage and the steady growth of lineages, the strangers came to be an accepted part of the borderland villages.

Many of their customs, particularly those most closely linked with their service to the *alusi*, held relatively firm against the forces of Igbonization. They continued, and continue to inherit their titles, and they are significant instruments of social control. Most important of all, however, is that they were accommodated by the Igbo lineages among whom they settled and live, so that the total effect of their occupation was simply to modify the old village geronto-cracy rather than develop anything distantly resembling Igala-style chiefship. Eldership, not chiefship or even priestcraft, finally dominated the borderland once again. The "conquered" triumphed over the colonializers, and we might now examine how and why.

8. Accommodation and Adaptation in the Nsukka Borderland

As we have seen throughout this study, the Nsukka borderland has been an area of culture contact for a long period of time, and this contact has been among numerous peoples, the more important being the Igbo, Igala, Umunri, and Okpoto. Moreover, with the possible exception of the Okpoto, all these peoples are composite groups: Igbo of the borderland have been intermixed with Okpoto, Igala, Umunri, and Onitsha; Igala are a mixture of Bini and other Edo-speaking peoples, Yoruba, Jukun, possibly Nupe, Okpoto, possibly Umunri, and some Igbo; Umunri are probably mixtures of Igbo, Bini, and other Edo-speaking peoples, and others; Okpoto are a group of westerly Idoma intermixed with Igbo, and other peoples. Yet there has been a fair degree of ethnic coalescing, so today one can speak of the Igala and the Igbo as constituting the two "tribes" of people inhabiting either side of the border. Along with such ethnic and linguistic coalescence there are other characteristics which differentiate the two groups: the Igala are monarchic and hierarchic in their politics whereas the Igbo are gerontocratic and democratic; in descent systems (although not always in title inheritance) the Igala practise a clearcut agnatic patrilineality, but because of the colonialization by Igala the Igbo in much of the borderland have traced descent matrilaterally as well as patrilineally; in religious behavior the Igala mesh ancestralism with the *attah*'s official divinity and with the functions of the various gods, whereas the Igbo—again because of the presence among them of Igala shrine priests—distinctly separate familial religion from that concerning the *alusi*. This is all more complicated than I have stated here, and it would require further study to elucidate in detail. Integrally related to these relationships are the processes of accommodation and adaptation of cultural elements and social institutions. Particularly important are the changed emphases in Igbo village religion whereby the Igbo tried to strengthen the non-Igala spiritual support of their lineages, and the adjustments which were required in family, household, and village organization.

Changed Emphases in Igbo Religion

The importance of Igala and Okpoto priests in borderland Igbo villages results less from their immediate political influence—at least in the earlier days of the occupation—than from their control of divination and their mediation between the Igbo and the *alusi*. As Meek has said (1937:159), the real rulers of those villages always were spirits and ancestors, not civil or even military authorities whether the latter were Igala and Okpoto war leaders, holders of such titles as *ashadu, asogwa, eze,* or even the British conquerors and their warrant chiefs. Accordingly, he who "controlled" the most powerful spiritual forces was likely to be the person with most practical influence among the ordinary people. This leaves out of consideration many titled persons, certainly so long as older customs remained strong in the Igbo villages, and even the modern version of these—the local councillor—ascends chiefly when there is a decline in traditional priestly power, whether the latter is dependent upon ancestors or other spiritual beings. Modern politics, as distinct from ethnically oriented politics or religion-oriented politics, works best when people are experiencing some degree of anomie, not when they are still resident among and controlled by their ancestors and gods.

The establishment of their own shrine priests, then, in the border-land villages was a brilliant maneuver by the Igala, although it was bound to arouse some reactions among the Igbo. The Igbo knew where power lay, for they realized full well that Igala colonialization was backed by Igala military force, and they feared the powers of the *alusi* for whom the Igala priests spoke, so the Igbo sought ways to regain their former control over their own native places.

Problems of rivalry over status and prestige arose early because of the presence, growth, and obvious power of Igala and Okpoto descent groups among the Igbo. Igala lines quickly became prestigi-ous at the expense of the Igbo, who probably had contended previ-ously only with one another. The settling Igala possessed several avenues to prestige, whereas the Igbo found some of their routes blocked, for priesthood henceforth was to be inherited within Igala lines, and the priests were to be in charge of the most important secret society, the *omabe*. As agents (the formality of this term varies with the personal differences among *attama*) of the military conquer-ors and collectors of tribute, the *attama* and their *olokpu* patriline possessed several sorts of power, political as well as indirectly mili-tary. Moreover, prior to Igala settlement, Igbo social controls were relatively equalitarian with status achieved through the open title societies and government largely by titled persons and elders. The Igala introduced distinctly authoritarian social controls (while per-mitting the older Igbo system to remain and atrophy) and possessed ascribed status through their own system of inherited titles which effectively closed out Igbo aspirants (see Broom, 1954:973-1000). The Igala could also accumulate more than Igbo, for shrines receive offerings and chiefs receive tribute as a matter of course, and such upset in competition was disgruntling to the acquisitive and diligent Igbo. Although many chiefs later on may have been Igbo, they had to have their titles confirmed by Igala authorities, which meant their prestige came only because of Igala power and willingness.

Igbo seem to have reacted in several ways as the situation and prudence permitted, for Igala colonialization was like later British and other control; behind the civil behavior of authorities lay the scarcely hidden threat of severe reprisal to any Igbo village offering open resistance. In the case of Igala control there was the added factor that resisters could simply be exported as slaves. The means apparently used by Igbo to restore control included first, an increased emphasis upon ancestral worship to raise the status of the village *ndishi* (headmen);[1] second, an increased emphasis on worship of Earth and the High God in an attempt, which generally failed, to establish the *ndishi* as priests of general non-ancestral spirits in direct competition with the Igala *attama*; and third, adoption of new Igbo medicine shrines to the district, and the increase in Umunri medicines such as *Ncheonye* and *Akwari* to counteract Igala-controlled *alusi*— again a failure.

1. Strengthening of Ancestralism. Apparently deliberate attempts were made by Igbo lineages to increase the status of the *ndishi*, and to assert partial independence from Igala control, by an increased emphasis upon ancestralism. "In the olden times," said Ugwuja *Attama*, the priest of Ntiye of Ameegwu Village, "before our forefathers came here the Igbo people had their own *alusi*. But then they made more offerings to their fathers, and the *arua* became more important to them. But even *alusi* have *arua*, and their [i.e., *alusi*] *arua* became stronger than the *arua* of the fathers of the Igbo families. So the *ndishi* still had to bring things first to Ntiye before they gave them [i.e., first fruits at harvest festivals] to their forefathers."

Problems seem to have arisen in Igbo lineages and clans about the proper identification of male ancestors who must be worshipped and who possessed powers over the lineage, especially when some Igbo wives of Igala men placed greater emphasis upon their own *umunna* and their children's *umune* in reaction to the steadily growing Igala *omenekele* in which they were married. (See Chart IX: *Ancestral Lines of Umu Attama*.) Where generational clashes had hitherto been diminished by the sense of family continuity—at least within a village or village group, where putative as well as real ancestry was accepted—

1. With the steady intermixing of lineage affiliations with Igala came also an emphasis upon *arua* worship as distinct from the worship of specific individual ancestors; related to this was an increased mythicizing of specific ancestors— a process occurring elsewhere in the world, of course, often for different reasons.

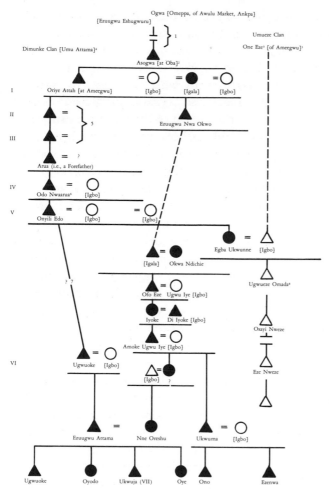

CHART IX. *Ancestral Lines of Umu Attama*

Notes

1. *Asogwa* is a title meaning "elder brother"; it probably refers to an official subordinate to the *Ashadu* controlling Ankpa; the number of generations here is unknown.

2. *Asogwa* is said to have been the first of the Okpoto at Oba Market.

3. The founding father of Umueze. One Eze means "Freeborn Man [who was] Chief."

4. Umu Attama begins with the establishment of Oriye Attah as first *Attama* of Ntiye in Ameegwu Village.

5. Names of these ancestors have been forgotten; informants could only guess at the number of them, but all agreed that they must not have been very illustrious.

6. Odo was *Attama* when Beke (W. B. Baikie [?]) was at Lokoja—i.e., the 1850s.

7. Ugwuoke was *Attama* after Odo, but whether another *Attama* preceded him my informants did not know.

8. Umueze claims to be Igbo, but traces ancestry not only through the Igbo male descendant of One Eze, but through Egba Ukwunne to Igala forefathers in Umu Attama.

now the problem was compounded by the felt loyalty toward Igbo ancestors on one side and partly Igala descendants on the other. Because it had been common within Igbo-Igbo marriages to have an affective relationship with one's *umune* (mother's agnates) and a generally formal respect relationship with one's *umunna* (father's agnates), and because the Igala had agnatic patrilineal descent groups, it would seem that continuation of the older pattern would be assured. In matters of ancestralism, however, with the Igbo it had been customary to emphasize one's *umunna*, which in fact did not now exist for the children of mixed unions, who became caught in the conflict of loyalties between Igala father's *omenekele* and Igbo mother's *umune*. In such a system, the child of the mixed marriage theoretically would be Igala, although his Igbo mother under constant urging of her people tended to emphasize the child's relationship to her own *umunna* (the child's *umune*) in order that the Igbo lineages would be able to claim as many consanguines as possible, including those with ties to the Igala. The Igala of course were interested in creating as broad a loyalty base as possible, so they did not strongly oppose the deepening ties between their progeny by Igbo women and the *umune* of those children, for by this means they avoided more direct conflict than might otherwise occur. Furthermore, they wished to keep inheritance and control of the *attama* title in the most direct line identified as Igala as possible, even switching through the "line" of a usually unmarried senior daughter analogous to *amom'ukpaihi* ("children of power") and reverting afterwards to the male Igala line, rather than passing the title through the children of any or all of the wives. This reduced the chances that the children of an Igbo junior wife might inherit the title of *attama* and relaxed the actual conflict of loyalties in ancestralism. The children could worship their mother's forefathers, while giving perfunctory acknowledgment of powers to their father's Igala ancestors without fear of offending father's ancestors, who apparently were more concerned with control of the title than with the normal matters of ancestors elsewhere.

The headman (*onyishi*) was the eldest competent man of the *umunna*, and any given consanguine could easily enough trace relationship to and through him, some through agnatic and others through uterine lines. With such a potentially huge descent group dependent upon him, the headman tended to emphasize Igbo fore-fathers presumably in attempts to strengthen the role of the Igbo lineage leader vis-a-vis the village *attama*. Modifications and con-fusions of ancestry, however, seem to have arisen later, sometimes because of forgetting and at other times because of the natural desire among some Igbo to associate themselves more closely with Igala. Nonetheless, in general Igbo emphasized Igbo spiritual forces, there-by maintaining strong Igbo identity over the generations. We might turn to Ameegwu Village as an example of some of these emphases.

As we have seen, Ameegwu Village consists of two *arua* clans, Dimunke, which is Igala, and Umueze, which is Igbo. Umueze tends to emphasize traditional Igbo control forces: "Group who own the earth" (I, 1; II, 1, 2, 3, 23, 26), which has reference to Igbo ancestors, is repeated in the *arua* prayers of this clan often over a dozen times— thrice at the beginning and ending of washing, as many as six times at the presentation of kola, and from three to six times during the kola ceremony and at its close. Ebonyeze's explanation of this was simple: "Our people are the senior ones, because we were here first, so our forefathers own the land; the *attama*'s people [i.e., Dimunke] do not make prayers to our forefathers. They have their own." Dimunke for parallel reasons stresses non-human spiritual forces and makes frequent reference to potentates and powers of the Igala; in their *arua* prayers, "owner of the land" is the *alusi*, Ntiye. The head man, Ugwooke Attama, explained these matters in part by saying:

> We are the people who furnish the *attama* for Ntiye. That was how it began in the olden times, when *attama* were first sent to Oba and other places in Nsukka by the *attah*. The most impor-tant thing our forefathers did was that [i.e., furnish the shrine priests], so the Igbo people would have to come to Igala men to make their offerings, and they could not make any war without the *alusi*. That was how it was in the olden times. Now it is important for me to invite all the spirits for kola when I offer to our *arua*, but other people invite only their own forefathers.

What their forefathers did is important to them, and what my forefathers did is important to me.

Significantly, the worship of *arua* is linked throughout the border-land with the coming of those forefathers whom the various groups claim as their own (e.g., Ezuugwu Eshugwuru at Ameegwu Village, the *Nshie* at Umu Mkpume, the "forefathers" at Umugoji Village), although as we have seen in Obimo the *arua* is virtually a staff of chieftancy and at Nkpologu the *arua* are used both as title staffs and as ancestral symbols. This latter variation, indeed, helps to explain the function of *arua* in the borderland: the so-called *arua* belonging to the *alusi* have nothing to do with ancestors, but represent authority as such, whereas the clan *arua* are symbols of ancestral power and sometimes represent individual forefathers (although this usage seems to be different from the original). The influence of the *ndishi* depended upon the powers of the *arua* for whom they spoke and which they worshipped, as well as the numbers of living descendants who claimed membership in the particular descent group identified by one bundle of *arua*—one *ukwaarua*. The larger the Igbo clans, the more strength the forefathers and their living representatives, the elders were presumed to have. Accordingly, worship of the ancestors and the *arua* increased while at the same time Igbo steadily developed modifications in their descent systems, urging their *okele* (daughter's children) to revere the ancestral power of their mother's patriline.

The elders of Igbo lineages in other ways attempted to maintain Igbo identity and to regain their former positions as leaders in the borderland society. These methods included increased worship of Earth and the High God, and the adoption of more nuclear Igbo gods and even ancestors in various areas.

2. Earth and High God Worship. Although worship of *Ane*, the deified Earth, is common in much of Igboland, worship of the High God, *Chukwu*, tends to be rather perfunctory at best. In the border-land matters are reversed; High God worship is an important aspect of familial religion (although not so important as ancestralism), whereas the Earth-Goddess-Mother has been replaced in importance by the *alusi*. One need not seek far for a reason. As Herskovits has pointed out, the earth deity is considered to favor the original occupants of the land, so it is obviously politically expedient for their successors to play down the importance of such a deity (Herskovits, 1962:145–146). "Precisely what does Ane do?" I asked Ugwuja *Attama*. He replied:

> Every person lives on the surface of the earth. Without the earth, we cannot grow food to eat. A man lives on the surface of the earth until he dies. He does not live in the sky or in the waters, and he goes inside the earth only after he dies. So the earth is here, and Ane owns it. We do proper things for Ane because she owns the earth and is the Great Mother [*Nne Ochukwu*: Mother's MoMo] of our fathers.

Meek described rites to Ane at yam harvest time in southeastern Nsukka District, some distance from the Igala and Okpoto borders, where she is worshipped fairly much (see Meek, 1937: 26–27). In the borderland each individual compound head within Igbo lineages has an altar to Ane in his compound, associated commonly with Ushuajiokwo (the yam barn spirit) and with his chi (High God) altar. It consists of a small pot which derives its power from a slightly larger village shrine to Ane and to Ezechitoke, the *Onu Chukwu* ("mouth [of the] High God").

Like other major gods, Ane is generally considered to have no kin group in the usual sense. She is eternal and uncreated, like her physical manifestation, the earth, and thus she resembles the High God, although as his consort rather than as his rival. The saying,

Ane na Chukwu ra,

"Ane and God sleep together and copulate," means that Earth and the High God are equal. But beyond this and rather scarce occasional references, little is made of this notion. Ane functions chiefly as a supporter of the ancestors and of the High God rather than as a power in herself.

The relatively strong belief in the ascendancy of the High God—certainly not the standard pattern in Igboland or in West African religions in general—results probably from Igbo reaction to the fact that Igala *attama* took charge of *alusi* worship, which weakened Ane worship by removing those shrine priests who originally had conducted such worship along with worship of the *alusi*. But because High God worship had always been in control of the family head, increased worship of the High God and attribution to him of ever-increasing powers strengthened Igbo control over Igbo affairs (compare Shelton, 1965b). A contrary argument about the general importance of the High God among the Igbo might be developed from the remarks of the 1841 commissioners about the worship of the High God at Aboh on the Niger River: The "Tshuku" (i.e., Chukwu) shrine is described as a large earthen "idol" placed in a thicket surrounded by high trees. "This we believe," say the commissioners, "to be the image to which most of their sacrifices are offered." And of the High God:

> His votaries believe him to exist far off in the bush; that he has the power of speaking and understanding all languages; is cognizant of everything that takes place in the world, and that he can punish evil doers. The priest whilst holding communion with Tshuku, is surrounded miraculously with water, and will perish instantaneously if he attempts to deceive (1841 Expedition: 244–245; compare Schon, 1842:50–51, who also refers to the importance of Tshuku).

It must be remembered, however, that the Aboh Igbo certainly are not nuclear Igbo, but rather Edonized Igbo because of their long contact with the Benin Empire, and that nuclear Igbo do not emphasize Chukwu.

The importance of increased worship of the High God was that it placed more power in the hands of the *ndishi* who were the priests and intermediaries of both Ezechitoke and Ane. Although such worship increased the stature of the High God and of Earth in the Nsukkan belief, these spiritual forces could not compete personally or politically against the *alusi*. The people could not conceive of them seriously as capricious beings, but only as protective deities who, like the ancestors, watched over their living "children" and, although they punished wrongdoers they were relatively forgiving.

Most important of all, they were not aggressive spirits; they did not "seek offerings." Predictable, protecting, dependable, trustworthy—however long I might make this list of positive virtues of God and Earth merely emphasizes the actual situation, that power was bound to remain with the man who spoke for the aggressive, hostile, and unpredictable god and had come from the aggressive, hostile conqueror.

3. Other Igbo Religious Developments. There appear to have been other reactions to conquest made by some Igbo clans and villages. Like the foregoing, these involved adaptation of religious elements in attempts to gain Igbo control over powerful gods who might then support greater Igbo prestige and political power. Most important, perhaps, were the adoption of new Igbo medicine shrines, as at Aro-Uno Nsukka, and the increase in the number of Umunri medicines, such as Nshie-one (ncheonye) and Akwari, as attempts to counterbalance Igala-controlled *alusi*. These attempts, too, failed in part of their object.

Adoro ("daughter who remains"—i.e., with the people of her father's lineage rather than going off to marry outsiders) of Aro-Uno (*Aruuno* in actual pronunciation) is a definitely atypical shrine for the borderland, controlled not by an *attama* at all but by Igbo slave-priests, *osu*. Basden said of this shrine:

> There is a small area where certain "osus" seem to enjoy privileges similar to those stated to have originally belonged to the priests in the Owerri and Okigwi Districts. This is situated in the north-east corner of the Nsukka Division on the extreme border of the Ibo country. A god named "Adolo" holds sway in this part. His priest is held in great respect and he, the priest, exercises considerable influence and authority. It is a lucrative post by virtue of the many sacrifices presented to the god and there is no doubt that, prior to his activities being curbed by Government, it was common to offer children as human sacrifices to "Adolo". All children so dedicated were, of course, "osu." The chief point of interest in this case is that the priest is called "Osu," and that he has maintained his authority. Further,

that it is a profitable profession, so much so, that there is no lack of candidates, especially from among the younger sons of chiefs who are willing to become "osus" with a view to becoming agents for "Adolo." (Basden, 1938:252.)

Ugwu, an Nsukkan himself, says that

what boosts the power of Adoro . . . is a mixture prepared by the great ancestors of this family [i.e., Umueze Oweye Ugwu] in Edem. The part of the sacrifice they claim is a token of remembrance of and respect for the uncommon magical powers that their grandfathers were endowed with (1958:34, 35).

Adoro was disseminated to some other villages from its central location, apparently in an attempt by Igbo clans to offset the power of village *alusi*. For example, Adoro shrines are found in Ujobo Obigbo, where the shrine receives very few offerings nowadays, and in Ameegwu Village, where the Adoro was established at the behest of ancestors in Umueze Clan but has received only two offerings during the past five years (as of 1963).

Umunri-related medicines, furthermore, were introduced in some villages in which certain clans or lineages claim *Nshie* ancestry. The more common of these is *nshieone* ("medicine-person"). According to *Attama* Iye Owo Uno of Imilikenu, these shrines are installed only by *nshie* (Umunri): "The *nshie* brought those shrines a long time ago, and then they went away." This is corroborated by informants in villages which claim partial *nshie* ancestry, such as Ohebe and Umu Mkpume in Oba.

Akwari ("raffia hides it") is a special medicine made by the *nshie* for the people of Umu Mkpume and intended particularly to ward off the oncoming British colonialists, although it is said to be based upon a much older medicine which long ago had been created to ward off other enemies. I could not elicit from my Umu Mkpume informants whether they considered these earlier enemies to have been the Igala or Okpoto: they played off my inquiries with explanations that people nowadays are trying to think of unity rather than of difference of ethnic stocks. The medicine itself is placed in a public location— in the village square—so it is seen by all and thus is a reminder of non-Igala spiritual powers. Akwari is considered to be a male medicine, which would make it potentially aggressive, although all the informants referred to it solely as a protective medicine which does not seek offerings. The name of this medicine is suspiciously like *akwali* ("cloth [or *cord*] tied around"), a fertility medicine made for women in the Awka District (see Basden, 1938:49) and even more like *akwali-omumu* ("cord tied around-fertility"), a mound of earth in which is buried a sacrificed animal and which exists as fertility medicine (see Basden, 1938:167). The *akwari* at Umu Mkpume resembles this, except that over the mound is built an enclosing raffia cage (*akwali*: palm branch) which almost completely obscures the small white-wrapped human form lying on its back atop the mound. The form inside more than symbolically resembles, moreover, the *ibwudu* wickerwork dummy which is made in the same size as a deceased person and is covered with a grass mat and white cloth and is buried in the same grave as the person's corpse, enabling the dead to rest in peace (compare Basden, 1921:120ff.). The medicine is possibly an amalgam of other medicines, or its original purpose may have become distorted by overemphasis given its power to ward off anti-fertility or trickster demons, as well as by some forgetting during its spread from nuclear to fringe-area Igboland.

Like the increased emphasis upon High God worship and the *arua*, the adoption and attempted use of non-Igala controlled shrines and medicine failed to change the base of power, which continued to be held by the *attama* who controlled the most powerful and least manipulable or predictable spirits. Power has its devotees, certainly among borderland Igbo, who prefer *ukwu* ("large") to *nta* ("small") and *oke* ("male") to *mgbe* ("female"), accordingly, Igala "giants" to *Nshie* dwarfs. Even though the latter made medicines, the former controlled the *alusi* shrines, did most of the divining in the borderland, and had behind them the conquering powers of the Igala. Changed emphases in Igbo religion did not result in any noticeable weakening of Igala power. But what of changes in the Igbo and Igala households and families which were almost bound to develop under the conditions of occupation?

Problems and Adjustments in Family and Household

"Our family names used to be those of our mothers," explained Elias Eze, one of my linguistic informants from Imilikenu. "A man would have people call him by his mother's name, not his father's. Nowadays [i.e., 1962–1963] this is being changed, and it is almost gone down in Nsukka and places farther south. Many people in Imilike now are changing their names, taking their father's name." In this context, "mothers" refers to one's *umune* (mother's consanguines), who whether male or female are classified as "mothers." *Attama* Ugwu Okanye, priest of Iye Owo Uno, added: "Where my fathers went and made offerings to the *alusi* they married Igbo women, and they wanted their sons to be Igala, but many of the Igbo wanted the sons to make offerings to the Igbo fathers instead of the Igala fathers." What is indicated here is simply that the new Igala descent groups required adjustments and accommodations by the Igbo, but that these adjustments were accompanied by Igbo resistance to Igalicization. After conquest and occupation, the Igala began Igala lineages in Igbo villages, their descent groups growing until they became *ukwaarua* clans in their own right. Only from these clans would be chosen the *attama*, his selection being by divination from candidates linked to direct descendants of the *attama*'s patriline. If the Igbo continued defining their groups agnatically they could never regain control of the influential *alusi* shrines in the occupied villages. By reckoning descent through the *umune* (mother's agnates), although they could not in this manner regain control of the *alusi* shrines, they at least could strengthen support for Igbo-controlled spirits; and by recognizing matrilateral descent, indeed, they could have the best of both worlds.

Mixed Igbo-Igala marriages—usually important ones—created problems of social control and land rights as well as problems of conduct in a mixed system where numerous institutions were alien and suspect from either tribal perspective. The Igala and Okpoto brought with them patrilineality and a theoretical tendency to stress the agnatic patriline (*omenekele*) but under some circumstances they had, in fact, a moderate inclination to emphasize uterine relationships and descent through an unmarried senior daughter ("child of power"—which actually kept descent within the patriline) or even descent through the matriline (*omonobule*: "sons of females"), especially for the transmission of rank (see Boston, 1964:122). Igala were acutely aware of problems of inheritance, yet they seem not to have defined the descendants of mixed marriages according to the strict patrilineality which would have perpetuated and increased Igala control. Byng-Hall (Temple, 1919) pointed out one means by which the Apa under Ayegba had gained control of Okpoto country through a strict definition of ethnic stock according to patrilines: the descendants of Apa men and Okpoto women were Igala, but the children of Okpoto men and Apa women were Okpoto even though they referred to themselves as Igala. A similar mode of definition, although not so strictly adhered to, characterized the Igala control of Nsukka villages.

The Igala need to obtain wives and their general desire to avoid unnecessary conflict, along with their willingness to trace descent through females under some circumstances, gave Nsukka Igbo means whereby they could strengthen their position in the pluralistic villages and not only successfully regain Igbo control over their Igbo lineages but even Igbonize many descendants of the Igala, particularly the children of junior Igbo wives of Igala *attama*. Igala could have deterred the Igbonization process by consistently insisting on agnatic patrilineal descent. But this would give rightful claim to the title to possibly too many descendants, when in fact inheritance was ideally through the eldest sons rather than through any or all sons: "The senior sibling is the person to succeed" (Boston, 1968:36). The Igala were caught up in their own needs, so Igbonization of their own descendants and steady renewal of Igbo influence proceeded apace. Let us survey the processes.

The descent groups, first, became very complicated. If we posit the case of an Igala shrine priest originally marrying one Igbo woman (see Chart X: *Varying Relationships in Igala-Igbo Descent—Simplified*), and presume for the sake of simplicity that they had one son and one daughter who each married exogamously, the results will shortly

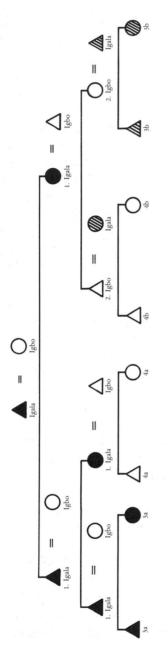

Notes

1. Son, Daughter, SoSo, and SoDa have Igala *omenkele* (patri-lineal *alokpa*) and Igbo *umune* (maternal agnates). Mother's Igbo people thus are further separated from Father's people because of the element of "strangeness"—the presence of the alien line.

2. DaSo and DaDa have Igbo *umuma* and Igala *omonobule*, and thus have reversed descent group loyalties from Mother's Senior Brother's children.

3. SoSoSo and DaDaSo, and SoSoDa and DaDaDa have Igala *omenkele* and Igbo *umune*, as well as Igala FaFaFa and Igbo MoFaFa; 3a offspring have Igbo FaMoFa; 3b offspring have Igala FaMoFa.

4. These children have Igbo *umuma*, Igbo FaFaFa, and Igala MoFaFa; 4a offspring have Igbo FaMoFa, but 4b offspring have Igala FaMoFa.

CHART X. *Varying Relationships in Igala-Igbo Descent* (Simplified) take on the appearance—to outsiders—of a hodgepodge. The son's *omenekele* (olokpu) will be Igala, and his Igbo wife's *umunna* will be Igbo; similarly the daughter's patriline will be Igala and her husband's patriline Igbo. The son's son will have an Igala *omenekele* but an Igbo *umune* or matriline (mother's agnates). The daughter's son, on the other hand, will have an Igbo *umunna* and an Igala *omonobule*. From this point downward in the descent system the relationships become increasingly more complex, and the opportunities for conflicts of interest more numerous. In actual fact, most *attama* married polygynously, thus compounding the complexities of interrelationships in the formerly Igbo village groups.

The core problem of such complications of descent and ancestry involved title inheritance, especially of *attama*, and it became steadily more obvious that modifications of the mode of descent were necessary. If the *attama*'s lineage were to trace descent solely through the males of the line (which is not in fact what occurred), the sons of daughters would automatically be excluded from consideration in the inheritance of *attama*ship. In such rigid patrilineality too many possible title heirs would be lost to the lineage of the *attama*—quite the wrong situation for people intent upon maintaining tribute control over occupied villages. It would necessitate the constant and unfailing production of sons in the *attama*'s line and, should no males be produced in the direct or collateral lines in a given generation or two (relatively unlikely, although not impossible, and certainly a worrying thought even today) the new *attama* would have to be selected from among children of the Igala daughters—that is to say, from among Igbo children, and thus control of the title would fall into the hands of the Igbo. In fact, when the line of the eldest son failed to produce a likely candidate, normally the collateral sublineage of a junior son produced someone suitable. But the problem *in potentia* remained.

Another factor tended to modify strict Igala patrilineality: the belief that the best person (the one most suited as the lineage elders defined the term) should serve the *alusi*, rather than simply any male in the direct line. There is indeed a certain vocation—a "calling" or a mission—involved in being *attama*, aside from its obvious advantages in making one wealthy and relatively powerful in the locality (see Seton, 1929:44–45). The merely greedy, it is generally understood, is not suitable for the office, which requires several abilities beside the desire to succeed in life, if that is an ability. In many larger Igala lineages a combination of dream-possession and divination, involving of necessity some selection, determined the new *attama* from a group of suitable candidates. It was and is therefore conceivable that the best candidate for the title when an older *attama* has died may not even be one of the males directly descended from the original *attama*, but one from a "non-Igala" line, the son of a daughter.

Of course, Igala notions of inheritance could accommodate the selection of a candidate from a line of the daughters under necessary circumstances, although this poses problems for the Igala lineage in other respects, particularly if the part-Igbo *attama* personally maintains a patrilineal filiation, for control could theoretically fall into Igbo hands. But by reference to the matriline ("Igbo" EGO's Igala mother's agnates, thus classifying EGO as Igala although his father may have been Igbo) when it suited their needs and purposes, the Igala lineages gained broad bases of support, for the children of daughters could be classified as Igala should they seem to be suitable heirs to titles. In marriages in which the wife was Igala, descent tended to be uterine especially if she was descended from a lineage possessing *attama*ship, even where the man himself was Igala, although if his own lineage were one of *attama*, descent was agnatic. The lineages of *attama* usually controlled the definition of *attama* and the mode of inheritance of the title, and Igbo by and large adapted to it.

The borderland Igbo seem already to have possessed a flexible descent system which the Igala could use largely to their own advantage. The influx of Igala men who married Igbo women required that Igbo claim descent from mother to maintain identity with Igbo lines, and that Igala identify with father and his ancestors. Even in those cases where Igala lineages traced their descent by strict agnatic patrilineality, by identifying themselves also with their mother's agnates the Igbo could benefit further. The child of an Igbo mother and Igala father might be claimed by the Igala, yet through the Igbo mother he would have extremely close ties with the Igbo lineages. They could thenceforth claim relationship (and all it entailed) with the Igala and—in the child's generation—develop or demand a certain loyalty on the part of that "Igala" child toward the Igbo elders and ancestors. The Igala could not object strongly, for they were quick enough to trace descent through a uterine line when it suited their own needs, as in the case of children of an Igala daughter married to an Igbo man. Such a situation is revealed in the case of Ameegwu Village (see Chart IX: *The Ancestral Lines of Umu Attama*).

In the case of an Igbo man's marriage to an Igala woman, the child would reckon descent matrilaterally to maintain Igala ties chiefly for the sake of title inheritance. An Igbo man's marriage to an Igbo woman raised fewer problems, and although descent could be reckoned through both or either line, normally it was agnatic and patrilineal; similarly, children of an Igala father and mother usually reckoned descent through the father's agnates. Igbo practised partial matrilateral descent to broaden the base of support for their ancestors and elders, and because the sons of junior Igbo wives of *attama* normally possessed no chance of effectively Igalicizing. This practice of matrilateral descent resulted in complexly interrelated families, the complexity increased, perhaps, because of continued ethnic identification of the two main groups as Igala and Igbo.

Other more or less "visible" results of overall Igbo reaction to Igala occupation appear in the borderland. These include dual divisions of villages and symbolism differentiating Igbo and Igala. Dual division of communities is common to several peoples of the lower Niger area, including both Igala and Igbo, but in the borderland the divisions are increased by their representing not merely junior and senior sections, but native and alien groups. For example, in Ameegwu Village (see Map V and Chart IX), the senior clan is Umueze, which claims to be Igbo in origin; the junior clan is Dimunke, which claims to be Igala. Similarly, in Umune Ngwa Village, the senior and Igbo lineage is Umu Iyoke, whereas the junior and Igala is Umakechi; and in Umugoji Village the junior

Igala lineage is Umu Attama Elele, and there are four senior Igbo lineages comprising the clan. Although it is common for these peoples to distinguish clearly between older and newer residents and between descendants of senior or junior brothers of a forefather, such divisions tend to sharpen the distinctions between "native" or Igbo and "foreigner" or Igala, and between what is "normal" and "understandable" and potentially sympathetic (that which is Igbo and linked with Igbo forefathers) and that which is "different" and "strange" and potentially antagonistic or hostile (the Igala as former conquerors and as agents of the *alusi*). Under such circumstances rivalries intensified, and when these occurred among co-wives over their children and the children's inheritance the antagonisms could endanger the community by increasing narrow group definition and perpetuating pluralism despite the high incidence of interrelationship through marriage.

This separation of groups is often apparent in names and symbols customarily, often consciously, employed in borderland villages. One of the more obvious examples is the strange name of one village, Umune Ngwa. Here *Ngwa* means "son" as "owner", implying "owner of the land occupied and claimed by the Igbo people resident there." *Umune* refers to "mother's consanguines," especially mother's agnates. The village name, therefore, refers to the people descended from the matriline of the original Igbo owner of the land, as opposed to later, "stranger," Igala agents who claimed that they, instead of the Igbo, were the controllers and thus the owners of the land. In this particular village the ancestral altar which is the "pathway of the spirits" of birth is divided in form to indicate basic differences among the human groups "entering" the village by means of it (see Figure XIV: *Ancestral Altar at Umune Ngwa*). This altar consists of a large rectangular block—the rectangle is a typical Igbo symbol—holding a staff called *Iyoke Ewolo* through which the senior and Igbo lineage is believed to have descended. The name means, "Iyoke [i.e., 'Mother of males'] did not take back the people, but let them remain in the lineage." Alongside the rectangular block is a smaller round block— the circle being a typical Igala symbol—named *Agodi Egwu* through which the junior and Igala lineage is believed to have descended. The name means, appropriately, "the new people have the masquerade" —i.e., control of the major spirits.

There were, then, several results of Igala colonialization of the northern Nsukka Igbo, which continued fairly effective certainly for as long as the slave trade lasted. The continuation of the slave trade in the interior was one of the important reasons for the subsequent British colonialization of this hinterland area. Igala colonial control steadily diminished since the ending of the slave trade (that is, about 1860–1880, and with greater rapidity after the British conquest of Nsukka). From that time until World War II, there was nominal Igala control over Nsukka (within the context of British colonialism, of course), and one might well wonder if the slave trade alone accounts for the Igala control of the area. Even at the present time, *attama* possess a fair degree of power in the northern Nsukka villages, yet none of them will deny that the powers of *attama* have decreased greatly during the past several generations. What accounts for this diminution of power is not merely the ending of the slave trade and the general lessening of Idah Igala interest in controlling the hinterland, but rather the Igbonizing of the Igala shrine priests' descendants through mixed marriages and, more important, through the constant shifting of methods of reckoning descent.

Igbonization

What brought about the most profound change and a return of Igbo control over most Igbo affairs was not conscious Igbo reaction. It was, instead, a combination of time and the non-Igbo matrilateral descent reckoning which the Igbo had adopted perforce to maintain a base of supporters for Igbo ancestors. Through intermarriage and the constant mixing of descent groups brought about by acceptance of both matrilateral and patrilineal descent, the lineages of the *attama* Igbonized sufficiently to decrease potential conflict along tribal lines. At present, reference to Igala forefathers by *attama* is almost completely a matter of ancient history which is not at all relevant to current events.

It is not remarkable, of course, that an occupying group who inter-marry with the native peoples among whom they settle will in the course of time lose much of their effective group identity. What offers resistance to such loss of group identity is anything which somehow institutionalizes or otherwise formalizes that identity. Among the borderland Igbo, there was formal identity of Igala lineages in order to maintain control of the *attama* title. Originally political and economic control of the Igbo motivated this separate Igala identity but later the original military-colonial purpose lost importance or was forgotten. Modifications steadily crept into the descent system. The most important of these was the case of *attama* of mixed parentage, as is shown in part in the example of Ameegwu Village (see Chart IX).

Although mixing of Igala and Igbo allegedly began with the first *attama* at Ameegwu, Oriye *Attah*, who married two Igbo and one Igala woman, mixing which resulted in actual crossing of descent groups occurred in the genealogy with *Attama* V, Onyili Edo. The daughter of his junior wife married an Igbo man of Umueze and became a remembered ancestress in Umueze even though her hus-band, who introduced her into the lineage, is forgotten. What is indicated by this is that the particular ancestress, Egba Ukwunne, was more important to Umueze than the Umueze man whom she married, even though after that generation Umueze traced descent through its males, as it had done previously. It shifted its pattern slightly at this point so that it could claim uterine relationship with the Igala lineage.

More central to the situation of Umu Attama, however, is the descent of the present generation out of the woman, Oreshu, who was a descendant of the junior son of Oriye *Attah*, but who regard-less was Igbo, tracing descent to the female "Widow of the Ances-tor" (Okwa Ndichie). Her son traced descent to Ezuugwu (*Ofo Eze*: "political power [of] *Eze*," a descriptive rather than proper name), and married an Igbo woman who is known as "Important Mother" (Ugwu Iye). Iyoke is the next descendant, her Igbo husband being remembered as "Husband [of] Iyoke" (Di Iyoke). Their male child, Amoke, married an Igbo woman, who bore the mother of

Oreshu. So the mother of the present generation of this lineage was Igbo because of general uterine descent tracing. But what of the father—was he Igbo or Igala according to borderland definition?

Ezuugwu Attama is considered to have been Igala because he was the father of a shrine priest, who *must* be Igala because, by definition, *attama* are all Igala. His father, who was *Attama* VI, was of course Igala, and ascending in the system the ancestors who are traced were Igala. But this is the descent system viewed largely as an inheritance system, so agnatic patrilineality is naturally emphasized. But were there no other children even of the generations mentioned? Ezuugwu Nwa Okwo is referred to because he was a uterine ancestor in Umu Attama and was also an ancestor of the other lineage of Dimunke, Umu Ezuugwu, who consider themselves to be as much Igbo as Igala. But other children are not mentioned because the title did not pass through their hands. They were "children of the mothers," persons claimed by the Igbo clans and lineages from which their mothers came. Genealogies are not true indices of consanguineous relationships, but rather charts of inheritance by which a given generation's claim to a title is affirmed. The majority of consanguines (*ikwu*) of Umu Attama in fact refer to themselves as Igbo, and Igbo is their native language. Igbo furthermore is the native language even of the people in the *attama*'s lineage, although these people also know Igala language. But the use of Igala is not common, and the claim of Igala descent other than to maintain the title is no more than a ritual chant whose function has long been lost. Umu Attama nowadays are Igbo men for all practical purposes save title inheritance. The Igbo, who were colonialized and colonized by strangers, have after all absorbed the strangers and become one with them, and the only persistent change was the necessity of placing Igala shrine priests in control of the *alusi*. This one institution remained through all the years of change and accommodation and adaptation, yet the very insistence upon tracing the line of *attama* strictly, at times led to a broad definition of "father's agnates" which in turn abetted eventual Igbonization.

Conclusion

THIS STUDY has been an ethno-historical survey of the northern Nsukka borderland, focusing particularly upon the mode by which the Igala colonialized the Igbo villages through the introduction of Igala and Okpoto lineages of shrine priests. These *attama* monopolized divination and were the only mediators between the Igbo people and the powerful, often hostile, and certainly unpredictable *alusi* spirits. Broadly similar contact situations of course exist, although like other human similarities these reveal differences upon close examination. Peculiar if not unique to the Nsukka borderland is that the central factor in social control by the colonializers was not political but religious and that the contact groups were of distinctly different political types—monarchic centralized as opposed to gerontocratic acephalous.

Much has been said about cultural borrowing and addition rather than substitution and replacement in African culture change, so questions naturally arise about this Nsukka borderland experience. Although this study cannot presume to answer such problems—indeed, its focus is largely description rather than argument, particularly argument over theory—perhaps it may add a bit of fat for the fire. The Igala shrine priests were all male, they were few in number for colonial agents (usually one to a village), they had obvious military support; so initial Igala contact with the Igbo was hostile. There was no equality between the new Igala settler minority and the older Igbo landowners, and immediately or shortly after the initial replacement of Igbo priests by Igala agents the contest for political control of the occupied villages began. One cannot presume from this, however, that the model proposed by Fernandez (1967, 11–14) applies. In discussing the general shift from patriliny to matriliny in the late 19th century, he relates the changes to colonialism, indicating that male competence was called into question by colonial dominance and that Christian mission evangelization attacked the means of male assertion by which fathers assured their lineage superiority. Although this may or may not apply in the contact between some Europeans and some Africans, it does not work in the Nsukka borderland. The borderland Igbo certainly were controlled in large part by the Igala settler priests and engaged in contra-acculturative movements as compensations for a certain sort of imposed inferiority, insofar as they had lost a great deal of political power in their own villages (see Redfield, *et al.*, 1936:152), yet they nevertheless retained control over their own lineages and their own *arua*, and their competence as males certainly was not called into question. Indeed, the colonialized man does not necessarily "lose his manhood" as many European ideologies suggest; this notion is all too often an easy solution to a complex situation, one in which social control is not necessarily linked with manhood, maleness, or any other matters having to do with sexual roles in a society.

In the case of the borderland Igbo, acculturation and interculturation are best understood by reference to the new Igbo methods for coping with new familial and social problems resulting from the Igala occupation. These coping techniques were related to social control deriving from religious and ritual power, some of which the Igala shrine priests had usurped, and caused the Igbo to change emphases in their worship. Although it was impossible in fact to deny the powers of the Igala-controlled *alusi*, who had become increasingly more capricious under the Igala, the Igbo attempted to regain power by increasing their worship of the High God and Earth, the ancestors and arua, and by adopting certain central Igbo medicines. These attempts failed, not because such spiritual forces could not be so powerful as the *alusi*, nor because the Igbo were so crushed or "emasculated" by the Igala that they were unable to develop this different worship sufficiently to offset the *alusi* powers, but because the Igala had physical control of the villages, and because of the hostile and capricious nature of the *alusi*. The Igbo in attempting to offset *alusi* powers—actually powers of the Igala shrine priests—were involved in a hopeless struggle, for such familiar spirits as God and Earth and the ancestors could not be effectively redefined. For this reason the Igbo adopted central Igbo medicines which in theory could act capriciously, but with few exceptions these simply did not fire the popular imagination sufficiently to work, save in Aro-uno, where *Adoro* replaced the *attama*-controlled *alusi*.

The Igbo also recognized the changes occurring among Igala lineages because of the complexities of affinity. The Igala had altered their mode of defining consanguineous kin largely to preserve proper *attama* descent so occasionally sons of daughters were named *attama*, with the title presumably reverting to the original patriline after a generation or two. The children of junior Igbo wives usually had little hope of gaining the title, so ancestral tracing often was matrilateral as well as patrilineal, with the stronger inclination of EGO toward mother's agnates. Such descent reckoning, following no set plan but only expediency, resulted in confusion of lineages and loyalties, as well as the steady weakening of original Igala boundary-maintaining mechanisms including language, land-holdings, occupational specialization, and the "purity" of ancestral groups. Accordingly, the Nsukka borderland Igbo and Igala both underwent much change. Was this change additive or substitutive or both?

The Igala-descended shrine priests remain today, although Igala colonialization—never strongly systematized—has ended. These priests still mediate for the *alusi*, which in turn has changed social control from what it once was. Originally control had been gerontocratically determined, Igbo titled men of course having much influence as well as Igbo elders. After the Igala came, the shrine priest with an inherited rather than acquired title—thus representing a special elite group not truly subject to the restrictions of Igbo village ancestors or even of Igbo gods—possessed powers equal to those of the gathered Igbo elders. His influence, too, remained until the present time, and his presence indicates a change in the system, not merely an addition to what already existed. What already existed was gerontocratic democracy; what developed afterwards was plural representationalism, the Igala being a privileged group usually with more power than the gathered and otherwise "democratically" represented Igbo headmen. The Igbo attempted to offset the special power and privileged status of the Igala priests, but to no avail. They came to accept the presence of the settlers, which changed the villages into politically and ethnically plural societies, but gradually over generations of intermarriage the villages became relatively unitary societies once again (at least ethnically, if not so clearly politically). But the factor that will finally fuse powers and reduce the Igala lineages to ordinary lineages rather than kingroups with special status, is alteration of the belief system. Once the people become sufficiently "modernized," which in this sense means European-oriented (not necessarily Christian but areligious or agnostic), not only will their ancestors become simply the dead, but the *arua* will become museum-piece spears, the *alusi* will become powerless old dead gods remaining only perhaps as spooks and hobgoblins in children's stories, and the once influential priests will merge with the ordinary people, politically powerless, no longer the agents of a once-powerful empire, but simply settlers whose forefathers once controlled the people among whom they now live.

Appendix

Supplementary Legendary Material

I. *Umunri*

The Umunri have intriguingly rich origin legends which sometimes overlap with certain Igala and northern Nsukka myths and origin legends. M. D. W. Jeffreys collected several of the Umunri tales, which are partly relevant to the history and religious institutions of the borderland. The "Aguku" version tells of God's having sent to earth Eri and his wife Namaku, who had several children, including Nri. Eri's second wife is said to have been the mother of Idah (the capital city of the Igala). Idah's mother sent her child across the Niger with instructions to settle there, which is meant to explain how the city of Idah was begun. Idah's eldest son was Onojo Obori, who figures importantly in borderland legends. Because the earth was watersoaked when Eri descended, God sent Awka the smith to dry it. Later God taught the people how to grow yams and kokoyams, and taught people the *ichi* title marks. The "Oreri" version repeats much of the same material, and adds further explanation of the *ozo* title. The "Obu Mmo" version introduces Adama, who was on the earth when Ndrinamoke [Nri, rather than Eri] first came from the sky, indicating the importance of *adama* as a title (see Jeffreys, 1956:120–130), which is often confused with the borderland title *attama*. These fragments of origin legends indicate that the Umunri people were itinerant medicine men (see Shelton, 1965, for their relationship with the borderland) and that the Umunri have links with Awka Igbo, with the Igala, and possibly with the Bini (see also Jeffreys, 1935:350).

II. *Onojo Ogboni*

Among the Igala, Nsukka Igbo, Okpoto, and even the Umunri there are several legends about or mentioning Onojo Ogboni. The *Nigeria Magazine* account (1964:17) quotes the present Attah Ali Obaje as saying that Onoja Oboni was the son of the Hausa princess, Amina. Seton (1928:267) argued that Onojo Ogboni was the son of an Igala woman, Obudali, and a chief of Ogurugu named Abatamu, and was thus called "son of a woman," from *obu* (Igala, "vagina"). The name thus derived is *ogbone* ("female person"), which is also the name for the sacred slit log drum used in ancestral and other rituals in the Nsukka borderland. Some of my own informants said that the name refers more mundanely to this hero's relationship with a descent group: *onojo* ("chieftain") and *ogbone* ("poor person"), thus: "the chief who did not inherit" (because he was the child of a woman). This may be only an interpretation of his situation, not so accurate as "the chief who was of the uterine side."

The names or titles *Onojo, Onu Ojo, Onoja*, and *Anaja* appear frequently in Igala and northern Igbo history. An Onojo Ogboni appears to have led Igala armies of conquest against some of the Edo-speaking peoples west of the Niger, who still use the title *anaja* to designate a chief. (Personal communication from Mr. Joseph Itotoh.) This title was reported by Allen and Thomson (1841 Expedition), who described a sub-chief named Ame Abokko, the *anaja* in the district on the east bank of the Niger north of Idah and chief of the Igbobi people who were then subject to the attah of the Igala. The Igbirra, led by their own anaja, had earlier invaded the eastern Igala.

There are several Igala and Igbo tales about an Onojo Ogboni who was an actual Igala war chief. John Boston pointed out that he was a "legendary Igala hero, who lived mainly at Ogurugu and from there raided the Ibo country as far as the villages on the Nsukka escarpment and as far west as the Niger"; he said there is strong evidence that Ogboni conquered Asaba, on the west bank of the Niger across from Onitsha, and referred to an unpublished manuscript by Charles K. Meek, "An Ethnographic Report on the Peoples of Nsukka Division" (1931) saying that most of the Division had been "overrun by an Igala chief known as Onu (chief) Ojo Ogbonyi" (Boston, 1960:56). Ugwu writes that Onoja Oboni was a son of an attah of Igala and he "over-ran the whole of Akpoto tribe which he conquered for his father. He was said to be a giant with six fingers, six toes. He was said to have later settled at Ogrugru from where he carried his attacks as far south as Opi" (1958:12).

Testimonies about Onojo Ogboni which I have gathered tend to bear out the foregoing, and fall into two classes: those which mythicize the hero, and those which describe him as a historical war leader.

The Ankpa Account

Informants: Alhaji Yacubu, Onu Ankpa (King of Ankpa)
Onoja Ogwuuche Ekwoh (Earth Chief of Ankpa)
Chiefmakers for both of these leaders
Gathered clan heads, etc.

"Onojo Ogbone" is a proverb in Igala. It is said: *Onojo Ogbone*, by itself, just like that. In the olden times a strong man went to heaven and then fell back to earth. On the tops of flat-topped hills you can see prints of his hands, because he landed very hard and left his handprints in the stone of the mountaintops. He was Onojo Ogbone. He was strong and brave, and he thought he could go to heaven all by himself, so he built a ladder and climbed very high, but he fell down to earth again, because he was not so strong as the spirits [an obvious cliche. See Gabel, 1967:58–59]. This saying is spoken by the Igala to recall the memories of their history in the olden times, and to tell about their bravery in trying to do very great things.

Onojo Ogbone was the son of Egbele Ejuona and Igala Mela [i.e., a proper royal descendant, out of the combined attah and, possibly, ashadu lines], but he left no children of his own, because he died when he fell down from the sky.

The Ogurugu Account

Informants: Attah Ago'fa Att'Idah Ogurugu, the traditional ruler.
His Council of Kingmakers.
Assorted elders.

[At Ogurugu a shrine building is dedicated to Onojo Ogboni, but only the Ago, the traditional ruler, is permitted inside it. Here sacrifices are made for kingship, and Onojo Ogboni is given regular ancestral-type worship.]

This man you speak of is the same one who was at Idah. He came from the time when God was on the earth: that was the time when he was king of the Igala. He came down from the heavens like a spiritual being. During the first war, he built a round wall of mud and put all the Igala people of Ogurugu inside it. This wall was built around the whole area of the Onojo's palace. That fence which you saw when you came into this part of Ogurugu is the mud wall made by Onojo Ogboni to protect the people.

There is a saying among the people which is his name: Onojo Ogboni. It tells children about our history, and it reminds grown men about Igala history, and what our fathers did, because he led the people who went into Nsukka and conquered the Igbo. He was very mighty, and the saying tells us about this, too. There is one big tree called "war medicine of Onojo Ogboni" [*ogwugwu*, which is the name of certain common Igala and Okpoto shrines], because he turned it upside down. He was so strong that he was able to do that, and now others grow that way, after he began it. [This is another common folktale heroic motif in African origin legends. In some versions the tree is *ibobo*, the baobab.]

One time he was wrapped in iron by the people, and he was thrown into the Anambra River close to Ogurugu, but he twisted the iron, and now only the iron remains in the water.

Informant: Omusa One, Igala from Idah, oral historian.

Onojo Ogbone was not chosen by the kingmakers to be king [according to Seton, 1928:259, because he could claim his right only through his mother]. He was from northern Igala, beyond Idah [i.e., the land of the Igbirra], but he left Idah and came to Ogurugu, which became his place, and which afterwards belonged to the Igala. He took warriors into the land of the Igbo of Nsukka.

After that, Nsukka was called *Ashado* [i.e., under the control of the Ashadu] and Ibagwa was called *Att'Igala* [owned by the Igala]. The old boundary line of Igala was as far as Nine-Mile Corner, in Udi Division [i.e., the northwest limits of actual Aro Chuku power]. Some of the old names of places in Igboland were *Enugu-Ezike amuushu, Nsukka amuushu, Ogurugu amuushu*, meaning that all of them belonged to the attah.

The Nkpologu Account

Informants: Onyishi Iga Attah Idu, Headman (age 105)
　　　　　Clan and major patrilineage elders

Attama
Major title holders.

We know that name well. We know about that man, but no one of us ever saw him. He was from Idah, and he was very famous and warlike. He conquered all of Nsukka division, but when he came to Nkpologu he left it because the people became brothers to Igala.

During those wars one of the strongest warriors of the Igala came through Nkpologu. After fighting the people of Nimbo, those Igala came to Nkpologu. This strong Igala was like a giant and was extremely fierce and powerful. The son of Okpogoro ["herald announces that civil war will not occur"] hid in a bush, but the Igala giant killed the young man. This was a masquerade and the son of Okpogoro saw the mask coming, and this masquerade, called Mmonwuofia ["spirit-son of the forest"], killed the boy. There is such a mask in Nkpologu today, with the same name, and by it we remember the past.

[Problem arises about actual details and reason for the mask killing the youth.]

I will tell you what happened. I know what happened, because my father told me. The masquerade was really a huge Igala warrior, who was inside the mask. You see, inside that mask it was an Igala man, but the mask was the Igala war medicine which we call *udenebe* ["vultures will not perch upon it"]. The son of Okpogoro didn't hide in a bush, but ran at the Igala warrior inside the mask and succeeded in pulling the mask off the man. But that was the medicine mask of the whole Igala army, and when it was taken off the giant Igala man became afraid that he lost his power and he couldn't fight, and the other Igala thought the same. In a way, the people of Nkpologu won over the Igala because of that, because the Igala made a truce with us, and they didn't burn down Nkpologu like the other Igbo towns, and they gave us much land. After this truce with us, they went to the east and conquered Nsukka, after they conquered Ibagwa. That is really what happened—not some Igala masquerade killing the son of Okpogoro.

"The Walls of Onojo Ogbone" is the name of the demarcation at Ogurugu: they are the walls that Onojo Ogbone built there, around the old town. He built walls at Nsukka, Ibagwa, and other places, too. He finally conquered Nkpologu [i.e., made the truce] and put his own men in charge of the people here, and our leaders descend from those Igala men [except for the onyishi himself, who descends from the Igbo hero, Okpogoro]. The most powerful people in the world in those days were Igala, and their leader who came here was Onojo Ogbone. They gave Nkpologu people land, more land than the people of Nsukka, Nimbo, Adani, Aku, and Ugbeni.

Bibliography

C. A. ABANGWU, 1960. *Nsukka Handbook*. Enugu: Federated Nsukka
 District Union.

J. C. ANENE, 1966. *Southern Nigeria in Transition, 1885–1906/Theory and
 Practice in a Colonial Protectorate*. Cambridge: At the University
 Press.

EDWIN W. ARDENER, 1954. "The Kinship Terminology of a Group of
 Southern Ibo," *Africa*, XXIV, No. 2 (April), 85–99.

———1959. "Lineage and Locality Among the Mba-Ise Ibo," *Africa*,
 24, No. 2 (April), 113–133.

ROBERT G. ARMSTRONG, 1967. *A Comparative Wordlist of Five Igbo Dialects*.
 Ibadan University Press.

———1961. "The Religions of the Idoma," *Ibadan*, 13 (Nov.), 5–9.

———1966. "Prolegomena to the Study of the Idoma Concept of God,"
 African Notes, 4, No. 1 (Oct.), 11–17.

KENNETH W. BACK, 1965. "A Social Psychologist Looks at Kinship
 Structure," in Shanas, 1965:326–340.

WILLIAM B. BAIKIE, 1856. *Narrative of an Exploring Voyage up the Rivers
 Kwora and Binue (Commonly Known as the Niger and Tsadda) in 1854*.
 London: John Murray.

MICHAEL BANTON (ed.), 1966. *Anthropological Approaches to the Study of
 Religion*. New York: F. A. Praeger.

WILLIAM BASCOM, 1966. "Odu Ifa: The Names of the Signs," *Africa*, 36,
 No. 4 (October), 408–421.

WILLIAM BASCOM & MELVILLE J. HERSKOVITS (eds.), 1959. *Continuity and
 Change in African Cultures*. Chicago: University Press.

GEORGE T. BASDEN, 1921. *Among the Ibos of Nigeria/An Account of the
 Curious and Interesting Habits, Customs and Beliefs of a Little Known
 African People*. New Impression. London: F. Cass, 1966.

———1938. *Niger Ibos. A Description of the Primitive Life, Customs, and Animistic Beliefs . . . of the Ibo People of Nigeria*. New Impression. London: F. Cass, 1966.

D. R. BENDER, 1967. "A Refinement of the Concept of Household: Families, Co-residence, and Domestic Functions," *American Anthropologist*, 69, No. 5 (October), 493–504.

E. BENZ, 1954. "On Understanding Non-Christian Religions," *Journal of Bible and Religion*, 22, No. 2. Included in M. Eliade and J. Kitagawa, *The History of Religions/Essays in Methodology*. Chicago: University Press, 1959.

OKOT P'BITEK, 1964. "The Self in African Imagery," *Transition*, 4, No. 15, 32–35.

JOHN S. BOSTON, 1959. "*Alosi* Shrines in Udi Division," *Nigeria Magazine*, No. 61, 157–165.

———1960. "Notes on Contact Between the Igala and the Ibo," *Journal of the Historical Society of Nigeria*, 2, No. 1, 52–58.

———1960. "Some Northern Ibo Masquerades," *Jour. of the Royal Anthrop. Inst.*, 90, Part I, 54–65.

———1962. "Notes on the Origin of Igala Kingship," *Journal of the Historical Society of Nigeria*, 2, No. 3, 373–382.

———1963. Communication to *African Notes*, 1, No. 1 (Oct.), 11.

———1964. "The Hunter in Igala Legends of Origin," *Africa*, 34, No. 2 (April), 116–126.

———1964b. "Ceremonial Iron Gongs Among the Ibo and the Igala," *Man*, 64, No. 52 (Spring), 44–47.

———1967. "Igala Political Organisation," *African Notes*, 4, No. 2 (January), 18–31.

———1968. *The Igala Kingdom*. Ibadan: Oxford University Press.

———1969. "Oral Tradition and the History of Igala," *Journal of African History*, 10, No. 1, 29–43.

R. BRADBURY, 1957. *The Benin Kingdom and the Edo-Speaking Peoples of South-Western Nigeria*. London: International African Institute.

L. BROOM, 1954 and B. SIEGEL, E. VOGT, and J. WATSON. "Acculturation: An Exploratory Formulation," *American Anthropologist*, 56, 973–1000. Reprinted in P. Bohannon & F. Plog (eds.), *Beyond The Frontier*. Garden City: Natural History Press, 1967, 255–286.

L. T. CHUBB, 1947. *Ibo Land Tenure*. 2nd Edition, 1961. Ibadan Univ. Press.

MILES CLIFFORD, 1936. "A Nigerian Chiefdom. Some Notes on the Igala

Tribe in Nigeria and their 'Divine-King,' " *Journal of the Royal Anthropological Institute*, 66, 393–436.

RONALD COHEN and JOHN MIDDLETON, 1970. *From Tribe to Nation in Africa*. Scranton: Chandler.

COMMAND 505. Secretary of State for the Colonies, Colonial Office, Nigeria, *Report of the Commission Appointed to Enquire into the Fears of Minorities and the Means of Allaying Them*. London: HMSO, 1958.

EMILE DURKHEIM, 1926. *The Elementary Forms of the Religious Life*. Trans. J. W. Swain. New York: Macmillan.

JACOB EGHAREVBA, 1949. *Benin Law and Custom*. Third Edition. Privately Published. Printed by CMS Press, Port Harcourt, Nigeria.

———1960. *A Short History of Benin*. Third Edition. Ibadan University Press.

E. M. T. EPELLE, 1966. "Chieftaincy Titles in Igbo Land and Church Membership," *West African Religion*, 5 (Feb.), 3–6.

E. E. EVANS-PRITCHARD, 1965. *Theories of Primitive Religion*. Oxford: Clarendon Press.

S. N. EZEANYA, 1963. "The Place of the Supreme God in the Traditional Religion of the Igbo," *West African Religion*, 1 (May).

———1966. "The 'Sacred Place' in the Traditional Religion of the Igbo People of the Eastern Group of Provinces of Nigeria," *West African Religion*, 6 (August), 1–9.

JAMES W. FERNANDEZ, 1967. "The Shaka Complex," *Transition*, 6, No. 29 (March), 11–14.

DARYLL FORDE, P. BROWN, R. ARMSTRONG (eds.), 1955. *Peoples of the Niger-Benue Confluence*. London: International African Institute.

DARYLL FORDE and G. I. JONES, 1950. *The Ibo and Ibibio-Speaking Peoples of South-Eastern Nigeria*. London: International African Institute.

MEYER FORTES and G. DIETERLEN (eds.), 1965. *African Systems of Thought*. London: International African Institute.

CREIGHTON GABEL and NORMAN R. BENNETT (eds.), 1967. *Reconstructing African Culture History*. Boston: University Press.

WILLIAM N. M. GEARY, 1927. *Nigeria Under British Rule*. Reprint. London: F. Cass, 1965.

C. GEERTZ, 1958. "Ethos, World-View, and the Analysis of Sacred Symbols," *Antioch Review* (Winter), 421–437.

MARGARET M. GREEN, 1947. *Igbo Village Affairs*. London: Sidgwick & Jackson.

J. S. HARRIS, 1944. "Some Aspects of the Economics of Sixteen Ibo

Individuals," *Africa*, 14, No. 6 (April), 302–335.

DONALD D. HARTLE, 1967. "Archaeology in Eastern Nigeria," *Nigeria Magazine*, No. 93 (June), 134–143.

ALHAJI HASSAN and MALLAM SHUAIBU NA'IBI, 1962. *A Chronicle of Abuja*. Trans. Frank Heath. Lagos: African Universities Press.

MELVILE J. HERSKOVITS, 1962. *The Human Factor in Changing Africa*. New York; Random House.

W. ROBIN G. HORTON, 1954. "The Ohu System of Slavery in a Northern Ibo Village-Group," *Africa*, 24, No. 4, 311–336.

ROBIN HORTON, 1956. "God, Man, and the Land in a Northern Ibo Village-Group," *Africa*, 26, No. 1, 17–28.

———1967. "African Traditional Thought and Western Science. Part I: From Tradition to Science," *Africa*, 37, No. 1, 50–71; "Part II: The 'Closed' and 'Open' Predicaments," *Africa*, 37, No. 2, 155–187.

JAMES A. HORTON, 1868. *West African Countries and Peoples*. 2nd ed. Edinburgh University Press [1969].

F. L. K. HSU, 1965. "The Effect of Dominant Kinship Relationships on Kin and Non-Kin Behavior: a Hypothesis," *American Anthropologist*, 67, No. 3 (June), 638–661.

C. C. IFEMESIA, 1962. "The 'Civilizing' Mission of 1841: Aspects of an Episode in Anglo-Nigerian Relations," *Journal of the Historical Society of Nigeria*, 2, No. 3 (December), 291–310.

M. D. W. JEFFREYS, 1935. "The Divine Umundri King," *Africa*, 8, No. 3 (July), 346–354.

———1946. "Dual Organization in Africa," *African Studies*, 5, No. 2 (June), 82–105.

———1951. "The Origins of the Benin Bronzes," *African Studies*, 10, No. 2 (June), 87–92.

———1951b. "The Winged Solar Disk, or Ibo ITCHI Facial Scarification," *Africa*, 21, No. 2 (April), 93–111.

———1954. "Ikengga: The Ibo Ram-Headed God," *African Studies*, 13, 25–40.

———1956. "The Umundri Tradition of Origin," *African Studies*, 15, No. 3 (October), 119–131.

G. I. JONES, 1949. "Dual Organization in Ibo Social Structure," *Africa*, 19, No. 2 (April), 150–156.

———1961. "Ecology and Social Structure Among the Northeastern Ibo," *Africa*, 31, No. 2 (April), 117–134.

———1962. "Ibo Age Organization with Special Reference to the Cross

River and North-Eastern Ibo," *J. Royal Anthrop. Inst.*, 92, No. 2 (July), 191–211.

J. P. JORDAN, 1949. *Bishop Shanahan of Southern Nigeria*. Dublin: Clonmore and Reynolds.

SYLVIA LEITH-ROSS, 1939. *African Women*. London: Faber & Faber.

ROBERT LEVINE, 1965. "Intergenerational Tensions and Extended Family Structures in Africa," in Shanas, 1965: 188–204.

H. S. LEWIS, 1967. "Ethnology and African Culture History," in Gabel & Bennett, 1967:25–44.

CHARLES K. MEEK, 1931. *An Ethnological Report on the Peoples of the Nsukka Division, Onitsha Province*. Lagos: Manuscript.

———1931b. *A Sudanese Kingdom: An Ethnographical Study of the Jukun-Speaking Peoples of Nigeria*. London: K. Paul, Trench & Trubner. (See also Young, 1966).

———1937. *Law and Authority in a Nigerian Tribe/A study in Indirect Rule*. London: Oxford University Press.

K. C. MURRAY, 1949. "Idah Masks," *Nigerian Field*, 14, No. 3 (July), 85–92.

S. F. NADEL, 1954. *Nupe Religion*. London: Routledge & K. Paul.

NIGERIA, CENSUS SUPERINTENDENT, 1953. *Population Census of the Eastern Region of Nigeria*. Port Harcourt: CMS Press.

Nigeria Magazine, 1957. "Nri Traditions," No. 54, 273–288.

———1964. "The Rise and Fall of the Igala State," No. 80, 17–29.

Nsukka Handbook. See Abangwu, 1960.

SIMON OTTENBERG, 1968. *Double Descent in an African Society: The Afikpo Village-Group*. Seattle: University of Washington Press.

———1958. "Ibo Oracles and Intergroup Relations," *Southwestern Journal of Anthropology*, 14, 3 (1958), 295–307.

———1968. "Statement and Reality: The Renewal of an Igbo Protective Shrine," *International Archives of Ethnography*, 51, 143–162.

MARGERY PERHAM, 1937. *Native Administration in Nigeria*. London: Oxford University Press.

———and M. BULL (eds.), 1963. *The Diaries of Lord Lugard*. Volume IV, *Nigeria, 1894–5 and 1898*. London: Faber & Faber.

A. R. RADCLIFFE-BROWN, 1939. *Taboo*. Cambridge: University Press.

ROBERT REDFIELD, R. LINTON, & M. J. HERSKOVITS, 1936. "Memorandum for the Study of Acculturation," *American Anthropologist*, 38, 149–152.

JAMES F. SCHON, 1842. *Journals of the Rev. James Frederick Schon and Mr. Samuel Crowther, who, with the Sanction of Her Majesty's*

Government, Accompanied the Expedition up the Niger, in 1841, in Behalf of the Church Missionary Society. London: Hatchard & Son.

R. S. SETON, 1928. "The Installation of an Attah of Idah," *Journal of the Royal Anthropological Institute,* 58, 255–278.

———1929–1930. "Notes on the Igala Tribe, Northern Nigeria," *Journal of the African Society,* 29, 42–52, 149–163.

E. SHANAS and G. STREIB (eds.), 1965. *Social Structure and the Family) Generational Relations.* Englewood Cliffs: Prentice-Hall.

T. SHAW, 1966. Note on Radiocarbon Dating of Igbo-Ukwu. *African Notes,* 3, No. 3, 21.

———1967. "The Mystery of the Buried Bronzes/Discoveries at Igbo-Ukwu, Eastern Nigeria," *Nigeria Magazine,* No. 92 (March), 55–74.

AUSTIN J. SHELTON, 1965. "The Departure of the *Nshie*: A North Nsukka Igbo Origin Legend," *Journal of American Folklore,* 78, No. 308 (Spring), 115–129.

———1965b. "The Presence of the 'Withdrawn' High God in North Igbo Religious Belief and Worship," *Man,* 65, No. 4 (January), 15–18.

———1965c. "The Meaning and Method of Afa Divination among the Northern Nsukka Igbo," *American Anthropologist,* 67, No. 6 (December), 1441–1455.

———1968. "Onojo Ogboni: Problems of Identification and Historicity in the Oral Traditions of the Igala and Northern Nsukka Igbo of Nigeria," *Journal of American Folklore,* 81, No. 321 (Summer), 243–257.

———1968b. "Causality in African Thought: Igbo and Other," *Practical Anthropology,* 15, No. 4 (Summer), 157–169.

———1969. "Igbo Child-Raising, Eldership, and Dependence: Further Notes for Gerontologists and Others," *The Gerontologist,* 8, No. 4 (Winter), 236–241.

———1969b. "The Articulation of Traditional and Modern in Igbo Literature," *The Conch,* 1, 1 (March, 1969), 30–52.

———1971. "The Aged and Eldership Among the Igbo," in L. Holmes & C. Cowgill (eds.), *The Aged in Various Societies.* New York: Appleton-Century-Crofts.

ROY SIEBER, 1965. "The Insignia of the Igala Chief of Eteh, Eastern Nigeria," *Man,* 65, No. 65 (May), 80–82.

PARBATI SIRCAR (ed.), 1965. *Nsukka Division: A Geographical Appraisal.*

Nsukka: University of Nigeria, Annual Conference of the Nigerian Geographical Association Proceedings.

P. AMAURY TALBOT, 1926. *The Peoples of Southern Nigeria/A Sketch of Their History, Ethnology and Languages, with an Account of the 1921 Census.* Four Volumes. London: Oxford University Press. Vol. II: *Ethnology.* Vol. IV: *Linguistics and Statistics.*

———1927. *Some Nigerian Fertility Cults.* London: Oxford University Press.

C. L. TEMPLE (ed.), 1919. *Notes on the Tribes, Provinces, Emirates, and States of the Northern Provinces of Nigeria Compiled from Official Reports by O. Temple.* Lagos: CMS Press. Reprint, London: F. Cass, 1965.

LOUIS-VINCENT THOMAS, 1961. "A General Outline of the Schedule of Theoretical Studies," *Presence Africaine,* 9, No. 37, 115–151.

NORTHCOTT W. THOMAS, 1913. *Anthropological Report on the Ibo-Speaking Peoples of Nigeria.* London: Harrison & Sons. Vol. I: *Law and Custom of the Ibo of the Awka Neighbourhood, Southern Nigeria.*

VICTOR C. UCHENDU, 1964. "Kola Hospitality and Igbo Lineage Structure," *Man,* 64, No. 53 (March), 47–50.

———1965. *The Igbo of Southeast Nigeria.* New York: Holt, Rinehart & Winston.

———1964. "The Status Implications of Igbo Religious Beliefs," *Nigerian Field,* 29, No. 1, 27–37.

DANIEL C. UGWU, 1958. *This is Nsukka.* Apapa: Nigerian National Press.

S. C. UKPABI, 1965. "Nsukka Before the Establishment of British Administration," in Sircar, 1965:26–36.

JAN VANSINA, 1961. *Oral Tradition.* Chicago: Aldine.

JOHANN WACH, 1951. *Types of Religious Experience: Christian and Non-Christian.* Chicago: University Press.

DIEDRICH WESTERMANN and M. A. BRYAN, 1952. *Handbook of African Languages. Part II: Languages of West Africa.* London: Oxford University Press.

JOHN E. WILLMER, 1965. "The Evolution of the Political Framework of the Nsukka Division," in Sircar, 1965:37–50.

A. H. ST. JOHN WOOD, 1959. "Nigeria: Fifty Years of Political Development among the Ibos," in R. Apthorpe (ed.), *From Tribal Rule to Modern Government.* 13th Conference Proceedings of the Rhodes-Livingstone Institute, Lusaka, 121–136.

M. H. YOUNG, 1966. "The Divine Kingship of the Jukun: A Re-Evaluation of Some Theories," *Africa,* 36, No. 2 (April), 135–153.

Glossary of Terms
and Names

Pronunciation Guide and Diacritical Marks

Tones: High tone is marked with ´ upstroke.

Middle tone is not marked.

Low tone is marked with ˋ downstroke.

All tones are relative to the speaker's voice.

Specially marked letters:

ñ: nasalized, bordering on sound of *ng*.

s̃: nasalized and sibilated front palatar sound.

Vowel sounds:

a: as in English *Mama*.

e: as in Spanish, or in English *may, day*, etc.

ẹ: as in English *get, set*, etc.

i: as in Spanish, or in English *tree, be,* etc.

ị: as in highly accented Spanish *e*.

o: as in English *go, grow*, etc.

ọ: as in English *saw, bought*, etc.

u: as in English *do, to*, etc.

ụ: as in English *put, foot*, etc.

Special consonants:

gb: unaspirated implosive

kp: unaspirated implosive.

nw: labialized velar.

kw: labialized velar.

Note: alphabetical order

gb = b
kp = p
ngw = nw

Material in parentheses indicates language; *Bord.* refers to particular Nsukka borderland usage which may not be paralleled in Igbo, Igala, or Okpoto.

ágbá (Igbo): "feast"

Àbẹ̀rẹ̀ (Bord.): "maiden," senior *álụsi* daughter. From (Igala) ìgbẹ̀lẹ̀. See Àbùlé.

Àbùlé (Igala): mask of land chief.

àdá (Bord.): "senior daughter"

áda (Okpoto): "father"

ádà (Igbo): "he speaks"

Àdádá (Bord.): *álụsi* at Obimo

Àdámà (Igbo): person in Umunri myths; Umunri title

Àdọ́rọ́ (Igbo): "daughter who remains"—*álụsi* at Aro-Uno.

ádú (Igala): "slave"

àfà (Igbo): "name"=divination

áfifa (Bord.): "small forest"—usually sacred

Àgídìbẹ̀ọ̀há (Bord.): "May you return again as another," an honorific; also

Àgìdìgbwọ̀há, "ladder of ọ̀fọ́"=means of power

ágó (Igbo): "farm"=new section of community

ágọ̀ (Bord.): "leopard"=salutation for titled person

águ (Bord.): "leopard"=title and salutation

àjà (Igbo): "sacrifice"

áká (Igbo): hand

àká (Igbo): many

ákàrà (Bord.): male shrine slave. See òsú, ìgbẹ̀lẹ̀

ákwáli (Okpoto): "palm branch"=protective medicine

ákwálì (Igbo): "cloth tied around"=fertility medicine

Ákwáŕì (Igbo): "raffia hides it"= protective medicine

ákwà ọ̀jújú (Bord.): "Cloth-question"=Igala cloth wrapped on spear used for oathing

ákwébì [ákwà úgbì] (Okpoto): cloth cap with red feathers, insignia of Attah, Chiefs, and Attama

álágbàà (Igbo): "its return cannot be prevented"—a life tree; tonally confused at times with (Okpoto) àlàgbá, "prisoner" álu (Igbo): "forbidden"

álụsi (Igbo): "something prohibited spoken"—non-familiar and aggressive, often hostile spiritual being

ámá (Igbo): "path" and section of village; "path"=lineage of people; (Bord.) title society

Ámányè (Bord.): "our spirit"—*álụsi* at Ohebe

àmbèkwu (Okpoto): ancestral spirits

ámọ́m'ụ́kpáíhi (Igala): "children [who] manifest wealth"—"daughters of power"=unmarried senior daughters of attama and Igala nobility

àmọ̀zù (Igbo): "witch"

ànà (Igbo): "earth"=junior section of village

Ánẹ̀ (Igala): "Earth" as deified; "earth"; junior section of village

ànẹ̀ẹ̀zí (Igbo): "land [of the] family"=lineage land

ànẹ̀ ḿmụ́ọ̀ (Igbo): "land-spirits"=the underworld

ànì, Ànì (Igbo): "earth"=junior section of village; "Earth" as deified

ànígò (Bord.): "earth offering"—buffalo horn or antelope horn flute

ànọ́ (Igbo): four

ányáká (Igbo): "net"

Ányáñwù (Igbo): "Sun" as abode of God; sun

ànyẹ́, ànyí (Igbo): us, our

ányị̀ (Igbo): our

àkpá (Igbo): castor bean tree

ákpụ́ (Igbo): sacred silk-cotton tree

árò (Igbo): "spear"; "fortune"; "body"

árọ̀ (Igbo): "year"

àrówà (Bini): head of compound

áruà (Bord.): "spears"=ancestral staves representing the abstracted powers of the forefathers

Àshádú (Bord.): title of Igala king's councillors; clan of borderland people

Àsọ́gwà (Bord.): title of chief of maskers; (Igala): senior brother

átǒ̀ (Bord.): "buffalo"

àttá (Igala): "father"; King of Igala

àttámá (Igala): "lord of many"=shrine priest

àttánẹ́bo (Igala): "lord of magic"=diviner-priest

àttébo (Igala): "lord of magic"

Áwàmú (Bord.): "Emerged Spirit"—an *álụsi*

áwọ́ (Igbo): "feathers"

Ází (Igbo): "people"

ázì (Igbo): [the present] "generation"
àzọ́ (Bord.): "back"—support
àzụ́ (Igbo): "back"
àzụ́bọ́íké (Igbo): "those standing behind a person give him strength"
àzụ́m̀mọ́ (Igbo): "back spirits"=the spirits supporting a person

gbàm̀mánụ́, gbámánụ́ (Bord.): "demanded [as masked priest, and]
   drove away"
bẹ́, bẹ̀ (Bord.): "is"; "are"
béá (Igbo): [you] "come"
   béàwẹ̀lù (Igbo): [you] "come take"; [you] "come have"
bíko (Igbo): "be it"="please"

Chí (Igbo): God
chí m̀mádú (Igbo): personal god
Chúkwú (Igbo): "Chi-Great"—God

déẹ́ (Igbo): address to Mother's brothers
dí (Igbo): "husband"
dì (Igbo): "is"; "exists"
dìbẹ (Igbo): [it] "is enough"
díbéà (Igbo): herbalist, soothsayer, sorcerer
dì ébéa (Igbo): [you] are to come here
Díìgbó ùgọ̀lòdú (Igbo): "old one of the night"—a male *álụ̀si*
dílí (Igbo): [may it] "continue"; [may it] "come to pass"
Dímodì (Igbo): "my master endures"—honorific for Ezuugwu
Dímụ̀nkẹ́ (Bord.): "master [of] their own spirit"—clan in Ameegwu

ẹ̀gbà (Igala): "when"=source in time
égbà èjà (Igbo): "to tie sacrifice"—crossroads offering to spirits
ébééto, ébẹ́íto (Igbo): "place untying"; "place exchanging"—
   crossroads offering for spirits
ẹ̀bèfá (Igbo): "from now on"
ẹ̀bẹ̀ìnù (Igbo): "place [of the] house"—house unit
Ègbèlẹ́ Éjúọ́nà (Igala): "maiden [with] face of [proper] child"="a
   female proper descendant"—legendary first King of Igala
ègbò (Bord.): spiritual being; also ẹ́bo
égbù (Igbo): [he] "owns"
échí (Igbo): wooden xylophone reserved for religious ceremony

ẹchí (Okpoto): "medicine"; see also ìchí

édọga (Bord.): "leopard's child"=salutation for titled person

ẹdọ́ga (Bord.): "leopard's child"=salutation for titled person

éfí (Igbo): "cow"

ẹ̀gàlẹ̀ (Igbo): "wealth [of the] earth"=age group of mature men

égò (Igbo): "money"

égwu (Okpoto): ancestral masquerade

éjú (Igala): "face"

èjùlọsi, èjùlụsi (Igbo): "sacrifice of álụsi"—a life tree

ẹ́júọ́nà (Bord.): "one asked to remain"=adopted group of settlers or later arrivals=section of village group

ẹ̀kẹ́ (Igbo): first day/market of week

ẹ̀kẹ́ (Igala): fourth day/market of week

èkèté (Bord.): round Igala "basket"

Ékké (Igbo): "python" as deified being

ẹ̀kum éhà (Bord.): "not to call name"—a circumlocutory for some spirits

ékwé (Igbo): wooden slit ceremonial drum; see ògbónyè

ékwéné (Igbo): [you] "agree"

ékwú (Igbo): "kitchen"=mud cones=pot supports and kitchen medicine

énéné (Igbo): "millet"

énú (Igbo): "up"=section of village

èkpé (Igbo): "wall"

és'àthọ̀ (Igbo): "mask-wearers"

éshuà (Bord.): "forest," usually sacred

éshì (Bord.): "body"

éshiọ́kùkwú (Bord.): "body swells up"=the swelling sickness

ẹ́si (Igbo): "pig"

ètàr̂ìgbà (Bord.): "many are joined together"=clan cluster or village group

ẹ́tuawẹ (Bord.): [it] "is piled up" (such as goods, money)

éyá (Bord.): "senior son"

Ézẹ̀ (Igbo): "chief"; "important person"

Ézẹ̀chítóké (Igbo): "chief god creator male"=God

èzí (Igbo): "compound"=senior section of village

Ézúúgwù Ọ̀wùlù [Ọ́wùrù] (Igbo): "great chief of Awulu Market"; Omeppa; Ézúúgwù ẹ́ŝh'úgwù'rụ́ (Bord.) "great chief known for his forest-cunning/ at Awulu"—founder hero of Nsukka borderland ẹ́zéúkwú (Bord.): "teeth big"=age group of pre-initiation boys

fánẹ̀ nwòchi (Igala): [he] "cleansed the land"—said of Abule
gí, ghí, gị́, ghị́ (Igbo): "you"; "your" [2nd person singular]

ịgbààfà (Igbo): "to divine"
ígbáná n'òsú (Igbo): "to run away to the shrine slaves"
ígba n'íkwúńnẹ̀ (Igbo): "to run away to Mother's relatives"
íbẹ̀ (Igbo): "group"
íbé (Igbo): "side"—as of a family
ìgbẹlẹ́ (Igala): "maiden"; (Bord.): female shrine slaves
Ìgbò, Ìgbọ̀ (Bord.): "people of the forest"; the Igbo people
íbóbo (Okpoto): baobab tree
ìgbwẹ̀ (Bord.): "time"; see m̀gbè
ìbwùdù (Igbo): wickerwork dummy buried as symbol of titled person
íchááruà (Igbo; Bord.): "to offer [to] áruà"
ìchákà (Okpoto): wickerwork basket rattle used in worship, esp. of
    Àbẹ̀rẹ́
ìchí (Bord.): "medicine"; "poison"
íchí (Igbo): facial scarifications for ọ́zọ́ title
íchiè (Igbo): "to return"
íchíkérị́ (Igbo): "it becomes strong"; "it returns greater than . . ."=
    a life tree
Ídényì (Igbo): "gives support"=junior female tutelary spirit
íchọ àjà (Igbo): "to offer sacrifice"
ífẹ́ọma (Igbo): "good things"
ìfìtè (Igala): junior section of village
Ìgálà (Bord.): "people of earth"=the Igala people
Ìgálà Mẹ̀lá (Igala): "The Igala nine"=the indigenous clans of Igala;
    the Igala "kingmakers"
ígááruà (Igbo): "to offer [to] áruà"
ígwé (Igbo): "iron"=iron flute
ígwe (Igbo): "sky"
ị́kwa ọ̀jújú (Igbo): "to spread out question"=to divine
íkwú (Igbo): "relatives"; "consanguines"; "agnates"
ili (Okpoto): "cloth"
íló (Igbo): village plaza
ímé (Igbo): "inside"
    ímèànẹ̀: "inside earth"=the underworld

ímẹ́nná: "inside fathers"=entire agnatic descent group

íméóbí: "inside house"=household group

Ịnyiámá (Igbo): "gives people"—a female álụsi

ịkpakàchí (Bord.): "it returns like days"=a trickster "returner" spirit; see ọ̀gbánjè; compare (Okpoto): úpàkàchí, tree of a god

ìrókò (Yoruba?=Bord.): African teakwood tree

írumá (Igala): "to sacrifice [to the] lineage"

íshí (Igbo): "head"; "most important"

    íshíchí (Igbo): "head god"=senior wife [who has first chí staff in altar after husband's]

ísi (Igbo): "to say"

ìtàr̃ìgbà. See ètàr̃ìgbà.

ìtè (Igbo): "pot"

ìwú (Igbo): "law"

íyè (Igala): "mother"

Íyẹ́ Ọ̀wọ́ (Bord.): "mother god"=álụsi at Imilike

Íyí Ákpàlà (Igbo): "female stream-goddess glorifies earth"=álụsi at Umu Mkpume

íyí (Bord.): "female god," usually associated with a stream

ízè (Igbo): "toothed"=a small child

ízíágọ̀ (Bord.) "tooth [of] leopard"—necklace of title worn by **attama**

ízù (Igbo): "week" [four days]

'jàdèbẹ́lú (Bord.): "to show and to keep forever"—prayer formula

jí (Igbo): "yam"

ka (Igbo): "may"; "let"

káma (Igbo): "instead of"

kélékédé (Igbo): "decoration"=grass loops used to designate areas inhabited by non-human beings

kèlù (Igbo): [you] "created"

kw'árọ̀ kwà'm (Igbo): "as year, so I"=expression of continuance

kwọ́ (Igbo): [you] "wash"

làà (Igbo): [you] "drink"

'ma (Igbo): [it] "strikes"

Mází (Igbo): salutation

ḿbà (Igbo): "country"; "land"; "area"

m̀bálá ẹ́zí (Igbo): "breadth [of the] family"=compound family
m̀gbè (Igbo): "female"
m̀gbè (Igbo): "time"
    m̀gbè ńdíchiè (Igbo): "time [of the] ancestors"—the past
m̀bẹ̀kwù (Igbo): "tortoise shell"="tortoise"
m̀má (Bord.): "power"="spirit"
m̀mádù (Igbo): "person"
    mmàdù ágáìre ńnẹ́yá mụrụ (Igbo): "person must not sell mother his
    [who] bore him"
m̀mányá (Bord.): "palm wine"
m̀mínyé (Igbo): "water"
m̀mọ́ (Igbo): "spirit"; masker's society
Mmọ́ñwụ̀ọ́fià (Igbo): "spirit-son of the forest"—a masquerade
m̀mụ́ọ̀ (Igbo): "spirit"; "spiritual force"
    mmụ́ọ̀ ànyáshè (Igbo): "spirit [of the] night"=Abere
m̀pé (Igbo): "small"

na (Igbo): "in"; "and"; "to"; "for"
n'àn'Ìgbò nị̀nẹ̀ n'élì jí àhụ́bẹ̀'èm íhẹ́ dékà nkẹ̀à (Igbo): "In the land of
    the Igbo who eat yam never have I seen a thing like that"—
    expression of normalcy and astonishment at the different
ńgbùlù (Igbo): "stick"=iron staff of attama's office
ǹchẹ́ónyé (Igbo): "sentry"—protective shrine
ńdẹ́gàlè (Igbo): "group [who are] wealth of earth"—age group of
    grown men
ńdẹ́ nwẹ́ ànì (Igbo): "group [who] own the earth"—formula in
    prayers, with varying referents
ńd'òkólóbeà (Bord.): "group of youths"—age group of unmarried
    young men
ńdí (Igbo): "group"
ńdíámá (Bord.): "group of people"=members of ámá title society
ńdÌgbò (Igbo): the Igbo people
ńdígbó (Igbo): "group of old ones"=ancient forefathers; the
    especially wise; Europeans
ńdíchí, ńdííchí (Igbo): "group [with] íchí [scarifications]"
ńdíchiè (Igbo): "group of returners"=ancestors; elders
ńdídì (Igbo): "patience"
ńdímó, ńdímwọ́ (Igbo): "group of spirits"=the world of spirits
ńdíshí (Igbo): "headmen"

ńdọ̀ (Igbo): "life"

ńdólu (Igbo): "waterside people"

ńgúọ́lù (Igbo): [you] "drink"

níné (Igbo): "all"

ńkàshì (Igbo): "kokoyam"

ńkẹ́súálọ̀ (Igbo): "that one follows year"=junior brother

ńkwọ́ (Igbo): fourth day/market of week

ńlì (Igbo): "food"="cooked food," especially pounded yam

ńná (Igbo): "father"

ńné, ńnẹ̀ (Igbo): "mother"

   nnẹ́kwù (Igbo): "mother [of] kitchen"=head wife

ńnú (Igbo): "salt"=black salt used only for sacrifices

ńkpúlụ́ (Igbo): "heap"="town" or village group

   ńkpúlụ chí (Igbo): "pieces [of] god"=representations of one's ancestors

   ńkpúlụ́ọ́bi (Igbo): "seed of chest"=heart

ńshiè (Bord.): Umunri

   ńshiè ónẹ̀ (Bord.): "Nri person"=protective shrine

ǹtà (Igbo): "small"

Ntíyè (Bord.): "mother of destruction"; "little mother"—álụsi at Ameegwu

ńgwà (Igbo): "son"="owner"

ńgwá ónyé Ìgbò (Igbo): "son of Igbo person"=Onitsha saying

ńwà (Igbo): "son"="child"

   ńwááká (Igbo): "child of hand"—very small child

   ńwá ńkpónọ́bì (Igbo): "child of heart"—junior wife

   ńwándù (Igbo): "child of life"—small child who is carried

ńwàyị̀ ọ́mẹ n'ọ̀mụ́mụ́ (Igbo): "woman repeatedly gives birth"=a woman tormented by ogbanje

ńgwẹ̀ànè (Igbo): "owner of earth" [see nde nwe ani]

Ṅgwú (Igbo): male álụsi

Ṅgwúmádéshẹ̀ (Bord.): "Ngwu knows person of the forest" [i.e., Ezuugwu]—álusi at Umugoji

Ṅgwúmákéchí (Bord.): "Ngwu knows which god . . ." [i.e., is powerful]—álụsi at Umune Ngwa

ńwúnyè (Igbo): "woman"="wife"

   ńwúnyè ńmá (Igbo): "woman of love"=younger wife

   ńwúnyè ósọbẹ (Bord.): "woman [who] follows"=junior wife

ọ́ (Igbo): "he"; "she"; "it"

ọ́gbáágbò (Bord.): "he divines"=diviner

ọ́gbààfà (Bord.): "he divines"=diviner

ọ́gbánjé (Igbo): "[it] returns [as] enemy"="returner"=trickster spirit;
see Ikpakachi

ọ́gbàrà (Bord.): sacred bush near álusi shrines

ógbè (Igbo): "village"; "area"

óbì (Igbo): "chest"="heart"

ògbọ́ (Igbo): "age group"; "club"; "group"

ògbòdò (Igbo): "village"; "town"

ọ́ bọ̀nkẹ́ ńdíchiè (Igbo): "It is something [of the] ancestors"="it is
customary"

ọ́bọnọ́kọ́ (Bord.): "she prepares for wealth"—misapplication of
ọ́bonọ́kwọ́, "female-great," from (Igala) ọ́bonuku, "vagina-great,"
referring to senior wife

ógbónyè, ògbónyé (Bord.): "female person"=the slit log drum used
for ceremonial music

ọ́bọ ọ́shióru̧ (Bord.): "it clears bush" [i.e., by poisoning other plants
around it]—a sacred plant often used in making war medicine and
arrow poison

ọ́gbu (Igbo): "it kills"=life tree associated with ancestors

ọ́gbú éfí (Igbo): "he killed cow"—title

ọ̀bù̧la, ọ̀bú̧là (Igbo): "any"; "whatsoever"="unexpected"

ọ́búnwà ọ́kwú (Igbo): "she is child large"=junior wife

ọ́chà (Igbo): "pale"; "white"

ọ̀chákàtá (Okpoto), from ìchákà: "rattling for the king"—method of
worshipping Àbẹ̀rẹ́; ọ̀shákàtá

óchè (Igbo): "aged"

ọ́chege, ọ́chẹge (Bord., Okpoto): "she guards constantly"; "person
who listens" [i.e., to pleas]—market Abere at Oba

óchúkwú (Igbo): "aged-great"=grandparent

ọ́dàgbà (Bord.): "the other side"=the junior line in village

ọ̀dọ̀ (Igala): "heart"="life"; "wall"

òdò (Okpoto): "yellow"

odọ̀ (Igbo): "clay" [yellow]; "chalk" [yellow] used for ceremony

ọ́dódúñwà (Igbo): "last child"

ódúátù̧ (Igbo): "bell [which] orders"—staff of office

ọ̀fọ́ (Igbo): sacred tree; staff of political power

ọ́gà (Igbo): "lord"; "supervisor" [as of sacrifices at shrine] ógè (Igbo): "time"

ógg̣ènè (Igbo): clapperless bell; gong

ògílíshí. See èjùlụsi

ọ́gọ̀ (Igbo): "in-law"

ọ́gwà (Bord.): "first"; "ahead of"—name of "first" Igala, Omeppa

ọ́gwụ̀ (Igbo): "medicine"; "spiritually empowered substance"

 ọ́gwụ̀ dị̀ n'ámá (Igbo): "medicine of the people"—special medicine at Nkpologu

ọ́gwúgwú (Igala): "war medicine"

ọ̀há (Bord.): ọ̀fọ́ tree and staff; (Okpoto): "again"; "another"

ọ̀hà (Igbo): "public"; "assembly"

óhù (Igbo): domestic slave

ọ́jé (Igbo): kola nut; hospitality

òjè (Okpoto): "iron"=sacred rattle-iron staff used to summon spirits

ójí (Igala): "head"="above"

ọ́jì̀ (Igbo): iroko tree

ọ́jị́ (Igbo): kola

òjí (Igbo): "dark"; "black"

ọ́jọ́ (Igala): "day"; "god"; supreme god

ọ̀jósẹ́ (Okpoto): "iron carried in hand"—an arua staff

ọ́jọ́zi (Bord.): "goes with message"—an arua staff

ọ̀jújú (Bord.): "to ask"; compare (Okpoto) òjojé, "truth"

 ọ̀jújú ẹ́bo (Bord.): "to ask spirits"=to divine

ọ́káká (Bord.): "it grows old" [i.e., with title holder]—an arua staff

óké (Igbo): "male"

ọ́kẹ́lẹ́ (Igbo): mother's agnates; daughter's children

ókíг̃ó (Igbo): "enemy"

ọ́kọ́ (Igbo): "heat"; "fire"; (Igala): "wealth"

ọ́kọ́chí (Igbo): "hot days"=dry season

ókódú (Igala): millet

ókoógbóò, òko'óbhò (Okpoto): "fallow farm"=land held in common by a lineage

Ókùké (Igbo): a creator god

ọ̀kụ́kọ̀ (Igbo): "chicken"

òkùtè̀ (Igala, Okpoto): "ancestral staffs"

ọ̀kwà (Igbo): "widow"

ọ́kwájù (Bord.): wooden serving dish for attama

ọ̀kwọ̀ (Igala): "spear"=ceremonial spear of attama

ọ́kwọ́jí (Bord.): tortoise-shaped kola containers

ǫ́kwǫ̀jújú (Bord.): "he spreads out question"="he divines"=diviner

Ọ̀kwúúgwù (Bord.): "great Ugwu"—álụsi at Ujobo-obigbo

ólọ̀kpụ́ (Igala): patrilineal agnatic clan

ólùèbò (Igbo): "water bell"—clapperless bell for ceremonial use

ǫ́ma (Igbo): "good"

Ọ́mábẹ̀ (Bord.): "sons of village"=men's secret society

ómáńnẹ́ (Igbo): "mother's goodness"—kitchen symbol of woman as source of nourishment

ǫ́ménàlà (Igbo): "it is in the earth"="it is customary"

ómẹnẹkẹlẹ (Igala): "son of males"=descent referent for heir especially to title of attama

ǫ́monǫ̀bùlé (Igala): "son of females"—descent referent designating uterine relatives of attama; descent referent for heir to title of attama through a female line

ọ̀mụ́ (Igbo): green heart of palm; new palm frond—used for ceremonial purposes

ọ̀mụ́mụ́ (Igbo): "fertility"

ǫ́námá (Igbo): "it is one path"=house group of mother and her children; extended family

ónẹ̀ (Igala): "person"; "man" [freeborn]

ónú (Igala): "chief"

ǫ́nù, ǫ́nụ́ (Igbo): "mouth"="altar"

Ónúmụ́nọ̀ (Bord.): "chief of the people"—senior son of álụsi

ọ̀nụ̀nù, ọ̀nụ̀nǫ́ (Bord.): "spirit remaining"—women's festival

ǫ́ñwà, ǫ́ñwá (Igbo): "moon"="month" [lunar]

òñwóyá (Igbo): "itself"

ónyénákwulu (Igbo): "person who calls"="herald"

ọ̀nyị̀nyó (Igbo): "shade," "shadow"; alter ego; "spirit remaining"

ónyíshí (Igbo): "headman"

òkpà (Igala): "groundpea"

ọ́kpàkàchí. See íkpakàchí

ókpálá (Igbo): senior son; major heir

ọ̀kpé (Bord.): "wall"

ópì (Okpoto): [wooden] "flute"

Òkpò (Okpoto): álusi at Imilike

Ọ̀kpógórọ̀ (Bord.): "herald [who] announces that civil war will not occur"—forefather at Nkpologu; compare (Igbo): ọ́kpǫ́gọ́rọ́, "lock"

ǫ́riè (Igbo): "he eats"=aide in shrine sacrifices

ọ́rígúnnẹ (Igbo): "big"=an ancestor

ọ́rọ́'m̀mè (Bord.): "let it [fertility] remain"—invocation at ọ̀nụ̀nọ́
ceremony

ósàyé (Bord.): "our speaker"

ọ́sáyì (Bord.): "our foundling"

ọ́sha (Bord.): dance "rattles"

ọ̀shákàtá. See ọ̀chákàtá

ọ́shiórụ (Bord.): "plant of the bush"; see ọ́bo

ọ́shíshí (Igbo): "stick"=arua staff

ọ̀shó (Igbo): "foundling"; "lost child"

ọ́shụórụ́ (Bord.): "it clears bush"; see ọ́bọ

ọ́sọálò (Igbo): "next year"=senior brother

ọ́sọ́be (Igbo): "he follows"=junior sibling

ọ́su (Bord.): "it speaks"=wooden flute

òsú (Igbo): shrine slave

òtì, ùtì (Igbo): "bell"

Ọ̀tikpògbòdò (Igbo): "he burned towns"—name ascribed to Mr.
Aaron, D.O. in Nsukka

òtóbó (Igbo): village plaza

ọ́tọ́nshiè (Igbo): "bamboo"=sacred spears of Umunri

ọ́wa (Okpoto): "age group"

ọ̀wéáká, ọ́wéáká (Igbo): "it surpasses life"—power of existence in one's
heart

òwèlè (Igbo): "interior" section of village

ọ̀yímà (Igbo): "ghost"

ózhíókó (Igbo): "message-youth"=messenger

ózíósú (Igbo): "message-slave"—an arua staff

ọ́zọ́ (Igbo): a major title

rã (Igbo): "copulate"; "sleep together"=are equal

tàà (Igbo): [you] "eat"

táà (Igbo): "today"

ùgbá (Igbo): oil bean tree

ùbẹ́ (Igbo): "pear" tree

ùdènẹ́bé (Igbo): "vultures perch not" [i.e., on it]—a medicine tree

údúmmílí (Igbo): "fullness-water"=rainy season

úgwù (Igbo): "honor"; "prestige"="great"

úkwááruà (Bord.): "great arua"—a patrilineal agnatic clan

ụ́kwárà (Igbo): "cough"

úkwú (Igbo): "great"; "big"

ụ́lọ́ńnà (Igbo): "house [of] fathers"—ancestral shrine house

ụ́mází (Igbo): "children [of the] generation"—the living

úmẹ́ (Igbo): "breath"="life"

ụ́mù (Igbo): "children"="people"

ụ́mùàdá (Igbo): "children daughters"—women's lineage association

ụ́mù ḿgbọ́tọ́ (Igbo): females related to EGO

Ụ́mù Ḿkpụ́mè (Igbo): village in Oba

úmúnẹ̀ (Igbo): one's mother's agnates

Úmúnẹ̀ Ǹgwà (Igbo): village in Nsukka

ụ́mụ́ńnà (Igbo): patrilineal agnatic descent group; one's agnates

ụ́nọ̀ (Igbo): "compound"; "house"

únù (Igbo): [all of] "you" [2nd person plural]

únú (Igbo): "salt"—black salt used for sacrifices

ụ̀ñwù (Igbo): "famine"

úshù (Bord.): [it] "follows"="belongs to"

ụ́tàbà [útàrà] (Igbo): "pounded yam fufu"

ụ̀tụ́tù (Igbo): "morning"

ụ̀wà (Igbo): "world"

ụ́zìgbò (Igbo): "road [of the] Igbo"

úzọ̀mà (Igbo): "road [of the] spirits"

wẹ̀tẹ́bẹ́ (Igbo): "give"; "bring forth"

yá (Igbo): "he"; "she"; "it"

zoghéde (Igbo): "[may you] protect"

Index